PEOPLE IN GLASSHOUSES

M.R. O' DONNELL

Best Wishes

M.R.O'Donnell

ISBN: 978-1-7392899-1-1

CONTENTS

Acknowledgements

I would like to acknowledge all of those who kindly and most likely in some cases, unknowingly, contributed to this exploration and those who openly and willingly shared their precious time, knowledge and wisdom. I would also like to express my appreciation to all who generously made words or photographs available and who have permitted me to share them within this book. Below, in alphabetical order, is a list of those contributors.

Richard Andrews, Reverend Patrick Comerford, Stephen Darcy, Georgina Darroch, Jim Deeds, Ewen Donaldson, Stephen Douglas, Lord and Lady Dunleath, Robin Elliott, Gerry Gallagher, Okikiolu Oluwagbemiga George, Pastor Trevor Gillanders, Paul Harron, Iain Houton, Canon Norman Jardine, David Jones, Alexandra Ledward, Catherine Little, Pat Lynch, Francis Maude, Gerry Millar, Pascal Murphy, Darren Mulligan, John McClean, Edel McDonald, Maurice McKendry, Justin McMinn, Eimear O'Brien, Graham O'Sullivan, Kevin Reid, Jim Reynolds, Father Sean Rogan, Frances Sampayo, Father Michael Sheehan, Andrew Sinclair, Andrew Williams, Kirsten Walker.

Now, it is through his diligence, direction, expertise and hard work, that the day has arrived. So, a very special thank you goes to Niall MacGiolla Bhui of ShadowScript Ghostwriting and to his wife and Director of Book Hub Publishing, Susan McKenna, for all your hard work. And I am also very grateful to those who helped with the review, edit and design processes, namely Giselle Marrinan, Karen Gallen, Amy Harrington and Dorothy Dreyer. Special thanks also to Pippa Gray and Anna Gray. Pippa for her introduction to Anna, and Anna for initially ensuring the narrative was delivered in a meaningful and hopefully an interesting way; and for her subsequent introduction to Book Hub Publishing. And to all of the aforementioned who guided me through some minefields – personal and professional and *grammatical!*

I am also very grateful to you, the reader, for buying this book.

I know you will forgive me if my last (but not least!) word of thanks is to my family. To my beautiful wife Rachel and our wonderful children, Lydia and Ezra. Thank you for your belief and support throughout this project; to God be the glory.

I dedicate this book in loving memory of Private Sean Rooney.

SYNOPSIS

I once read that 'beauty doesn't have to be about anything. What's a vase about? What's a sunset or a flower about? What, for that matter, is Mozart's Twenty-third Piano Concerto about?' Yet, everybody appreciates beauty in one form or another. Beauty makes people stop. It can make people covet or gasp in eye widening awe and it can inspire and make people aspire, in equal measure. Beauty insists we share our precious time and enables us to ponder. In fact, it was Sir Clough Williams-Ellis, creator of the colourful Italianate village of Port Merrion in North Wales who once stated, 'I think that beauty, the strange necessity – as Rebecca West once called it – is something that matters profoundly to humanity.' In essence, beauty can mean different things to different people, at different times.

Yet, for me, architecturally and historically speaking, the unfading slender elegance of a Victorian curvilinear glasshouse glistening in the gentle seasonal sunshine is indeed, an object of ineffably sublime beauty. Whilst its inner self brings with it a quiet and calm beauty, it is often served by gentle breaths of wind, which are punctuated by sensual scents that emanate from the elaborate array of colourful botany, housed safely beneath the glazing.

Like a delicate catwalk model, a glasshouse's glazed curves flow with a stylized elegance, a timid grace and a fragility but not without substance or an overarching purpose. It is an appreciation of the visual and experiential nature of these triumphant historical structures that *initially* inspired me to embark upon this project.

My enjoyment of glasshouses, particularly those of a Victorian curvilinear variety, first started in 2011 when I was tasked with project managing the restoration of an 18th century Bishops Palace and a deconsecrated 18th Century Primate's Chapel located outside of Belfast. More-over and rather as a quaint add-on, I would also manage the restoration of a beautiful vacant south-facing, lean-to curvilinear glasshouse. It was erected against a traditional grey stone wall facing to the north, that was hidden behind some high, lush, green hedging. A few short years later, I would be heavily involved in the initial stages, of the proposed restoration of a larger, more iconic Palm House, heaping more fuel on the fire of my passion for all thing's conservation, restoration and heritage related.

Yet, as a Chartered Surveyor, I am not ashamed to say that I am less fascinated by the beautiful and exotic horticulture housed within, but more by the architectural wonder of the detail-rich structures in which the tropical botany resides. Surviving examples of Victorian glasshouses are a rich and vocal emblem of connectivity between Victorian historicism and their varied contemporary end-use. They embody a unique legacy not only from a design and construction perspective but also from a social one; and that in itself, I felt, warranted further exploration.

Such aesthetically pleasing, elemental elegance and multi-functional excellence, deserved a book of equal sophistication. Designed with quality and discernment in mind, I felt such a book would provide a platform for contemplation and pleasure for the reader. However, although I had initially planned to develop a stylish coffee table book, it quickly transpired that wasn't to be God's plan, because He had an entirely different proposal in mind for me. To say this book is merely about the restoration of *actual* glasshouses, would be a half truth, because like many of the rare Victorian glass houses that I would survey, there was a time when I, too, was in a state of obsolescence and desperately in need of restoration.

By witnessing, in the spirit of veracity, this book enables me to testify to the anxiety inducing obstacles that led to my personal life once becoming as fractured as an eighteenth-century terrazzo tiled floor. Externally my façade was always calm and in order, yet a spell of some highly questionable decision-making and a catalogue of challenging situations, led to my soul becoming as dark, filthy and as badly corroded, as a Victorian cast iron gutter. With my confidence as severely chipped as a two-hundred-year-old ashlar stone plinth, it was clear that I was defective and in desperate need of a transformational change and tranquillity of mind.

Using a self-formative function, this recollection provides a written chronological testimony that confesses to not only my own failings, but to those various vices and primary demons that attacked and tempted me throughout my life. It highlights my struggles with the flesh and with the world but in doing so, this book also brings with it the promise of purificatory value. For like many of the architectural glasshouse designers who borrowed heavily from previous designs, I would learn to *imitate* the Lord, who always met his attacker head on with testimonies from the Scriptures.

This book is a thematic literary diptych offering two stories juxtaposed, personal and professional, depicting key moments in my life. It is about paradigm shifts, and judgements shaped by perceptions. It is about the management of risk throughout a lifecycle. It is a little love story which not only gives an insight into the profession I adore but it enables me to reflect on the personal risks and pitfalls that await anyone of us at any time.

That said, it is less an elegant composition and more a book of practical help. For having committed to living a Christo-centric lifestyle some ten years ago, I pray this book offers an arsenal of effective words that will edify the reader to such an extent that it will inspire reading of scripture and the development of that essential, personal relationship with Christ, because although we might not realise it, reading scripture is an encounter with the living Jesus.

This book is about our spiritual struggles, but it is also an exhortation to white martyrdom and to a life of higher morals and of virtuous improvement. It is my hope that this book will be an aid to those aspiring to cultivate a tranquil disposition, for much like a glasshouse in need of restoration, you will find that with God's strengthening grace He can remove all fragility, restore you with integrity and instil an overarching purpose in your life. It is my hope that this book will enable those of you, whose need was as keen as my own, to recognise the powerful and effective nature of the words of Scripture. It is my Christological claim that God's Word can provide us with meaning and purpose in this landscape soaked in the sublime and the ridiculous.

This project is not an opportunity to fire poisonous darts in the direction of anyone who has blighted any part of my journey. It is a public testimony and an opportunity for me to share my life experiences, thoughts, and perceptions, but in a respectful and a constructive way.

I have travelled around the islands of Ireland and the UK, exploring many magnificent (and some very modest) glasshouse structures; and like the elements that go into the design and construction of a glasshouse, so too do the components of this book link together to offer a unique perspective. It is a book about conservation, heritage, preservation and restoration but it also is about a future born of the past.

It is a book that focuses on the very practical far-reaching risk of living a life of sin and Godlessness. However, with scope and precision it pays attention to the protection, safety and joy that can come from immersing oneself in God's Word. And all with the aim of helping us to become the Christians we are all called to be.

FOREWORD

When M.R. first spoke with me about this book, I wondered how he would weave his own story and testimony into a book about glasshouses. He has successfully achieved just that, and in the following pages – he has shared, opened up and been vulnerable to us the reader. And, alongside his own story, he has shared his knowledge of architecture and glasshouses. There is lots to learn about M.R., about faith and about glasshouses here.

M.R.'s enthusiasm for glasshouses is contagious. As you read you will find out about the structures, the places and the history that these majestic buildings inhabit. I'm always intrigued to the back story of buildings like these. Who was around at the beginning of the project to build a glasshouse? What did people think of them as they watched them being built? What impact did they have on the people that worked there, on those who enjoyed the food grown there, or appreciated the beauty and variety of the plants and flowers?

The story of faith and testimony that is weaved throughout had me asking similar questions, which M.R. answers openly. Who was around at the beginning of his journey? What did people think at the various significant moments in his life? What impact has this journey of faith had on the people closest to him over the years?

Glasshouses are things of beauty; they are an architectural wonder in many ways. Many have stood the test of time and yet they are still vulnerable. They have weathered storms and survived the elements thrown at them, yet they still need to be cared for and maintained. They could be a metaphor for each of us. We have stood the test of time; we have survived the elements and yet we need care and protection from those around us.

Glasshouses protect what is inside, they encourage deep roots to grow and develop, they nurture plants to reach their full potential. As individuals we need to grow deep roots, we need to develop and reach our potential. M.R. shares his story of faith in this book, he tells us about his journey to know and love Jesus and the Word of God.

Glasshouses take us back in time to an age forgotten, yet M.R. introduces us to many structures which are vibrant and in use in 2023. Many in society think that faith and church belong to a time gone by, yet M.R. shares of something that is vibrant and alive today. M.R. has a living faith that is rooted in the Bible and that is relevant and still in complete use today.

I met M.R. as he embarked on a project to encourage more people to engage with the Bible. He arrived at my office to discuss an idea, we had never met before and yet I knew that here was a man of integrity who wanted others to have what he has. He wanted others to grow in their understanding of the Bible by reading it regularly. He wanted others to grow in their knowledge of Jesus, as their Saviour. The Daily Bible Reading Guide, which M.R. subsequently produced, was a version of something we, at the Bible Society in Northern Ireland, were already doing. However, M.R.'s version had an altogether different reach than anything we produced. As M.R highlights later in this book, that project has had an impact beyond what any of us had hoped for, and many people have journeyed through the Bible as a result. The impact of this project continues, and we are so grateful to those brave first steps that M.R. took in popping into our office with an idea that day.

I commend M.R. for pursuing his professional passion for glasshouses and for sharing his personal faith here in these pages. It is my prayer that this book has an impact on you beyond an increased understanding of some unique Victorian architecture but provides the structure for you to grow in your own faith. Make the time to read beyond M.R.'s story to the story of Jesus – read the

Gospel of John and see how Jesus has come 'that we might have life and have it to the full'. (John 10: 10).

When you next stop to look at, or step inside a glasshouse, remember what it represents in you – a thing of beauty, something that needs to be protected, that needs to be looked after and something that is strong enough to stand up to the trials and storms of life and remain steadfast in its purpose.

Catherine Hillcox
General Secretary
Bible Society in Northern Ireland
February 2023

INTRODUCTION

"It is…no question of expediency or feeling whether we shall preserve the buildings of past times or not. We have no right whatever to touch them. They are not ours. They belong partly to those who built them, and partly to all the generations of mankind who are to follow us. The dead have still their right to them: that which they laboured for…we have no right to obliterate. What we have ourselves built, we are at liberty to throw down; but what other men gave their strength and wealth and life to accomplish, their right does not pass away with their death…'

—John Ruskin: *The Seven Lamps of Architecture* (1849)

Before we meaningfully commence, let us talk semantics. Historically, the words glasshouse, palm house, conservatory, greenhouse, hot house, peach house, orangery, glazed-lean-to or vineries are all largely interchangeable. These words will mean many things to many people, depending on existing use, function or the commonality of any given structure. However, throughout this book and for ease of reference, I will mainly be referring to these elegant structures as glasshouses, palm houses or conservatories.

The UK and Ireland has a glorious heritage of charming Victorian glasshouse structures some of which have, with sensitive and sympathetic restoration, withstood the rigorous tests of time. Whether in a public or a private setting, I found these celebrated buildings often exist in the most affluent and salubrious locations. Since this project commenced, I have been probing at the narratives inherent within these heritage structures, paying attention to their transformations, not only in terms of their structural restorations, but also in relation to their refined multi-functional end-use. This exploration has taken me on a privileged journey to many of the UK and Ireland's prominent botanical gardens, beautiful stately homes, historic castles, walled gardens and even an ambassador's private residence. All of which, you will agree, befit the magnificence of these structures.

Since the early days of the ancient Chinese and Roman Empires, we sought to protect fragile plants from harsh winter weather and to outwardly display prized exotic plant collections. The first greenhouses, orangeries and conservatories originated in the form of 'special shelters' designed in Europe to house orange and lemon trees and rare, precious species brought back during the great Age of Exploration. I read that there is evidence that Pompeiians were growing oranges behind mica windows before they had their 'run-in' with Mount Vesuvius, but it was from Italy that citrus trees and the aforementioned shelters that were constructed to house them, were brought northwards. Later, the Dutch would develop more sophisticated structures and the concept spread throughout Europe culminating in architectural splendour; Louis XIVs orangery at Versailles is a famous example.

Moving forward, Victorian-era glasshouse construction was largely established on the Victorian's fascination with observing the natural world and achieving connectivity with nature. It was to prove a triumph of art, design, construction and horticultural talent, over nature. Historically, glasshouses were only constructed for those wealthy enough to pay for the privilege. They were the ultimate stamp of wealth, which of course was diametrically opposed to the Victorian perception that one could be closer to God in a glasshouse.

Ownership of larger glasshouses or palm houses, especially those designed by the likes of Lanyon, Paxton or Burton, were glorified consumeristic and individualistic outward symbols of status, which demonstrated that one had succeeded in achieving society's materialistic success goals. Moreover, they were 'Celebrated beacons of an ability to explore and exploit foreign lands.'

Gradually, larger structures were designed and constructed to facilitate more sizeable plants collected by enthusiastic colonial botanists, such as tall Palms, which were a powerful symbol of Victorian exoticism. Transplanted to temperate climates, tropical palms could be domesticated in glasshouse structures and in some cases, vast collections could be rehoused in larger structures, such as the Great Palm House at Kew Gardens or The Crystal Palace London, both of which I will touch on later in this book.

Prior to the mid nineteenth century, ownership of a bespoke glasshouse filled with glamourous botanical plant life, was merely an aspiration for the vast majority of the population, as the horticultural hobbies enjoyed by wealthy romantic Victorians, were an intrinsic aspect of 19th century life. Window tax (on domestic properties) and glass tax (imposed by weight) ensured that even the most modest structure was completely unaffordable for the hoi polloi. The same applied to the global pool of rich exotic plant life from tropical and sub-tropical continents such as palms, hibiscus or orchids, with which one could fill a glass house. The penchant for Victorians to create their own bespoke, brightly coloured, paradisiacal 'tropical Eden' existed only for society's elite.

According to Landscape Architect, Maria E Iganatieva, "Gardenesque style was connected to the industrial revolution, geographical discoveries and the conquests of new lands by the British Empire. Victorian Gardens had always been based on Christian belief and philosophy that man was nearer to God in the garden (a reference to Eden and the Gethsemane gardens in

12

the Bible). For wealthy people, gardening was a source of agreeable domestic recreation and for the poor it was beneficial to physical, mental and spiritual well-being." Moreover, in the book Piety and Perversity: The Palms of Los Angeles, it highlighted that Victorians were mad about palms and it is to their invention of the greenhouse that we owe much of our palm legacy. These large structures built of cast iron, wrought iron and glass allowed the exotic flora of the world to grow and be seen throughout Europe and America – entire greenhouses were devoted to them. Evoking exotic climes, far off colonies and intrepid explorers, they were emblematic of Victorian aspirations, and their biblical associations stirred the pious Victorian soul.

In the early 19th century, glasshouse structures had always been the exclusive custom-built playthings of the aristocracy. However, new wealth generated by the industrial revolution, the repeal of glass tax (1845) and window tax (1851); alongside innovative technical advances in manufacturing, such as the availability of cast iron, were key factors that enabled social change.

'Around the turn of the 19th century, the availability of cast iron made possible stronger, higher, glass and steel structures allowing for a dazzling array of architecturally flamboyant, stylistic excesses to be achieved. In 1816 English horticulturalist J.C. Loudon discovered that a wrought iron sash bar, less brittle than cast iron and cheaper than wood, could be curved to construct large glass domes. This enabled a trend towards construction of large-scale public structures. It was also Loudon who championed 'ridge and furrow glazing' but as glazed structures increased in size, improvements in temperature control were also required.

There is something truly pleasurable and reassuring about visiting a European glasshouse during a crisp winter, consistently offering the type of warmth you would only expect from a continental climate such as Asia or South America. But it was the Dutch who pioneered the heating of larger glass houses, initially with the use of charcoal braziers. By the 1700's heating in hollow walls or flues which ran under the floor, enabled hot air or smoke to run the length of a building from a brick fire- place on one end, to a chimney located at the other end, thus providing necessary heat.

By the late 18th century, the British were providing plants with both heat and humidity by steaming them with perforated pipes laid under stone or rock, before steam gave way in the mid 1800's to hot water heat, which provided an efficient, evenly distributed heat. This of course was always complimented by the passive- solar- gain achieved directly from the sunlight via the thin curved glass.

To reduce the risk of condensation, which is a major factor in metal corrosion, glasshouse structures also require a means for heat and humidity to escape and this was achieved via ventilation systems. Ventilation can take any number of forms. For instance, these can be traditional low level manually openable vents or windows, or higher level 'skylight' vents, which can be openable via a traditional metal crank or a pulley system. Today a mechanical, electrical or computerised system can also provide alternate options for ventilation but know that such a recommendation may not be the preference of the puritan from a conservation, restoration or a heritage perspective.

As the price of glass plummeted, so demand for glasshouses increased, as did the supply, all of which provided an opportunity for aspiration to become a realisation for many. However, today, anyone restoring glass houses will likely replace damaged single panes with tempered or toughened glass, especially overhead and particularly in a public setting. Traditionally single paned glazing such as crown spun (possibly green tinted) glass would have been the pane of choice.

Today, given health and safety risk, either toughened, double glazed or 4mm 'agricultural' panes are recommended by conservation professionals, if there are no original panes remaining. It depends on a number of factors such as aesthetics, budget or end-use.

In my experience the combination of structure and setting only serves to enhance the reverential and spiritual atmosphere that comes from standing within something so powerful. It brings with it a drama, like standing beneath some glazed proscenium. In terms of end-use, I discovered that glass houses aren't always practical structures that exist solely to house botany or horticulture. Multi-functional in the extreme they can also serve as restaurants or coffee houses, as educational facilities used by schools and communities, or as venues for formal corporate happenings, informal functions, religious and non-religious ceremonies, key milestone celebrations, musical events and seasonal festivities. Throughout this book I will gently highlight how a glasshouse is for me, the perfect example of perpetual architectural excellence.

CHAPTER 1:
IN THE BEGINNING...

The Palm House, Belfast (1839-1840)

Belfast Bitter
(this poem may not be about beer)

There's no bitter like Belfast bitter
No better bitter
Brewed
No bitterer bitter
Begot

Belfast bitter begins Barely after birth Born and...
Boom! We're bitter

Beginning to back one band
Or another band
Of boyos and bogeymen
Out to bend our brains

Bringing
Bickering
Bruising, blitzing and battering
Between bothers
Brothers!

Bitterness
Belfast bitterness
Burning beneath the surface
Brought back by
Banter
Bout borders

Battles, bullets
Bombings
Brexit!
It was bad before...
But Brexit!?!
Bye bye balance
Hello bonanza of backwardness
And backwoodsmen from both sides
Banging on
Bumbling and mumbling their bigotry

Bitter Belfast bitter
Old buddy
Always been between us
Beyond bankrupt now
Bacteria blooming below
Biting at us
Brazen
Going berserk
Bad, bad
Blowing away
The bold and the benevolent and the bright
Belfast bitter is,
Baffling.

By Jim Deeds

BELFAST EUROPA HOTEL HAS HISTORICALLY and infamously been regarded as the most bombed hotel in Europe, if not the world, having been bombed a reported thirty-three times between 1970 and 1994. Both a landmark and a symbol of investment, it became an easy target during 'The Troubles' with its windows being blown out seemingly on a monthly basis.

In fact, it was once highlighted in a Belfast Telegraph newspaper article that there was a standing order with a warehouse that had every pane of glass duplicated or triplicated so they could be immediately replaced, but then the windows got blown out so many times that the steel window-frames got warped.

Ironically, located less than one mile away from this dark chaos was the veritable peace and tranquility of Belfast's iconic Botanic Gardens. And situated within its manicured grounds was another much-loved local landmark, The Belfast Palm House, which was constructed in 1839-1840. It was nothing short of a miracle that this stunning 19th Century Grade-A listed, Victorian curvilinear glasshouse structure, with circa 3,000 panes of single-paned glass, remained completely intact and unharmed throughout the whole of Belfast's brutal 'Troubles'. Today it sparkles proudly as one of the oldest surviving examples of a Victorian curvilinear glass house in the world.

Located at the north end of the Botanic Gardens, The Palm House is broadly orientated along an east to west axis and comprises of three separate environments. An 11.4-metre-high central ogival dome is flanked by two 22-metre-long, lower linear wings, all of which are situated on one level. The central dome or drum is formed by two semi-circular halves at the front and rear, connected by an elongated central section. The two linear wings are designed as lean-tos to two tall masonry spine walls.

This masonry wall exists in contrast to beautiful sandstone plinths, steps, and sill details, which are visible as you access the building at its frontage.

The West wing (pointing towards West Belfast as you look at it), which is the 'cool' wing, is home to plants such as begonia, fuchsia, geraniums alongside ever changing, sensual colourful displays. The East wing (pointing towards east Belfast as you look at it) is the 'hot' or 'tropical' wing, and it houses colourful bromeliads and heavily scented frangipani, alongside exotic plants such as the striking bird of paradise, which thrives on warmth and full sun. The central dome is home to ferns, fronds and, of course, palms, helping to create a mini jungle environment.

Its superstructure consists of an ornate framework of elegant slim cast and wrought iron columns, beams and curvilinear wrought iron ribs made of rectangular rolled sections that run radially through the dome. The principal (larger) ribs have within them four smaller ribs each measuring 38mm and these metal ribs are tied together with small 10mm diameter horizontal rods. Such symmetry creates a beautiful and constant cruciformity, which is a joy to behold, as you stand inside on the original existing terrazzo floor and look upwards through the glass toward the heavens.

The mullions and glazing bars are now mainly of replica mild steel, as opposed to original wrought iron. These support fix, clear over-lapping, sheet-glass panes, which enables ventilation to trickle into the glasshouse. These panes sit on the external side of the supports and are supported along their left and right sides only, where these days a modern mastic secures the curved glass to the ribs, instead of traditional putty bedding. The existing glazing is currently 3mm thick clear glass and not crown spun or traditional, green-tinted glass. It was likely added as part of refurbishment works carried out during the 1980s.

Every one of the aforementioned 3,000 sheets of curved glass in the Belfast Palm House provides protection and shelter for its impressive collection of plants and species. The combination of passive solar gain, the sun's energy and water enable photosynthesis to occur, like three Knights of St. Columbanus quietly going about their charitable business within their local community, selflessly serving those in need by helping the botany to flourish and the precious plant life to grow.

Author Eileen McCracken once wrote – "From the beginning of the nineteenth century Belfast men had dreams of a Botanic Garden for their town and plans for a Botanic Garden finally crystallised in 1827". Moving forward, the foundation stone of the Belfast Palm House was laid on 22nd June 1839 by the Marquis of Donegal at a ceremony 'at which no intoxicating drink was provided'. Then, as in now, this crown-jewel of horticultural Victoriana exists as an oasis in our city; a demonstrable continuity that embraces the darkness of our past and the light of our present and future.

Considered to be one of Belfast's most Iconic buildings, the Palm House was built to designs of Belfast based architect Sir Charles Lanyon. By profession, Sir Charles Lanyon was first and foremost an architect, but he was also a civil engineer and a well-known public figure having been a member of parliament in 1866. I read an on-line article which stated, "When the architect Charles Lanyon was campaigning to hold his seat as a conservative MP for Belfast in 1869, he fatally declared that 'I may say that the large increase in the constituency of Belfast is owing to my exertions"—and he was immediately lampooned as a begetter of numerous illegitimate children. However, far more legitimate are the numerous existing examples of built heritage that he left for us to enjoy.

Take a tour of Belfast today and you will observe many wonderful and influential heritage structures designed by Lanyon. Situated behind the Palm House and constructed in 1849, witness the grandeur of Queens University, with its aptly named, The Lanyon Building. Another example is the stunning Sinclair Seamen's Presbyterian Church, which was designed by Lanyon in 1856. The Belfast Custom House, which was designed in 1857, is now used for free concerts and public events; or the Crumlin Road Courthouse and Gaol, which were both designed from 1846-1850. Whilst the Gaol was restored and transformed into a popular tourist attraction, it is proposed that one day the Courthouse might be sympathetically preserved and restored to become an event space and a luxurious hotel.

Lanyon also designed many other less prominent public buildings in and around Belfast City Centre. The Marks and Spencer building in Donegall Square North and Queens Bridge, which owes to Lanyon's earlier talent as a civil engineer, are two examples which exist today. Moreover, it was during his time as Provincial Deputy Grand Master of the County Antrim Freemasons, that he enthusiastically commenced a project to design a Masonic Hall, in Corn Market on the corner of Ann Street in Belfast city centre. This was apparently one of the last projects undertaken by Lanyon.

Whilst Sir Charles Lanyon was responsible for the design of the Palm House, the cast iron frames and the actual construction were completed by celebrated ironmaster, Richard Turner of the Hammersmith Works of Ballsbridge, Dublin. The Palm House in Belfast may have been Turner's first known work, but he is also famous for carrying out some other high-profile commissions throughout Ireland and Britain. The National Botanic Gardens, inin

Glasnevin Dublin, the home of The Great Palm House of Glasnevin, is a wonderful example of his talents but his most spectacular work to survive is The Great Palm House at Kew Gardens in London.

In Fiona Grant's wonderfully snappy book, 'Glass Houses', she stated, the curvilinear glasshouses built by Irishman Richard Turner in the botanic gardens of Belfast in 1840, were effectively prototypes of the world- famous Great Palm House structure at Kew Gardens in London; with Turner's works at Kew only commencing several years later in 1844, before subsequent completion in 1848. Eileen McCracken echoed these sentiments when she said, 'The most striking and interesting feature of Belfast Botanic Gardens is the Palm House, with its two wings flanking a bold elliptical dome. One cannot but applaud the determination of the men who directed the garden in its early days and who, without outside financial help, built a curvilinear glass house before Kew or Glasnevin had one. And it was most likely a source of satisfaction to them that when Kew and Glasnevin put up their Palm Houses, they both chose the contractor who had built the wings of the Belfast house.'

However, in the spirit of truth, it cannot be glossed over that whilst works to Belfast's Palm House linear east and west wings successfully completed in 1839-1840, its existing central ogival dome built by Young & Co of Edinburgh, was the result of a design change that was only installed in 1853, some five years after the full completion of The Great Palm House at Kew. Although the scale differs considerably, conversely it is therefore also possible that Belfast Palm House's central dome was influenced by the design of the Great Palm House at Kew.

In terms of dimension, the final design of the Belfast Palm House's central elliptical dome measured at 46 foot high. The clue is in the title, but Palm Houses were designed to house palm trees. Palm trees have been described as tall, thin pillars of towering opulence and utterly ubiquitous; and given that palm trees grew in popularity during the Victorian era, there was a greater requirement for significantly larger and higher glass house structures. Such buildings would enable palms to flourish in environments that would otherwise be inhospitable. In an article entitled, Piety, Perversity and Palms its states, 'Palm trees encapsulated the Victorian ideals of exploration and conquest, enabling lovers of tropical species to fall under the embellished foreign allure of the palm tree.'

Belfast was once unenviably, albeit understandably, included alongside Beirut, Baghdad, and Bosnia as one of the four Bs on earth you should want to avoid at all costs. That said, Belfast as a culturally curious attraction, is presently regarded and recommended by Lonely Planet as, one of the most popular, must-visit tourist destinations on the planet. Regeneration in all its forms is still ongoing but Belfast, as complex as its history is, has been well and truly transformed by comparison. Restored, renewed, and refreshed it is reborn, no longer appearing to live in a state of outward darkness. On the contrary, much like the botany within its Palm House, everything exposed by the light becomes visible and everything that is illuminated becomes a light - and it is visibly flourishing.

IN THE EARLY DAYS OF THE TROUBLES, my grandparents were displaced from their family home in east Belfast, and subsequently rehoused by the Northern Ireland Housing Executive in a purpose-built council estate, which saw them polarised to the outskirts of west Belfast. This new estate would be a large-scale new build, phased housing development, that would quickly become one of the 'hotbeds' of the Northern Ireland troubles, as social exclusion, gross inequality and unfairness would blight the lives of many of the families who were forced to dwell there.

Having been born in a humble one-bedroomed, pebble dashed, new build council flat, a flat which my pregnant mother apparently squatted in before being allocated it, a couple of years later, we progressed to the nose-bleed heights of a three-bedroom pebble dashed council house, located on the other side of the very same estate. It is fair to say that my life commenced in a stigmatised environment and one which boasted a truly abysmal infrastructure, at that time.

In terms of my earliest childhood memories, I recall one evening when there was a knock on the external door of our first floor flat. I couldn't have been any more than three years of age at the time, but it is a memory that has stuck with me ever since. As I toddled to the letterbox I peered out from the inside and enquired, 'Is that you Uncle Rory?' To which the person on the other side of the door, replied with a muffled 'yes'. My mother hearing this opened the door only to find two masked men armed with guns, barging their way into the flat. Distressed she grabbed my younger brother and I and threw us behind our old seventies-style tanned leather sofa with its green and yellow patterned soft, foam seating.

A row broke out with my father who was there all along and there was a lot of coarse Belfast bellowing but I recall my mother's quick thinking. I recollect looking up from behind the sofa, witnessing her scream for help from the window of our first floor flat, yelling 'quick the British army are coming, they are outside!' At which point the fracas suddenly stopped and the two men made haste out the open door, down the grey concrete stairs, before turning right onto an existing alley way to make their escape. My father gave immediate chase. I know this because my mother was momentarily distracted by my younger brother and this enabled me to run after my father and witness the two assailants running away, making aggressive, sinister threats as they 'took to their heels'. When this scenario was later discussed, the two men in question were described as young and inexperienced teenage paramilitary members, which is probably just as well.

Without irony, the night-time clatter of metal bin-lids hitting the roads and pathways - used by women to raise the alarm when British soldiers were genuinely entering the vicinity - became an accepted social norm. The sight of armoured jeeps patrolling the streets or Saracens aggressively ramming through barriers in the form of burnt-out cars was de rigueur. For the uninitiated, a Saracen was a form of tank. Yes, every other day there were tanks and 'pop-up' jeeps, with armed soldiers pointing loaded rifles, as they drove past my mother's kitchen window, and this gradually became somewhat normalised.

That said, something else that was normalised at that time was the existence of God. Having been born into a Catholic family an abiding memory I have is of my mother reading a large A4 sized children's Bible to me before bedtime. It was full of colourful pictures. And one image that stayed with me most was of a red muscly, horned Satan sat atop of a mountain tempting a long haired, bearded Jesus to throw himself down from the pinnacle: before also tempting him by offering all the kingdoms of the world.

Looking back at that verse, which was taken from the Gospel of Matthew 4: 1-11. It is safe to say that the Christian seed had been planted in me early on. But little did I know then as a five-year-old boy, that I would have meaningful encounters with both of the aforementioned characters, later in life.

Moving forward, our humble off-white house was located on an elevated site at the top of a short, two-way vehicular access tarmacadam road. I believe for a period we lived in a house that had no paint on the walls and no carpet on the floor and when we did get carpet, we had no underlay. All of which would have been pretty grim for my parents. From my mother's kitchen window, you had an uninterrupted view, downhill onto a main road and right across an expansive green field. All the way to the other side of a dreary estate that comprised of grey block work and off-white pebble dashed elevations.

I recall one grey, damp autumn afternoon staring out of my mother's kitchen window. I couldn't have been any more than four or five years of age at the time. Suddenly, a car came speeding up the aforementioned hill, before sensationally skidding right onto an existing large turning head before dramatically screeching to a halt. As both back doors flung open, two masked men suddenly jumped from the back of the car and started randomly firing bullets from machine guns for a few seconds against the gable wall of an existing house, before jumping back into the car and speeding off down the hill again and out of sight.

This type of occurrence probably grew to be unremarkable in certain parts of Northern Ireland, as 'The Troubles' spiraled out of control. With both parents unemployed we could ill-afford to exist on anything other than different potato dishes for more than a year and this was only because we would receive large sacks of potatoes and a supply of dairy products that were 'charitably delivered' by an uncle, who happened to work for a popular purveyor of agricultural foods at that time.

However, I can say with confidence that none of this negatively impacted on me or my enjoyment of my early childhood years because, put simply, I was too young to know what exactly was going on. Although I do occasionally shudder to think what path my life might have taken had I been born into that environment ten years earlier; and I praise the Lord for that.

Regardless of what was happening at a societal level, I can say with confidence that I was blessed to have been born within the same locality as my grandparents and our large extended family that comprised of eight uncles and two aunties, all of whom I loved dearly. There was never much money in circulation at that time, but being the first grandchild born into such a large extended family brought a lot of love, affection and attention my way, along with much fun and laughter.

I am deviating for a moment, but the design of the houses in the estate were very generic. So, as you would imagine, my grandparent's house was very similar in design to our own home. It was a standard, modest three-bedroom, two receptions end terrace, with a flat roof canopy and timber cladding over the front door. It was literally the last property in the estate. So, to its left and straight ahead, you had views of green grass, with hills and trees in the distance. This property incredibly managed to house all of the aforementioned family members. To do this successfully a clever configuration of bunk beds, double beds and needs-must sleeping arrangements were employed. Yet, that house was also the venue for some sensational family parties, where generations would happily gather together like sardines in a tin, to celebrate my grandmother's birthday, which fell poignantly on Halloween.

As you would assume, the occasion often required fancy dress, when black bin liners and green face paint were used innovatively. But the occasion was even more renowned for my grandfather's 'Home Brew' and my grandmother's assembly line of delicious homemade, warm clove-kissed apple tarts, pizzas, and savoury mincemeat pies, served hot from the oven. Such sustenance was in constant supply to keep guests well fed, and to soak up the constant stream of alcohol that flowed like a spring throughout the night. Something else that were homemade, were the large glass bowls filled with delicious fresh-fruit punch that were spiked with an explosive array of alcoholic spirits, the strength of which was cleverly masked beneath a vast assortment of mixed fresh fruits.

These would sit comfortably beside a variety of canapés such as that staple seventies delight, cheese, pineapple, and pickled onions on a stick. In later years I would eventually sample that punch and I can testify first-hand to the power of its devious kick! My abiding hazy memory of those wonderful parties was the constant upbeat din of high-pitched conversation, laughter and the clinking of glasses and clunking of cans. With the front door left unlocked, well-loved neighbours would continuously come and go throughout the night to join in on the popular celebration. And all through a pea-soup-fog supplied by a mix of Park Drive, John Players and Majors cigarettes that could sting the eyes.

It was a time of light-hearted enjoyment and escapism for all concerned, where the only fireworks and rockets were those procured and set off by my uncle from the muddy back garden, as they fizzed, whistled and crackled, lighting up the cold, eerie pitch black, Halloween night sky. As the first-born grandchild, more than forty grandchildren and great grandchildren would follow. But I can say with great confidence that my grandparents were special to me. My grandfather was a man of faith. He was a clever, talented man who taught me how to play chess. When physically fit, he would work on personal projects. One of which included the construction of a small rowing boat, from scratch, which he worked on in his front garden. However, one of my favourite memories was of my grandmother and I spending simple quality time alone, at Belfast's Anderson and McCauley's department store, enjoying tea and scones together.

With both since gone, the world is undoubtedly, a poorer place. Sentimentality aside, as you would imagine, my parents were always desperate to leave the troubled toxic, risk filled milieu that existed at that location during that era. And by the time I had turned eight years of age, they had somehow managed to achieve their aspiration. They purchased a lovely, modest three bedroom, two and a half storey, traditional Belfast-red-brick property in popular south Belfast. The property was situated in a bustling yet pleasant, leafy location, where the pace of life was undoubtedly slower, quieter and a tad more balanced (if anywhere in Northern Ireland could be described as balanced at that time).

There were all kinds of shops and a wonderful infrastructure. It even had an Art Deco cinema right at the bottom of my street. There were youth facilities alongside dedicated, well maintained football pitches, playing fields and public parks. There were bars and eateries and several churches, including a selection of differing non-Catholic Christian denominations – something I knew absolutely zero about at that time. It was a buzzing hub of activity and a veritable breath of fresh air given the dramatic change of atmosphere. I loved it so much. I started a new school, joined a football team and a Gaelic team. I made new friends, one of whom was a fellow Arsenal fan (a relative rarity in Belfast in the nineteen eighties) who had ironically also started out life in the west of the city. It was a new beginning, and in a way, our lives would be transformed.

The atmosphere was immediately less intense and, put simply, the area had everything we would need and more, to live happily. That said, although we appeared to have escaped from the worst of Belfast's archetypal 'troubles' and although our lives appeared to be on the upward trajectory, this house move would unfortunately see the overt commencement of my family's very own dark troubles.

CHAPTER 2:
GENERATIONAL CURSES

Ballywalter Park, Ballywalter (1846-1852)

LOCATED ON THE EASTERN SHORES OF THE ARDS peninsula is Ballywalter Park, and the private stately home of Lord and Lady Dunleath, built in 1846 by Lord Andrew Mulholland (the first Baron Dunleath). This Grade-A Listed Georgian structure, was designed in the Italiante Palazzo style by Sir Charles Lanyon with work completed in 1852. The structure has been in their family for more than 170 years.

By 1863, Lanyon had returned to add what would become a historic conservatory and the Gentleman's Wing to the north-west corner; while in 1902 the architect, W J Fennell, added the Bachelor's Wing to provide accommodation for visiting cricketers. The Lanyon designed conservatory is glorious, but it wasn't until 2009 that a challenging restoration project was successfully completed.

'The work to the conservatory involved restoration of the entire glass roof, including the elegant cast- and wrought-iron dome, by a specialist metalwork company in Bradford. Other major aspects of the work included repairs to the intricate ashlar sandstone facades with their Corinthian columns and detailed cornices, refurbishment of the existing sash windows and an exact replica of the elaborately bordered polychromatic tile floor, replacing the severely damaged original'.

In her personal blog Lady Dunleath commented, 'we have this wonderful conservatory which we restored 2008-2009. I walk out through it every day on my way to the Walled Garden. This was designed by Charles Lanyon and constructed by Turner, just like the

Palm House in Belfast. We had been told that he designed ours before his Belfast effort of 1840, but I don't think that is possible because the Mulhollands did not buy this house until 1846. Still, I was keen to see the Palm House as there were bound to be interesting similarities.'

Similarities indeed. Externally, the eye will instantly be drawn towards the Ballywalter conservatory's beautifully impressive, ribbed, glazed dome, which has been immaculately restored. However, its low-level stone steps, impeccable external stonework and low-level sills certainly echo the design of Belfast's Palm House. Step over the threshold through its timber doors and witness tiled floors, a low-level heating system, restored- cranked ventilation and cast-iron columns and you will agree that microcosmic comparisons are evident.

It was a miserable, cold, and wet winters day in 2018 when I first arrived at Ballywalter Park. My drive had seen torrential rain follow me all the way from Belfast, but the grim weather paled in significance when I first caught sight of the magnificence that is

Ballywalter House. Having driven slowly along the gravel drive I arrived at a commanding porte cochere where I was warmly greeted at the door by Lady Dunleath. Once over the threshold, I was guided through the grand hallway, where I gazed in awe as an imposing oil painting of the Archangel Michael stared down on me from the large lime plastered wall. In a mere moment, we were joined by Lord Dunleath, and we instantly took to chatting about the structure, its history, its restoration projects, and its stunning surrounding environs. At this point, I was also invited to join them for a cup of black coffee and to help polish off the remainder of the previous nights delicious home-made tart-tatin, which was filled with the home grown produce from Lady Dunleath's very own walled garden.

Speaking with Lady Dunleath it was clear that home grown food and a health-conscious lifestyle was very much on her radar. I read that she had once eloquently stated that a 'Walled Garden was the supermarket of the 18th century'. Many of her projects involve and rely on produce grown within her walled garden, which aligns with her ethos to use produce from the Estate. The Walled Garden successfully supplies seasonal fruit and vegetables all year round. From potatoes, asparagus or 'nature's spears' and beetroot, to strawberries, quince, and apples. Lady Dunleath not only supplies Ballywalter Park, but is also known to supply one of Belfast's most popular Michelin Star restaurants with her home grown produce. Such is the quality.

Surrounded by 30 acres of pleasure grounds and situated within the walled demesne of some 270 acres, Ballywalter Park also comprises of beautiful woodland, scenic walkways, manicured lawns and rolling pastures. Its superb setting means the estate is now in demand as a film location and as a corporate venue for events, tours, and previously for food ventures such as their wonderfully biblical-evoking Loaves & Fishes Food Fair, which celebrated locally produced bread and fish during the annual Sea

Food Week. Much of what is grown is done so in the existing glasshouses. The glasshouses within the walled garden comprise of a lean-to glazing system within timber frames but unfortunately due to damage caused by 'Storm Ali' in 2018, the proposed Paradise Gardening Club was postponed until winter 2019. The storm did its best to demolish the rare 18th century glasshouses but plans for a proposed restoration project were already ongoing, with suitable craftsmen all but poised to commence works around the time of my visit.

Throughout my explorative research, I discovered a vast array of differing local glasshouses. For example, the Walled Garden at Glenarm Castle in Larne is one of Ireland's oldest walled gardens. It was originally developed to supply the Castle with fruit and vegetables, but the garden now blooms richly with vibrant flowers and herbaceous plants particularly throughout May to September. Flowers are not the only thing on display within the walled garden for today the garden and its impressive glass house are utilised in several diverse ways.

Enjoy art exhibitions or a relaxing afternoon tea, or a weather dependent picnic within a glorious setting. It has been the venue for an educational maths trail for primary school children. It has been the location for charitable musical events, where talented local traditional musicians can entertain guests, with their good works, helping to raise money for local foodbanks. There are historic, story-telling evenings exploring the existing linkage between Scots and Irish in Larne and the Glens of Antrim.

Fascinatingly, the castle and its surrounding environs has been the chosen venue for Ireland's premier Christian youth event – Summer Madness - by offering young people from all backgrounds, a long weekend of exciting faith building encounters with Christian bands, workshops, and activities.

It is an opportunity for the hundreds of teens in attendance to learn more about their faith by exploring God's Word and spending time with young like-minded individuals.

When mentioning links between Scotland and Northern Ireland, it would be slipshod of me to pass up the opportunity to briefly highlight a rather different glasshouse that I once visited in Wales. It was during this exploration that I discovered that not every glasshouse was indeed constructed of glass. Take the wonderful Roath Park Conservatory in Cardiff for example. The Conservatory was built on the site of two historic greenhouses - the Chrysanthemum House and the smaller Cactus House. It was also known as the New Plant House and the Tropical House. In the initial planting scheme, there was to be a pond and planting beds in the middle and staging all around the perimeter to hold a collection of tropical pot plants. The roof and staging were to be supported by purlins which were to be the supports for rampant climbers and vines.

After consideration, this was deemed too expensive and too labour-intensive, and an alternative plan was drawn up. In the revised plan there was to be a temperate glasshouse (55 degree winter night temperatures), with a fully landscaped interior including a larger pond and a waterfall. It would be mostly stocked with plants from the castle nursery, and it could be operated by a single person. It is thought to have been opened in the summer of 1975. In 1989 the original glass windows were replaced with cheaper triple polycarbonate. This material was also considered safer than the glass windows, which were subject to regular breakages.

The present-day conservatory, which measures a humble 43m x 19.5m excluding the foyer, is the focal point for the Botanic Garden and fulfills the educational role originally envisaged for the aquarium. It is heated and contains many unusual species of plants and trees. There is also a large fishpond, containing carp and turtles. Whilst it is not the 'lowliest potting shed' it does lack the quality and scale of its more aesthetically pleasing UK counterparts. Yet, that does not detract from the fact that it successfully achieves its overarching purpose as the home of a diverse range of botany, fish and as an educational hub. Therefore, in terms of functionality and versatility, I can say with confidence that it performs on par with any other macrocosmic glasshouse structures that I visited. It achieves this wonderfully well, and what's equally impressive is that it is only moments away from the stunning Scott Memorial Lighthouse and Clocktower, which was erected on the breathtaking Roath Park Lake. The Lighthouse's connection with Cardiff is that the famous Polar Explorer, Captain Scott (of Scott and Amundson fame) and his companions sailed from Cardiff in the Terra Nova in 1910. The structure commemorates Sir Robert Falcon Scott who lost his life in 1912 having embarked upon his own personal explorative journey.

Living in a South Belfast suburb on and off for more than twenty years, has given me great access to several local glass houses and conservatories of differing levels of scale, scope, and complexity. All are located within a reasonable distance and timeframe from my home; and each has their own particular story to tell. Take, for instance, the secluded Tyrella House, which is a listed luxury Georgian house located in the heart of picturesque County Down. It is a fine 18th century structure surrounded by glorious, wooded parkland and boasts access to a private beach just a short stroll away. Yet, abutting this impressive period house is a splendid original lean-to glass house, which has been sensitively refurbished and sympathetically restored by its talented former engineer owner, who I discovered was also a dab-hand when it came to joinery. With archetypal single glazed panes, timber frames and traditional crank and pulley ventilation system, this romantic little structure, lends itself tremendously for private formal or informal dining parties alike, during most seasons. My visit was random and impromptu. I happened to be in the vicinity and took advantage of the opportunity by pulling my car into their drive to introduce myself and to ask if I could inspect the structure in question. The owner could have said, 'sorry, too short notice, doesn't suit.' But he didn't. He trusted what was happening and operated in the spirit of helpfulness. The owner gave me his time and he did so willingly. It was during that inspection that the owner confirmed he was in poor health. So, my instantaneous reaction was to ask if he 'would mind if my wife and I prayed for him that evening'. He gave an unexpected smile and said he wouldn't mind, and he thanked me for my help.

This moment made me recall the second letter of St Paul to the Corinthians that states, 'Remember how generous the Lord Jesus was: he was rich but became poor for your sake: to make you rich out of his poverty. This does not mean that to give relief to others you ought to make life difficult for yourselves: it is a question of balancing what happens to be your surplus now against their present need, and one day they may have something to spare that will supply your own need. That is how we strike a balance: as scripture says.

Some fifteen minutes away from Tyrella and located within the historic village of Saintfield is the inspirational Rowallane Gardens. With its established and mature tree collection one can witness seasonal change in all its glory, with the rich palettes of colour creating transformation throughout any given month. Rowallane Gardens is a National Trust property, which is noted for its extensive collection of azaleas and rhododendrons.

It also boasts a period estate house, which doubles up as the National Trust NI's headquarters for Northern Ireland. This house exists within some 50 acres of walled garden, featuring a natural Rock Garden, wildflower meadows, a Farmland Walk (taking in the summit of Trio Hill) and a Woodland Walk, as well as a tea-room in the old farm stables, which features an impressive belltower. Yet, it was to a small generic glass house structure to which I was particularly drawn.

Abutting a stone cottage used for pottery classes is a modest timber and glass lean-to that is often used as a break-out space by those attending the aforementioned classes. Unlocked, it is also used by random passers- by, as a spot in which to take shelter when the weather turns inclement, which it often does. There is no pomp or ceremony with this relaxation space. Take a seat on its generic Ikea garden furniture to enjoy a coffee, whilst looking out through its imperfect glazing to take in the impressive plant and shrub collection planted within the picturesque walled garden. People come and go throughout the day and that's what I love about this little unit. It's multi-functionality. It is 'fit for purpose' on several levels and that's what makes its end-use so diverse, flexible and adaptable.

Situated a fifteen-minute drive from Rowallane is Montalto Estate, which is nestled in the hamlet of Spa, in the heart of County Down. Montalto, is a privately-owned demesne which dates to the early 1600s.

No longer a family home, the estate's listed 19th-century threshing mill has been converted and it opens as The Carriage Rooms at Montalto. This is a high-end, unique wedding venue, and a popular element of these rooms is its stunning walled garden, with its pristine, newly constructed, glasshouse. This popular glazed structure is not only used to grow flowers and botany but has become a focal point for wedding photographs.

Another somewhat local glasshouse I found hidden away in the Orchard County, in County Armagh. Located within the Armagh Palace Demesne and obscured behind a Bishops Palace and a deconsecrated Primates Chapel is a truly hidden gem. With my wife hailing from a nearby County, I had the privilege of being able to walk through that glasshouse on several occasions. In doing so I would almost always take a moment to stand beneath its curved glazing, often enjoying evidence of seasonal change or witnessing grey squirrels dashing up the established mature trees close by. In doing so I could appreciate its sense of history and value, its structural robustness but above else, I loved its multi-functional capabilities.

Having undergone a minor restoration, which involved replacement of the damaged single panes, repointing its stonework with a lime-mortar, making good its manually operated ventilation shutters and its subsequent redecoration. The structure would quickly become an outdoor classroom for primary school children with its sinks and sandpits. It also had vines successfully growing up its internal stone wall, which bore red grapes, albeit inedible ones. The structure would later become the venue for 'Dining Under the Stars'. This popular event was run by the patrons of the superb restaurant, The Moody Boar, which at that time, was located within the Demense's historic stables.

MY MOTHER WAS A BEAUTIFUL YOUNG WOMAN who had a very difficult upbringing. In the early nineteen sixties she had half a lung removed in an operation when she was twelve. This left her to battle with respiratory issues for the rest of her life. She was then sent a couple of years later to live away from her family home to help look after a sick elderly aunt. When she was allowed to return to the family fold, she was encouraged to leave school early to help my grandmother to look after and help raise her ten siblings, all of which must have been very challenging for a young teen. As confused as my mother could be, looking back she was put simply, someone who was very untidily scrambling around searching for answers to life's questions. She had a bubbly, curious, fun filled and mischievous personality and is the type of character who would have lit up any lecture hall or university campus, if she had the opportunity to attend. She was and is a genuine people person with a very loving and caring nature and she was and is a very affectionate mother, albeit a flawed one. Yet, throughout her life there are many instances when people will testify to her operating in the spirit of helpfulness and kindness. Today, as a woman of faith, who has long since made her peace with God, she is loved by many people. Especially her two grandchildren.

She was, however, understandably very troubled. Her difficult life experiences meant that she had to live with a lot of pain and turmoil and sometimes, that meant our home life was very problematic. There were times when her pain manifested as suspicion and insecurity in our household. I recall one warm summers day I came home from playing football to find my mother frantically taping pages she had ripped out of a jotter, around the perimeter of our living room walls. She had found a book belonging to my father with writing in it, writing which had her convinced that my father was having an affair. When he came home a screaming match ensued about his would-be affair with a lady called Clare Morris. However, it transpired the wording was apparently nothing more than his cringe-worthy attempt at writing poetry. Poetry about his time spent fishing with friends in the Mayo town of... Claremorris.

Not long after this incident, I arrived home one afternoon to find my mother wailing. She was on her knees in the middle of the kitchen floor, surrounded by what looked like every piece of crockery that we had previously owned, shattered all around her. As I crunched across the kitchen floor, I crouched down to give her a hug, but it was clear at that moment that the crockery wasn't the only thing that might be irreparably damaged.

There were times I wondered if my mother found her pain so hard to bear, that she didn't want to be here on this earth anymore. It certainly seemed that way to me at certain points, and as her son, that was very difficult to come to terms with. I wanted her to be well, to be present and happy in her life. I needed her to be my mother, in as much as she was capable of being. I often wondered, what was the root cause of this sadness?

She had many experiences in her time (we all have) that left her with trauma and confusion. I believe she spent a lot of time searching for enlightenment. For instance, when she wasn't getting those answers from the church, the rosary or prayer life, she might lapse by turning to alternative practices, that might have done her more harm than good. I recall she brought a crystal ball home, housed in a velvet purple draw string bag. This aligned well with the set of tarot cards she already owned, and tea leaf and palm readings she would occasionally do. To me, it seemed she was turning towards a direction, that even at nine years of age, deeply worried me. I was unfamiliar yet wary of these types of practices, and I certainly didn't feel it was the right way for her to find the strength and peace she so desperately needed.

Looking back, it was incredibly risk filled to use or even own such mysterious tools. In fact, from a spiritual perspective, it is safe to assume that by dabbling in such dark arts one could easily have opened up channels for all sorts of unwanted demonic spirits or generational curses.

That said, a number of months later, during the hot and bright summer days of nineteen eighty-four, the personal darkness would continue. Having spent the morning playing football with my friends in the sunshine, I came home one afternoon to find my mother accompanied by two strangers, who were helping her to load up a dented blue van with black-bin-bags filled with some of our personal belongings. It was at this point that my mother announced that she was leaving my father and that my brother and I would be leaving too.

I can say with confidence that this latest upheaval affected me very badly. Even with everything else that was happening, I was beyond happy in our South Belfast property, with my school and with my small circle of friends. My life wasn't complex. It comprised of playing a lot of football, buying Panini football stickers and going to the cinema most Saturdays with my friends to enjoy a matinee, but my brief taste of childhood joy was about to be stolen. For via a stint at my grandparent's house, we would move to a random, pokey summer residence situated by the County Down coast, for another supposed new beginning. In reality, my parents' separation would be the commencement of yet another phase of misery for all concerned.

CHAPTER 3:
SNAKES AND LADDERS

The Great Palm House, Glasnevin, Dublin (1883-1884)

"And there is so much glass, panes, and panes of it, flat and curved, all opaque with mist. It is one of the most ridiculous and gorgeous buildings we have ever been inside, if building is a word for such a light and delicate structure. Somewhere the chill sun of winter begins to shine and the drenched air glows and turns a turbid gold. We think of the people, grave frock-coated gentlemen, dundrearied, elaborately moustached, who designed and put up this perfectly calibrated, utterly mad caprice, this gay gazebo. Who says the Victorians were dull?"

—John Banville, *The Palm House* (2016)

EVERYONE SEEMS TO REMEMBER where they were when the 9/11 strikes happened in 2001 and I am no different. I was stood in the tiled lobby of the Civic Offices of Dublin City Council on the first day of my university placement, watching the whole bizarre scenario unfold on a large fifty-five-inch black plasma TV. In stark contrast to being in New York at that time, being in a vibrant Dublin from September 2001-2002 was to be a wonderful, enlightening experience that would be memorable for all the right reasons.

The "Celtic Tiger" meant the Irish economy was booming, marking the country's resurgence on this world's stage. The change-over currency was introduced, as Ireland said goodbye to the Punt and hello to the Euro and of course, Ireland would subsequently qualify for the World Cup Finals in Japan and South Korea. All of this combined meant that Dublin was an incredibly exciting and pulsating city in which to live and work; and right in the heart of it all was Dublin City Council.

I witnessed Dublin City Council and its dedicated staff embark upon many significant projects that would enhance the quality of life for its citizens, investors, and tourists alike. Major infrastructural projects such as the construction of the Port Tunnel, the Luas and the development of two new bridges spanning the River Liffey were all ongoing whilst I was there. Moreover, the public realm regeneration of O'Connell Street had commenced, including the installation of The Spire. The Spire was a 'marmite' structure (which I love actually) that would become an iconic symbol for Dublin.

I never really strayed far from Dublin City Centre during that year. Yet unbeknown to me at that time, located a few miles outside of the city was the picturesque Dublin suburb of Glasnevin. Glasnevin is famous for being the burial place of Michael Collins. Collins was the Irish volunteer who rose up in Easter 1916 to rebel against the British occupation of Ireland. He was a key member of the party who negotiated the treaty with the British government that controversially saw the thirty-two-county island of Ireland partitioned. This left six counties in the north of Ireland separated from the other twenty-six, which formed a new Republic.

However, the National Botanical Gardens of Glasnevin is also famous for its breathtaking Great Palm House (1883-1884), which is complimented by a beautiful range of bonus glasshouses comprising of, The Teak House, The Alpine House, The Cactus and Succulent House, The Great Palm House, The Orchid House, The Curvilinear Range, and The Victoria Waterlily House (1854). Upon my recent visit I found the collection to be immaculate.

Dublin Ironmaster Richard Turner was born in 1798 and died on 31st October 1881. He descended from a long line of Dublin ironmongers and is reputed to have become the greatest ironmonger of his day. Turner is principally associated with the construction of sophisticated glasshouse structures such as the Belfast Palm House (1839), Dublin's, Glasnevin (1843-1869) and Kew Gardens in London (1848). However, as you will discover later in this book, he was also responsible for the construction of other notable glass house structures in Ireland.

During my desk-based research I came across an article which stated that 'the curvilinear range (at Glasnevin) was originally developed in a piece-meal fashion between 1843 and 1869, although the involvement of Turner gave the design some coherence.' Turner's glasshouses embody the industrial age. Standardised materials and prefabricated elements that were manufactured off site could be assembled quickly on site. His use of wrought and cast iron was at the forefront of construction technology by the mid-nineteenth century and with 'French innovation in glass production, this enabled curved glass to be manufactured successfully. Alongside the intrinsic architectural and engineering properties of wrought and cast iron, this enabled Turner to develop a sophisticated yet aesthetically pleasing curvilinear range, which were described as avant-garde in their design and innovative in their technology.'

Dating from 1884, the Great Palm House at the National Botanic Gardens was magnificently and faithfully restored over a two-year period before subsequently reopening in 2004. Prior to its restoration the range had become utterly corroded and unstable, before the decision was finally made to close it to the public in the early 2000s. After more than 100 years, its wrought and cast iron and its timber construction had deteriorated to such an extent that many panes of glass were breaking each year due to the structure's instability.

The structure was disassembled into more than 7,000 parts and tagged for repair and restoration off-site. Its twenty-metre-tall cast iron columns that were situated within the structure were replaced by new cast iron columns that were modelled on molds made from the original columns. Using an innovative process called 'drop forging', recycled original wrought iron was reheated and reshaped and used to replace other corroded parts of the building.

Moreover, new modern paint technology was specified to develop long-term protection for the Palm House from future corrosion caused by condensation, high humidity and a tropical climate and I would later discover that 'Turner white' was the obvious, specified color of choice at Glasnevin for its metal and timber. In terms of health and safety compliance, replacement overhead glass was laminated, and vertical panes toughened. A specialised form of mastic was used to fix the panes, replacing original linseed oil putty that had contributed to the decay of the building over the century.

Dr. Peter Wyse Jackson, Director of the National Botanic Gardens, said "The restored Palm House complex provides ideal conditions for the Gardens' internationally important collection of tropical plants, many of which are threatened by extinction in the wild. The restoration of the full curvilinear range has protected and renewed a magnificent building that was seriously at risk, safeguarding a valuable educational, scientific and cultural resource for the future" and like a 'city on a hilltop that cannot be hidden', they stand out boldly from the moment they come into view. After the restoration project was successfully completed it went on to receive the top Europa Nostra award, representing the first and only award of its kind for a project in Ireland.

Turner was incredibly impactful, in the world of glasshouse design and construction. Yet I believe the architect Thomas Drew described his influence perfectly when he recounted, Turner was 'in his vigorous days as ubiquitous, with a stock of daring and original projects always on hand, remarkable for his rough and ready powers of illustration of them and his sanguine belief in them, and his eloquent, plausible and humourous advocacy of them.'

In the Dictionary of Irish Architects 1720-1940, Turner was described as a man of great energy and enterprise, who built up a thriving business and carried out commissions throughout Britain and Ireland, and perhaps even as far as Russia. This talented

Irishman's legacy lives on, in every one of these existing memorable structures.

One such structure can be found at Ballyfin House in County Laois. Here exists a beautiful conservatory that was constructed by Turner c1850-1855. In 2019, my wife and I would embark upon a smooth two-hour drive from Powerscourt, in County Wicklow, to the remote County Laois countryside to what, it would transpire, had apparently been voted as the best hotel in the world. Described as a place of history and romance, of tranquility and great natural beauty, this lavish noble mansion is securely set within 600 acres of parkland. It has a lake and ancient woods; all of which ensures it slips comfortably below the radar, far away in absolutely every capacity from the island of Ireland's established, popular tourist traps.

Having pulled up outside its daunting black wrought iron gates, I leaned out of my driver's window to press the buzzer, introduce myself and request access. As the automatic gates slowly opened, we gently set off along a dreamy mile long drive, whereby you apparently 'see nothing' that is, until you suddenly 'see everything'. In this case, 'everything' was in the form of a mind-blowingly opulent Irish Regency mansion set amidst its own exclusive private landscape. The mansion faced onto a stunning private lake, which sat peacefully but imperfectly like a long sheet of tinted crown spun glass.

I digress for a moment, but in the mid-nineteen eighties, I attended a secondary school in Belfast called Lagan College. Lagan College was ground-breaking, because it was the first ever integrated school in the north of Ireland where Catholics and Protestants, boys, and girls, were educated together, co-existing in relative peace and harmony. Aware always of course that in any 'normal' society an integrated school would simply be known as... a school. Although I say 'peace and harmony' ironically because most months the buses taking Lagan's pupils to school, would be attacked with bricks and stones, having been targeted by children

47

attending both 'rival' all-Catholic or all-Protestant schools. Nestled in the Castlereagh Hills, a few miles outside of Belfast City centre, Lagan College was unlike any school I had ever experienced. Comprising of several temporary, medium-term mobile huts, its pupils were taught in structures that were anything but salubrious.

In stark contrast to Lagan College, Ballyfin had been the highly impressive location for a 'much loved' former Catholic boy's secondary school. Designed by the father and son team of Sir Richard and William Morrison and constructed for the aristocratic Coote family in the 1820s, it was the Coote's grand family home for 100 years before it became a school. However, in the subsequent years that followed, it would fall into a state of veritable obsolescence. Before it was sensitively and sympathetically restored in 2011 and transformed into a select and very secluded, five-star hotel. With twenty bedrooms, which are regarded as the most exclusive in Ireland, it was reportedly the sanctuary of choice for a super-rich American celebrity couple, to enjoy as their super-private historic, honeymoon haven.

With the car parked, we were greeted by a charming gentleman who guided us across mosaic floored hallways and through rooms with incredible parquetry and stone floor finishes before we settled in a sumptuously carpeted library, for rich hot coffee and sublime lemon biscuits.

The 'library' was of course very opulent. As you would imagine there were a plethora of books, but these books were housed in crafted mahogany glass-fronted bookcases, with horned Grecian pediments recessed into the wall spaces. There was also sumptuous interior design, alongside classical black scagliola columns, complete with gilded capitals at the base of each column. There also classically detailed 'ghostly' white marble chimney pieces at either end of the room, which merely added to the extravagant grandeur. In Kevin V Mulligan's book Ballyfin he states, 'While the book filled cases were intended to issue a sense of the scholarly taste of the house, the soothing rows of leather bindings within them also contributed to a warm and calm environment, attractive to even the non-bookish.' With antiques and fine Irish artwork visibly on display, this and all the aforementioned history was really something to behold. However, for me, the best was still yet to come.

Respectfully bound by previously unmentioned time constraints, we stood up and made our way to the corner of the room towards the library where craftily hidden behind the bookcase was a secret mirrored doorway that opened, leading into a wrought iron and glazed corridor, which created a perfect linkage to an airy Victorian conservatory, located externally.

'The proposal to erect a conservatory at Ballyfin may be traced to a comment referring to the old house in 1801, during William Wellesley Pole's time, where it was said one of the wings was intended for conversion to a 'green house'.

It is written that plans for a conservatory were designed into Richard Morrison's early drawings. However, good things come to those who wait, for approximately thirty years later in circa 1855, ironmaster Richard Turner, who had previously developed the Great Palm House at Kew in London, was procured to construct one of his magical feats of engineering, by developing yet another splendid wrought iron ribbed, curvilinear glasshouse structure.

According to Kevin V Mulligan, "In its architecture and materials, the conservatory departs from any direct association with those of the house, presenting a masterful curvilinear cage that, like the Palm House at Kew, possesses an elegance 'as gracious as a crinolined lady, as smooth as a camelia.'"

Positioned impeccably, this white, floaty, elegant structure was enhanced further by its magical setting and celestial environs. However, the conservatory was to fall into a horrendous state of disrepair. Its metal work corroded and rusted so severely that it had to be deconstructed and transported off site to England for

49

restoration of each element. The glazing too was either shattered, cracked, or missing as water ingress became a major issue. Fortunately, the glazing work was undertaken closer to home at Tullamore in County Offaly.

In essence, most Victorian glass house structures of the world are painted in some form of off white, but like an Irish Salmon that swims upstream, the good people of Ballyfin had an impactful solution that would create the perfect juxtaposition. By bravely reverting to painting the metal work an almost charcoal black colour, it contrasts perfectly with its glazing, by creating a shimmering shining light, that shines more and more unto each perfect day that one gets to spend at Ballyfin. The glasshouse is used today for everything from breakfasts to private fine dining and it is perhaps, out of all the prominent conservatories that I would explore, one of my favorite glasshouse structures.

HAVING SEPARATED FROM MY FATHER, my mother moved my brother and I into a pokey, dated summer house. It was located in a small coastal fishing village in County Down, less than an hour away from Belfast. It was summertime when we arrived, and the decent weather briefly masked the grim nature of the tiny mid terrace rented property in which we now resided. In reality there was very little to do, and we knew no one.

To entertain ourselves, my younger brother and I would spend most of our balmy summer days five minutes away from the house, walking about the pier or hanging out amongst the rugged rocks getting lightly sprayed by the salty Irish sea. The rocks were situated below the first tee box of an established golf club. So, when the tide was out, and armed with a couple of cheap children's bamboo-stick-fishing-nets that were purchased from a local shop down by the pier; we would fish for golf balls that had been badly shanked or sliced by golfers onto the rocks or into the sea.

Although some of the golf balls were often slightly scraped or dirty, the majority were still close to perfect and still very useable. So, we would take them home and scrub them with nail brushes in a basin of hot soapy water, before rubbing them dry and polishing them with cloths to make them as good as new. Looking back, there must have been some *seriously poor* golfers teeing off from that first tee box each week because when our father came to collect us, we would take bulging plastic carrier bags full of golf balls that we had saved, back up to south Belfast to sell them to a local sweet shop owner, Bertie.

We would exchange the golf balls for money, confectionary or Panini football stickers. It was during these Saturday trips that our father would also successfully buy our affections. New watches, burgers, football tops, you name it – we got it. This sort of attention was something we had never got from him before because he had always been incredibly tight with the purse strings. I recall one Saturday opting for a black electronic Casio musical watch, which I believe played Vivaldi, but what wasn't classical was having to return from the city each Saturday night, to the dank coastal summer house, which was super-depressing.

Come September, we started yet another new primary school. This would be our third primary school in four years. It was my eleven plus year but needless to say, I would fail miserably. The school itself was small and dated. Friendships had already been forged and for the most part as 'city slickers' with our Belfast accents, we were not particularly welcomed by some of our rural counterparts. The upshot was some minor bullying that would lead to a few instances of school yard or after school 'scraps.' This would in turn, result in either detention, or the horrible headmaster happily administering 'the strap'.

With summer having all but ended, after school my mother used to take us for pleasant but boring walks of an evening along country roads, towards Coney Island, where we would pick blackberries that were later baked in a crumble. But after a couple of walks the novelty very quickly wore off.

The onset of a cold and wet autumn and a dark, freezing winter only exacerbated the depression. The single paned summer house was just that. It had a coal fire but no central heating, so the water was always cold unless we used the immersion or boiled a kettle. It was a musty old house, and we would be occasionally visited by mice. My brother and I had to sleep on very old, rock solid, horse-hair mattresses that were located in a dark, damp, and dingy back bedroom and all of this started to take its toll on me. In fact, the stress led me to sleepwalk and on one occasion I fell down the stairs in my sleep, fortunate to end up with only a bit of bruising, stiffness and some carpet burns.

In the months running up to Christmas, communications and negotiations had been ongoing behind the scenes and my father had slowly but surely managed to worm his way back into my mother's affections. Eventually convincing her to move back to Belfast by the New Year. 'The Power of Love' by 'Frankie Goes to Hollywood' was the Christmas number one in the charts that year. And I recall my father and mother awkwardly slow dancing around the cramped living room floor together, as the song played on Top of the Pops, which we watched on the small portable tv that always had irritating interference. It was horrible, and I couldn't listen to that song for many years after. That Christmas was a complete nightmare, and I spent a lot of time randomly crying.

The New Year wouldn't be much better. Having eventually left the coastal village we initially moved to my grandparent's house for a brief spell before reverting to our house in south Belfast. However, it was at this point that my parents then decided to sell up again, you guessed it, for another fresh start in yet another new house.

That said, with our property being situated in a sought-after location, it sold quickly before we had something else to move into. So, as a consequence of this, we had to temporarily relocate to an extended family member's, compact and bijou two-bedroom house, located down the road towards the inner city. Now, the distance from our existing property to the house in question was literally just over a mile away, but metaphorically speaking the localities were a million miles apart; polar opposite in fact. Our dwelling house was situated in a sought after, balanced, leafy location, whilst the location down the road was, well, none of those things. Both properties were separated by a landmark bridge beneath which the river Lagan flows, but it was tantamount to us finding ourselves on the wrong side of the tracks.

Like a game of snakes and ladders, we had briefly climbed up the ladder only to encounter a serpent, that saw us slide right back towards the lower end of the board. It was awful.

The aforementioned family member, who would come and go from time to time, was pretty uncouth. I recall him picking his nose and flicking it against his unpainted grey plastered living room walls and opening up his park-ray fire and spitting his thick green mucus onto the hot coals and watching it sizzle - vile. As much as we got on, I was thankful he was not always there. But either way, this latest move meant my brother and I would have to sleep on bunk beds in the same room as my parents for several months, whilst they attempted to buy yet another house.

It was a dreadful experience for an eleven-year-old. In fact, it would be nine months before they purchased a large three storey, four-bedroom, traditional Belfast-red-brick, end-terrace. It was a proper fixer upper, which they slowly refurbished one room at a time. It had potential but the only saving grace was that it was once again located a few streets away from our previous house and that made me happy, albeit for a little while.

CHAPTER 4:
WHO WANTS TO BE AN AMBASSADOR

Malahide Castle, Talbot Botanic Gardens, Malahide (1800)

I T WAS DURING MY RESEARCH FOR THIS BOOK that I stumbled across some other fine Victorian glass house structures. Having lived in Dublin for a year, I never strayed much beyond the city centre areas to far flung places such as Blackrock, Howth, or Malahide. However, located in the greater Dublin area, is the stunning Talbot Botanical Gardens and hidden away within the historic Malahide Castle Demesne, is a special walled garden with its seven glasshouses of differing levels of scale and complexity. These structures apparently contain some 5,000 different botanical species, with a particular focus on rare and delicate plants from the Southern Hemisphere. The gardens cover an area of just over 8 hectares, with 7 hectares of shrubbery and the remainder contained a walled garden. Olearia, Hebe, Escallonia, Nothofagus, Syringia, Hypericum, Clematis species, Euphorbia, Eryngium, Hosta and Crocosmia all thrive in the Talbot Botanic Gardens. The first glasshouse you encounter is the beautiful butterfly house, and you should expect to see it gracefully guarded by fabulously proud peacocks parading peacefully, at its entrance.

A tradition of ornamental gardening has been associated with Malahide Castle since the late 1800s. The Former Dublin County Council was anxious that such a tradition should continue when it first learned of the impending sale of the estate in 1975, and so it was acquired by Dublin City Council the following year. It had been a kitchen garden supplying fruit and vegetables to the Castle and replaced an even earlier garden to the south-east of the castle. But the Ordnance Survey map of 1872 notes an ornamental garden when the triangular section at the North-West was sectioned off for flowers. This area was extended by Lady Isabel Talbot, a very keen gardener, after she arrived at the Castle in 1902. It was again extended in 1946 by Lord Milo Talbot in order to contain his burgeoning plant collection.

There are also some notable trees in the gardens including a large Cedar of Lebanon, and an Oak as well as many magnolias, pines, junipers, and acers. Its collection of glass house structures includes beautiful teak outhouses and pot houses. These units complement their outstanding 'peacock patrolled' Victorian conservatory, which is the structure that forms the great centerpiece, of the Talbot Botanic Gardens at Malahide Castle. The 100-year-old glasshouse was acquired by Fingal County Council and it is believed to have been originally part of a convent garden in Killiney, County Dublin.

This linkage takes me very nicely onto my next curvilinear glasshouse structure. Killiney is an affluent seaside resort and suburb located in Dun Laoghaire, Rathdown. It was during my extensive desk-based research that I stumbled upon a truly stunning example of modern-day glasshouse renovation. Situated to the rear of the then Australian Ambassador's residence, sits an immaculately reconstructed glasshouse. This stunning structure had previously fallen into a state of obsolescence, before a commitment was made by the previous Ambassador in residence, to bring the structure back to its former glory.

I openly approached the Ambassador via his assistant to introduce myself, and approval was granted for me to visit his residence, to carry out a visual inspection and to survey the successfully completed project.

Having stayed in a hotel outside of Killiney the night before, the next morning, I took a private taxi to the residence, having scheduled an 8.30am meeting. It was a gorgeously warm, sunny summer morning. However, the Monday morning road traffic that I was anticipating didn't materialize, as we arrived at the entrance of the property at around 8.05am.

So, with twenty-five minutes to spare and seeing as it was a beautiful morning, my taxi driver suggested he take me on a tour of the mansions owned by Killiney's rich and famous, before stopping at an elevated height to momentarily soak-in the heavenly views of the blue-green Irish Sea. As we sailed away like Enya round Killiney, my fleeting Chauffeur, complete with a brilliant archetypal Irish brogue accent, demonstrated an extraordinary facility as he regaled me with tales of 'Bono drinking here and 'The Edge' shopping there; of Formula One's Eddie Irvine residing there and Van Morrison occasionally holidaying here'. It was tremendous.

When my brief, impromptu but enjoyable tour ended, I re-arrived at my destination, upon which I was greeted warmly by the Ambassador. As he walked me round his glasshouse, he happily answered any questions I had about its restoration project. Having previously only seen photographs of the restoration, I was suitably impressed by the immaculate end result. One element of the rehabilitation related to the badly rusted and corroded cast iron columns. Its structural frame was cautiously disassembled before each element was numbered and tagged before being shipped off to Telford in England, to be made good; before being re-transported and reassembled, ensuring the return of its structural integrity. Any replacement constituent parts had been individually cast, where required, and these corresponded perfectly with the original elements.

All of the original glass was now gone, only to be sensitively replaced by acceptable toughened glass, which gleamed superbly. There were an apparent seven coats of paint sympathetically applied to the cast iron features but this did not detract from the detail richness of the structure. The original low level manually operated windows for ventilation were upgraded as part of the electrical installation, and sensitive granite resurfacing was in place around its perimeter. When all was said and done, the structure stood respectably, complementing its salubrious surroundings. Today, this glasshouse offers the Ambassador the perfect location for cloistered weekend relaxation, but it is also used for hosting elegant intimate functions and even I am told, the occasional private wine tasting event. Once the host left for his meeting in Ballsbridge, I spent the remainder of my time with his gardener, who also shared his knowledge of the restoration project. What he also admitted was that he originally hailed from County Kildare, at which point it quickly transpired that he was actually an old acquaintance of my uncle and cousin who also lived there - it is indeed a small world we live in.

Having completed my survey inspection I said my goodbyes and commenced a short walk downhill towards the pristine Killiney Dart Station, which was located by the aforementioned Irish sea. Once on board an immaculately clean Dart, I took my seat, but was immediately joined by a debonair white-haired gentleman and it wasn't long before he introduced himself and we started talking. Patrick was a seventy-year-old retired accountant and a local Killiney resident. He was on his way to Dublin city to engage in final preparations before he and his wife of fifty years would meet the Pope that forthcoming Saturday morning. This was fascinating because I was also scheduled to work as an acolyte at Phoenix Park in Dublin, for what would be the Holy See's first Papal visit to Ireland since 1977.

He was a relaxed, well dressed, well-spoken gentleman, the exact type of man I would have loved to have as a father of my own, but above all else he spoke calmly and with transparency. He quickly confirmed that he had prepared a speech that he would be giving the following weekend in front of the Holy Father. Now as a Liturgical Minster of the Word myself, I was used to proclaiming God's Word at a packed Mass of a weekend, so I asked him if he was nervous and if not, how he controlled his nerves? I loved his response. 'One must postpone the panic!' he effortlessly exclaimed. This was brilliant. Simply, delay the dread because once you have read what you are called to read, the moment will have passed, as will the unnecessary need for nervousness. Sage advice if it can be implemented.

Having initially delighted him with my reason for being in Killiney, referring to the once destitute glass house that had now been saved, it wasn't long before we started talking about family and about God. He admitted he was concerned that his daughter, who it seemed had a successful career and family life, was distant from God. He didn't believe his daughter was atheist but suggested that she might be agnostic. We talked about the church, Jesus, and the power of the holy-spirit and in doing so, I reassured Patrick that I would pray for his daughter and that in my experience, once God came calling and if his daughter responded accordingly to God's call, there would be no turning back.

It was a very pleasant journey, and I was disappointed that we didn't get to ride all the way to my stop at Tara Street station. I have no idea how Patrick's meeting with the Pope went but I am sure that if it happened, it would have gone wonderfully well. I was also certain that with Patrick's influence and through the power of scripture and prayer that his daughter, like the ambassador's glass house, might also one day, experience a wonderful transformation.

IT WAS THE SUMMER OF 1985 when I travelled with my family to London for a summer holiday. It was the first time my brother and I would be anywhere other than Ireland and this was an amazing thing. As previously stated, if there was a challenging route to traverse, my parents would traverse it. I am guessing flying must have been cost prohibitive, because we travelled on the Larne to Stranraer ferry from N. Ireland to Scotland, and then took a bus from Scotland to London to get there. It was an arduous trek. When we arrived, it was already late evening, but it was instantly obvious that London was unlike anything I had ever experienced before. With its ongoing 'troubles', Belfast City Centre in 1985 was like a ghost town after 6pm, but not London. It was bustling, fast, vibrant, and alive with multicultural diversity.

That said, unthinkably, my father hadn't booked a hotel in advance of our trip. So, like many other tourists we then began to tramp around London with our travel bags and heavy suitcases with no wheels, looking for vacancies. It was the first time I recalled gazing upon the beautiful external façades of those stunning white Regency style hotels that are commonplace in London. They were like nothing I had seen before, all white painted stucco frontage with hand painted black numbers on the tall resplendent columns. However, before I could meaningfully comment, my father looked me in the eye, raised his voice and aggressively cut me off. "Forget it!" He snarled through gritted teeth, "poor-people don't get to stay in places like that."

I can say with confidence that his negative defeatism resonated with me then as a twelve-year-old boy, as much as it does now that I am a father myself. For knowingly and willfully planting such a damaging seed, in the mind of a young twelve-year-old boy that you brought into the world, would be *absolutely* unthinkable to me. For as parents we should aspire to absolutely nothing other than the out-and-out finest for our children. The sky must be the limit; in so far as is reasonably practicable.

Yet, under pressure from his tired, moaning family members, my father reluctantly ended up paying over the odds to stay in the exact type of hotel I had earlier tried to comment on. The hotel, complete with archetypal grandiose white pillars, had looked magnificent from the outside but alas all that glitters is not gold, as it would be rather mundane on the inside. I recall the curtains in our room had bird poo on them. A deposit possibly left by the flock of opportunistic cockney pigeons who were flapping about outside, near the lush green trees that swayed above our balcony. Either way, when we pulled back the curtains and opened the large single paned sash windows, my brother and I clambered straight out through them and onto the aforementioned balcony, and immediately began to unleash our boxes of "devil banger explosives" onto the unsuspecting passers-by below. Now you could be forgiven for thinking 'Oh hear-we-go again with those young Belfast boys and their explosives' but for the uninitiated, "devil bangers" were also less sensationally known as 'fun snaps' which we procured from a Belfast joke shop. They were, in essence, tantamount to little off-white cigarette papers filled with potassium nitrate that were rolled up tightly and once thrown, they would make a loud crack or a snapping sound the second they came into contact with a pavement or hard surface. If timed perfectly, they would successfully scare the wits out of any unsuspecting passer-by, at which point hilarity would ensue! The best thing about it was that our mum joined us on the balcony to lob the bangers, before ducking out of sight. It was great craic. Little amuses the innocent, as they say.

The holiday was off and running and my brother and I would want for nothing on that trip, getting to see absolutely every tourist trap that London had to offer. It was magical and it was the beginning of a life-long love affair I'd have with London. In fact, today having been blessed to have seen many of the countries and cities in the world that I have wanted to see, I still believe London is easily one of the best cities in the world.

My mother and father had obviously been to London before. In 1972, before they eventually married, they had broken up for a period of time. My mother had moved to London to work as a legal secretary and although initially lodging in a convent run by nuns, she would occasionally regale us with her memories of that time, spent hanging out on Carnaby Street and Notting Hill market, or sneaking out with friends to enjoy the London night life. However, after a period of time my father had apparently travelled over to London to 'win back her heart' and the rest it seems, was history.

Weirdly, I loved the sound and smell of the London Underground and I adored the pace and freedom of the city. It was the home of TV celebrities and walking through the West End one evening, I would catch a glimpse of soap star Letitia Dean, who was better known as Sharon from EastEnders. This completely blew my mind at the time because there were only four channels on TV and EastEnders, with viewers of twenty million or more, was rather a big deal in 1985. At almost twelve years old even I could appreciate London's history and its obvious multiculturalism. It was the home of Paddington Bear, Mary Poppins, Sherlock Holmes, and the Queen of England but above else it was also home to my favorite thing in the world – Arsenal Football Club.

It was a scorching hot August in 1985 but it was during this holiday that I would get to realize a childhood dream by going to Highbury Stadium to watch Arsenal play football for the very first time. Late on the Friday afternoon before the Saturday game, we took the Piccadilly line to the Arsenal tube station and once we egressed, we walked up towards Arsenal's hallowed, art deco Highbury Marble Halls to buy tickets for the match the next day. It was almost 4pm. However, before we got there, we were approached by an old archetypal cockney geezer. He was wearing a trilby hat and smoking a roll up cigarette. He was a ticket tout and out of his trouser pocket he magically produced four tickets. "Last four tickets for the big match" he gloated out the side of his mouth. My eyes lit up like Charlie Bucket about to unwrap the Wonka bar that had within it the golden ticket to Willy Wonka's Chocolate Factory. 'Buy them, buy them!' I whispered beneath my breath to my dad. "I tell you what" said the cockney- geezer, "seeing as your big Arsenal fans, I'll do them for £40 each." I could see the color drain from my father's face because in reality £160 in 1985 was tantamount to almost £500 now. However, as we were only moments away from the ticket office, my father spotted an immaculately dressed man in uniform egressing from the Art Deco splendor that was also the Arsenal ticket office entrance. It transpired he was the Highbury Commissioner.

My father quickly excused himself from the geezer and scurried towards the Commissioner and after they had a quiet word, the commissioner went back inside the historical halls to approach the ticket office booth, which had only just closed. None the less, after a quick chat with the lovely lady behind the counter, she agreed to pull up the horizontal blind and reopen to sell us four tickets for the big match. I still have the used tickets to this day, so can confirm that the purchase price was £4.50 each or a grand total of £18.

We would arrive back at Arsenal the next day ahead of the 3pm kick off. The buzz outside the ground was unreal. Arsenal merchandise stalls, flags and banners and thousands of fans chanting, police on horse-back and the smell of burger fans all fueled my excitement. Once inside the ground, our old worn wooden seats were excellent, as I sat flicking through my match-day programme. They were located relatively near the pitch side in the West stand close to the North Bank end, where the Arsenal home fans stood. A guy was walking round selling white paper bags filled with monkey nuts, and I duly purchased. They were

Percy Dalton monkey nuts, the type which were still in their shells – apparently proper match day fayre back then. I was like a rabbit caught in headlights; frozen from kick off to the final whistle, and even though we lost the game 1-2 (my then idol Charlie Nicholas missed a penalty), that day and the whole holiday actually, would be the best memory I have of my entire childhood.

Throughout my lifetime I would idolize Arsenal; I was obsessed by it. It distracted me from basically everything else in the world. God, Church, school, family, and friends - its importance superseded everything and everyone and it took over my mind and my life. The moment the new season's fixtures were released in July, I would learn the fixture list to such an extent that I already knew where I would be watching Arsenal on Boxing Day. Later as an adult, the fixture list would also dictate when I would take a foreign summer holiday. This was to ensure that anytime spent abroad would also include me watching at least two if not three live games, if timed correctly. I would desire much of the new merchandise and know everything about the history of a club that was formed in 1886. As I got older, I would travel to England to watch Arsenal a few times a season, home and away. If they won, then great I had bragging rights for a week but if they lost it could also affect my mood for a week. In fact, it was and probably still is, something that many people identify with me to this day. But I wasn't alone.

I recall an old school friend who also supported Arsenal as passionately as I did. He had elderly parents who innocently thought nothing of buying a then sixteen-year-old boy, ten Silk Cut and a tin of Coca-Cola every day for him coming home from technical college. However, on this one occasion Arsenal were on the wrong end of a heavy midweek 2-6 home defeat. He didn't turn into college on the Thursday or Friday and was even unapproachable by phone that weekend, until the following Monday morning when he sheepishly returned to class, at which point his retrospective mocking commenced anyway. Depressed by the defeat his mother had agreed to give him time off from 'tech' to recover. The only difference between he and I then was that my mother wasn't elderly, and she would never have tolerated my mood being impacted to this extent. However, the truth is that such a defeat did also affect me to the same extent. I idolized that club and have been an avid follower for forty years.

After I returned from that holiday, I recalled boasting to an uncle about my new preference to buy my Arsenal top directly from the club itself rather than from a locally based Belfast sports shop. He looked at me strangely before saying "Yeah, because Arsenal really needs your twenty quid?" I didn't see it at the time obviously, but he was of course correct. This club didn't know me and certainly didn't need or care about me. As a club member I was merely a number or more crudely, an occasional bum on a seat and my infrequent purchases in reality made little or no impact to the club's very major global cash flow. That said, if football were a God that I worshipped at that time then Arsenal was my preferred church and with my enhanced knowledge of the club, I was less a fan and more a disciple. But it wasn't until later in life that I started to see things in a different way.

I hadn't realized what was happening because I was living a worldly life blinded by the Americanistic, consumeristic, materialistic, well-oiled global money-making juggernaut that Arsenal had become.

Of course, the signs were literally already hidden in plain sight in the early eighties when foreign sponsorship first meaningfully entered the game. The first noticeable sponsorship deal Arsenal had was with electronic giants JVC. JVC was emblazoned across their top and across the huge famous sign on their East Stand which read, 'JVC and Arsenal the Perfect Match'. This stood out boldly for all stadium fans and fans watching on TV at home. The power of advertising took no time in manipulating me as a young primary school boy, as I encouraged my parents to only consider buying JVC branded electrical goods. In fact, we owned a JVC video recorder, camcorder, and stereo. I was preoccupied with Arsenal, even though it didn't mean anything in the grand scheme of the entire world. Never yet having the time to consider or seek the truth about life.

Today, football, like American football, basketball, or baseball, has long since extended beyond being a grass roots working class sport and has subsequently morphed into the realm of celebrity culture. With some multi-million-pound superstars earning upwards of two million pounds per month, this can equate to an estimated twenty five million pound per year, which over the term of a four-year contract can earn a footballer an unimaginable one hundred million pounds during one contract term.

Aware at all times that we live in a capitalist society driven by a free market economy, I have become a critic of worldliness and the richer world, because when I look at the gross and overt socio-economic issues which blight society today such as homelessness, poverty, and unemployment; grotesque sums of money do not sit easily with me. The players of today, often highlighted on social media, are as much if not much more focused on money and materialism, than the pleasure that comes from enjoying a healthy career playing a game they love.

I will elaborate further on the risks of consumerism and materialism throughout this book but meeting the Australian ambassador in Killiney that day made me think of scripture and of God's promises to me. When we discover the power of God's infallible Word, we can also learn how to pray properly and to speak comfortably into God's silence. We can grow and develop spiritually and in doing so we can discern our ministry passions, spiritual gifts, and talents. We can discover our true purpose in life. We can turn our backs on living a consumeristic, individualistic, materialistic, worldly existence by living a Christocentric lifestyle and operating in the correct spirit, by walking in the spirit of truth. In doing so we not only become witnesses to the power of the Gospel but serving others becomes second nature, and this I believe, enables us to become an ambassador of Christ.

2 Corinthians Chapter 5:20 the Apostle Paul states, 'we are therefore Christ's ambassadors', as though God we're making his appeal through our witness. In being reconciled with God, Paul described himself and those who work with him as Christ's Ambassadors. Why does Paul describe those who live and work for God as ambassadors? To explain this, we must first consider what is meant by the 'Kingdom'.

When Jesus walked the earth, he often spoke of 'the Kingdom of God' and he always proclaimed that he was a King. This differs from the worldly perception of Jesus which looks at him through the eyes of religiosity and as only a religious leader. Yet, again, he always claimed to be a King. For instance, in John 18:36 Jesus proclaimed that "my kingdom is not of this world." Moreover, in Matthew 6:33 its states, "seek first his kingdom and his righteousness... ", and also in the Gospel according to Luke 22:29 it states, "I confer on you a kingdom, just as my father conferred one on me."

In this respect it was as though Jesus was declaring that he was a government figure, a ruler of a kingdom or a type of government. A kingdom has a King as its ruler and one who oversees its citizens. So, in essence, Jesus came and declared he was a King of a kingdom that was not of this world because his Kingdom was the Kingdom of Heaven. Therefore, if you and I are citizens of that Kingdom and God has called us to represent him on earth, wouldn't that make us ambassadors?

An ambassador by definition is described as an official of the highest rank who represents their head of state whilst in a foreign territory – an authorized messenger or representative. According to the AoC Network, as Christians, we are born into a new family where our ruler, head of government or head of state is King Jesus and we are citizens of his government, the government of Heaven. When we successfully convert, we become citizens of God's Heaven. As Paul states in Ephesians 2:19, "Consequently, you are no longer foreigners and strangers, but fellow citizens with God's people and also members of his household...". Also, in Colossians 1:13 it proclaims that He has delivered us from the domain of darkness and has transferred us into the kingdom of his beloved Son..."

This is why the Bible states that we are no longer foreigners in Heaven but are foreigners on earth. To put it another way, we are in this world (earth), but we are not of this world, because we are merely passing through on our way to our true home (Heaven). So, when God calls us to turn away from our sinful lives and to authentically repent of our sins, we become a new creation, and in doing so we can become a literal ambassador of heaven, living the gospel and being a witness for Jesus. Moreover, when an ambassador is in a foreign territory, the head of state gives the ambassador authority to represent his government.

This is why Jesus says in Luke 10:19, "I have given you authority to trample on snakes and scorpions and to overcome all the power of the enemy; nothing will ever harm you."

Nothing can ever harm us if we repent of our sins and lay all of our transgressions and inequities at the foot of the cross because by doing so, we can remove ourselves from the wide road, the road that leads to destruction (the road taken by many), and embark upon a journey, through the narrow gate and along the smooth path (the path taken by the few). Such a Holy Spirit driven journey may see us enter the true world of apostleship and discipleship, growing spiritually to such an extent that we can become a powerful witness and an actual ambassador for God's kingdom.

Knowing this, do you aspire to be an ambassador for Christ? Do you aspire to be removed from the wide road and to live a life on the narrow path? Do you aspire to live a life like Jesus? If so, take a moment to consider if your life is affected by the following thematics of sin – Alcoholism, blasphemy, consumerism, divisions, evil-thoughts, functioning alcoholism, greed, high-mindedness, individualism, judging, laying up treasures on earth, materialism, neglect of care, outbursts of rage, profanity, quarrelling, riotous behavior, swearing, trusting in riches, (being) unmerciful, voluntary humility, worshipping other Gods.

Such sins have impacted upon my time on earth. How do you or your nuclear and extended family and friends, stand with regard to such sins?

CHAPTER 5: MODERN DAY IDOLS

The Great Palm House at Kew, London (1844-1848)
& The Temperate House (1863)

IN KEW, 'THE PLANTING WOULDN'T APPEAR anywhere as spectacular were it not for the architecture of the Palm House itself. The soaring arches and seemingly impossibly narrow ribs of wrought iron create and ornate a backdrop to the plants. It may look like an upturned hull from the outside but on the inside there's more than a whiff of Paddington Station.'

As part of my research, I recall flying from Belfast City Airport to London Heathrow in 2018. When I disembarked, I speed-walked towards the exit, at which point I was immediately attracted by a brightly lit advertising hoarding which read, "You never actually own a Patek Philippe. You merely look after it for the next generation." How apt. Any professional tasked with conserving and sensitively restoring these stunning Victorian glasshouses, also has the privilege of knowing that these historical, heritage structures remain protected for the pleasure and enjoyment of generations to come. Comparison could be drawn with those privileged, God-fearing Victorians who could effortlessly spree on a glass house then, with those today who can frivolously splurge on an eye wateringly expensive timepiece, now. It made me think of the words of the Apostle James who wrote, 'your gold and silver will corrode'. This metaphor highlights that corrosion and rust destroys any transitory items constructed with metals, just as greed corrodes the soul.

Although as we will see, decay and pollution does not have to mean the end. On the contrary, it is often an opportunity for what is broken, to be restored and saved.

Having taken the Heathrow Express train to the frenetic Paddington Station, I alighted, and upon doing so, I quickly gazed upwards recognizing the similarity of the design of the station roof to those elements used in the construction of Victorian curvilinear glass houses. I read the following wonderful quotation on-line. 'Looking is what is required at Paddington Station – so that you see all the exciting shapes of the steel arches and notice the detailing of the pillars, the capitals and the ribs of the roof. In this frantic world in which we live these days, places like Paddington Station are busy, as you are surrounded by crowds leaving no time to 'stand and stare.'

Paddington Station was designed by Isambard Brunel and took four years to complete, opening on 29 May 1854. This was around the same time the construction of Kew Gardens was completed, and a visit to Kew Gardens to explore its newly restored Temperate House Conservatory (1863) and its existing Great Palm House (1848), was to be my next destination.

Getting off the over-ground train at Richmond, I was transported into what can only be described as a quintessentially beautiful English suburban scape. Immediately greeted by little fresh fruit stalls, pastry stands and artisan shops, I stopped to glance at the expensive properties for sale in a local estate agent's window. At that point I would have been forgiven for thinking that at any moment a bumbling, floppy haired Hugh Grant might egress awkwardly from a quaint coffee shop - playing on his Englishness with his 'received pronunciation' twittery. Alas, Hugh didn't appear and so I commenced my short but pleasant walk towards the Victoria Gate entrance, of Kew Gardens. The world-famous Kew Gardens, with its winding walkways and mind-blowing vistas, is without doubt somewhere I could easily imagine an affluent Victorian dandy meandering foppishly. Marvel today at the grandeur of its exemplar structures, instantly evoking an image of prosperous Victorian London. Witness in wonder at the historic Temperate House

Conservatory (1863) and the Great Palm House (1848) and it is easy to imagine the Victorian crowds that flocked to gaze in bewilderment, at the scale and technical complexity of the structures and the extensive collections of exotic botany housed within.

I read that Kew Gardens was one of 'Europe's earliest adopters of new technologies. The Palm House (1848), which we will discuss next, was one of the first buildings to use curved glass, setting a trend for architectural innovation. The Temperate House, which started construction in 1860, was even more ambitious: twice the size of the Palm House and much more ornate in style.' At 4880 square metres in size, the Temperate House is the largest public glass house at Kew. In 2013 a project commenced to restore the structure before successful completion was achieved in 2018. In an article from The Guardian I read, "After five years, 10,000 plants uprooted and replanted, 15,000 panes of glass replaced, 69,000 sections of metal, stone, and timber, repaired or replaced, enough scaffolding to stretch the length of the M25, and £41m spent, the largest Victorian glasshouse in the world is ready to open its doors again."

Kew's Grade 1 listed Temperate House, which was designed by architect Decimus Burton and constructed by William Cubitt & Co. has been reawakened and restored to its former glory. Using crushed-garnet blasting techniques, corrosion was removed, and the building was cleaned; repainted with a form of 'Turner white'. This has enabled previously hidden Victorian casting marks, stamps, and lozenges to reappear. It is truly special, and it has been transformed. New and pristine, as white as light with the new glazing providing a purity of light transmission. Its restoration is of course complimented with generic, modern inclusions, such as improved accessibility, interpretative signage, and mechanically operated ventilation.

Altruistically, this project was as much about conservation, restoration, and heritage as it was about ensuring the Temperate House remained dedicated to its original intent; to show its visitors some of the rarest temperate plants in the world. These include a rare cycad (Encephalaratos woodii) which harks back to a time 'When dinosaurs roamed the earth'. Richard Barley, director of horticulture stated, "The theme of rarity is at the heart of the newly opened building. It will open the door to a lot of Kew's work as a scientific (and a botanical research) organisation... conservation work and the science that's going on behind understanding these plants better and working with communities where they grow naturally around the world."

Home to previously immoveable species, earlier decanted plants, and an array of completely new floras, its temperate zone houses specimens from South Africa, the Americas, Asia, Australia, New Zealand, and oceanic islands, whilst some of its best-known ferns have been in Kew's collection, incredibly, since the glass house first opened.

Filled to the brim with species and with 260 years of plant expertise alongside a significant focus on botanical scientific research, Royal Botanic Gardens, Kew works in partnership and collaboration with shampoo giants Herbal Essence, to 'celebrate beauty rooted in plant science'. With collective scientific, biological and botanical expertise, this partnership believes that 'plants lift our spirits and fill our senses with beauty and wonder'. A leading authority on the potency and purity of plants, Royal Botanic Gardens, Kew is home to over 30,000 different plant and seed species from around the globe. It has therefore become a place where its scientists believe in a world where a rich diversity of plants and fungi need to be better understood and respected and that is to be commended. Visit the beautiful Kew Gardens today and I assure you it will leave you no less than awestruck when you witness its grandiosity and the extent of the botany included within.

While expansion of the British Empire in the nineteenth century had fueled an interest in the exotic plants from overseas amongst aspirational Victorians, developments in engineering made it possible to build huge glasshouses from which one could tend to the many species of Palms and their crops. Kew Gardens was established as a *botanical garden* in 1840 and director William Hooker's master plan envisioned a grand glass palm house. He enlisted architect Decimus Burton and engineer and builder Richard Turner to design a radical state-of-the-art modern building. Using ship building technology and wrought rather than cast iron, huge span spaces with little or no apparent support and unusually slender structural metal work, gave a feeling of immense lightness to the vast building. At 36ft long, 100ft wide and a soaring 66ft high it was, at that time, the largest glasshouse structure in the world.

The project to construct an elegant and ornate, curvilinear Palm House commenced in 1844 before it was successfully completed and opened to great acclaim, in 1848. The palm house, which recreates a rainforest climate, resembles an upturned hull of a ship, and comprises of 16,000 panes of glass and 5,500 components. Following refinement of Burton's design, Turner also recommended wrought iron for the metal ribs, which helped create its soaring arches. Its lightness and tensile strength enabled the roof to span 15.2 metres between columns. I read an article in the Financial Times, "At the end of the 19th century it was nothing short of miraculous, an augmented reality defined by technological revolution and imperial grandeur. This was the century of glasshouses – beasts of glass and steel, delicate hulks perched in the middle of imperial parks and gardens and the best known among them today include Kew's Palm House."

A wrought iron rolling technique patented by Kennedy and Vernon and designed originally for ship decks, was used to construct its frame and the curved profile maximized sunlight. However, it transpired that those large areas of clear glazing were not appropriate for light-sensitive rainforest species, creating the risk of leaf-burn. Therefore, following experiments from Robert Hunt, the existing glazing was replaced by 'manganese oxide-free glass tinted green with copper oxide, to diffuse solar gain and approximate the light conditions in a tropical rainforest.'

The Palm House recreates a rainforest climate and emulates a multi-layered exuberant, yet shadowy forest of swaying ferns and palms. A tropical habitat including canopy palms, dwarf palms, hibiscus, orchids, and bamboo grows alongside bananas, coconuts, macadamia and Brazil nuts, sugar cane and spices such as pepper and vanilla. Truly a wonder.

In July 2003 the Royal Botanic Gardens at Kew rightly achieved UNESCO World Heritage status and was described as a 'historic landscape with elements that illustrate significant periods of the art of gardens from the 18th to the 20th centuries. In fact, it is safe to assume that the Great Palm House and the Temperate House have become models for many such prominent conservatories around the world.

DURING THE LATE 1980S AND EARLY 1990S increased terrorist activity in Belfast saw tensions ratchetted up to another level by paramilitaries. There were tit-for-tat killings between Loyalist and Republican terrorists and bombs going off around Belfast city – things were getting risky again. My brother and I were in secondary school at this stage and were both attending Lagan College. As mentioned previously, Catholic and Protestant children were educated together here. One morning, we were queued at a bus stop waiting on our school bus to arrive as normal. The bus stop was situated in South Belfast, located directly outside of a longstanding Church of Ireland church. It was a traditional old stone church constructed in the late 1800s and its boundary wall comprised of the very same stonework and was constructed using a lime mortar. Behind that wall lay several manicured grass verges and some small, colourful flowerbeds. Although unimaginable, as we will discover later in this book, this church would have another part to play in my story, many years later.

Looking up the road you could see a couple of large Catholic churches, one of which I attended as a parishioner and as an altar boy. Looking down the road there was a Police station and rows of shops and bars. All of the aforementioned were surrounded by and densely populated with traditional Belfast-red-brick residential housing. However, as I looked down the road this morning, my brother, school friends and I heard a commotion before witnessing a number of panicked Police Officers fleeing in terror from the station entrance. Some of them tried to cordon off the road, dragging red and white tape behind them as they ran, but seconds later a bomb exploded loudly. As the ground shook violently, I witnessed one of the officers stumble to the ground. Next thing, I remember hearing a loud thud on the grass verge behind the stone wall, where we stood. Police officers had been trying to scream at us school children to run up the road, but we hadn't understood what was happening. Once we realised what was happening, we immediately made an excited dash towards the Catholic church, to safety.

It wasn't long before news broke that the IRA had attempted to launch a mortar bomb attack on the local Police station but had missed their intended target entirely. It transpired the loud thud that I heard was one of the bombs. It had arched its way over the Police station, missing its target, before landing on one of the Church's soft grass verges. It was a miracle that it hadn't detonated. Looking back at old newspaper cut outs that my mother had in a scrap book, it later emerged that there were six mortar bombs fired that morning, none of which hit their proposed target. One hit a vacant house, two had landed in the grounds of the Anglican Church and two had landed in private gardens. Only a 100lb booby trap device in a wheelie bin was detonated that morning.

We lived in a relaxed neighbourhood that was friendly and integrated. It was rush-hour and many civilians could have been killed or maimed that morning. I do not believe it is twee to suggest that it is by the grace of God that I am alive today and able to write these words.

I returned to school the next day to regale my colleagues of my near miss, but I never really dwelled on it after that. I guess I got on with life and buried the experience deep in my subconscious, to be stored and never again retrieved, until now. Following this incident, my parents who had tolerated Belfast for most of their lives, decided they wanted to move out of the city towards the countryside. We had lived in our second south Belfast house for only three years, but it had been refurbished and redecorated to such an extent that my parents were ready to trade up and sell once again. I was now fifteen and as a teenager, the thought of leaving our property which was located two miles from the city centre, to live in some depressing, grey 'backwater' was gut-wrenching.

In reality property-wise, there was much better value for money to be had further outside of the city but ultimately for scant regard for little other than the monetary benefits, we would be moving yet again. It was a time before mobile phones, social media, or internet, so most of my mates and I would drift apart, as our friendships gradually fizzled out. Yet again, I would be the stranger, forced into making new friends and acquaintances in a place where many friendships had already long since been forged. Moreover, it would become clear that many of the people I would meet would not be like-minded.

Although my parents had purchased a nice 'detached-villa' on an elevated site with undulating countryside views, the County Down village was drab and lifeless. It was located only twenty miles or so from Belfast, but it was a stark contrast to the buzz in south Belfast. For a start, I would have to take four buses a day to get to and from Lagan College, every day. This inconvenience wasn't ideal but at least I only had a year to go before school ended for good. Thankfully that year came and went quickly, but unsurprisingly, having shown little in the way of intellectual promise at that time, my GCSE results were underwhelming. So, I joined a local technical college to repeat those GSCEs that I failed.

I quickly got my first-ever part time Saturday job stacking shelves in a supermarket but that aside, there was very little for teenagers to do in the town. I dressed differently to most teens who lived there. I was into electronic dance music whilst the vast majority were into guitar-based music and youth cultures that I had no interest in, but it wasn't long before I was sought out by relative like minds.

That summer, as a fifteen-year-old, I would go on a trip to Donegal with an old Lagan College school friend. His older sister and her family hired a summer house in Downings, but my mate and I would camp in a tent which was pitched on its bumpy lawn. It was all very nice, with days spent between the sandy beaches, the sea, and fresh hilly walks - harmless stuff. However, there would be one unexpected part of this trip that would have a major influence on my early life. Having 'blagged' our way into a local 'night club', we subsequently met and linked in with three teenagers from London. They were eighteen and nineteen respectively, which meant they were veritable adults compared to us fifteen-year olds. They dressed and sounded different from us. Not in terms of their accent but in terms of their street language. They were relaxed and completely cool. We would get chatting and I was able to impress them with my newly developed knowledge of London, due to me having holidayed there two years in a row. This appeared to go down well.

Although the music being played at the nightclub was tantamount to what you would expect to hear at a wedding reception, remarkably the DJ did manage to dig out a couple of electronic tracks that would see our new London friends hit the dance floor. We would join them and throw some really questionable shapes, but I would quickly discover the dance music was Acid House. We also noticed they were not drinking alcohol but had shown us and we subsequently witnessed them swallowing, what it later transpired, were LSD tablets. At that time, we knew zero about hallucinogenic drugs or any type of illegal drugs in fact, but we were certainly intrigued by what we had seen.

When our trip to Donegal ended, I returned home and by coincidence watched the ITV current affairs show, World in Action. Unbelievably, it focused on the Acid House Party scene that was raging in London and throughout England. It showed footage of hundreds of sweaty party goers dancing to futuristic electronic dance music, in illegal dark warehouses filled with strobe lighting and dried ice and as a teen at that time, it excited me. The Acid House scene also made the front pages of the tabloids, but the media's attempt at scaremongering backfired badly as it simply made my friends and I all the more curious. From briefly meeting our new friends from London, who we'd never see again, we had got the inside track on how to dress, how to dance and what music to listen to. We had also got an inkling of what we needed to do to enhance this new experience, should the opportunity ever present itself.

It would only be a matter of months later, December 1989 to be exact, when I would attend a dance music event for the very first time. And as I left with the music ringing in my ears, it was a scene that I would become fully immersed in. It was pure escapism. I was incorrigible, as being part of such a scene gave me confidence to get away from archetypal teenage insecurities. Like many of my peers, this hyped-energetic sub-culture was somewhere that we could all fit in. The acid house scene, the rave scene, or the club scene, whatever your preferred nomenclature, also brought together positively like-minded Catholics, Protestants, and unbelievers alike, who happily set aside their perspectives. This enabled us to share in something at a sub-cultural level that we all had in common.

My school friends and I would go to these parties religiously and come Monday morning on the school bus we would evangelise about the experiences of the Saturday night before. Parties would happen in the most unlikely places. Dried-ice and strobe filled derelict buildings, art colleges, rural barns, or warehouses but this only enhanced the mystery. It was a unique generational movement and a once in a lifetime scene, where the excitable tension was often palpable.

Our love of obscure electronic dance music, fashion and all things club related, created a feverish, liberal culture of individualistic hedonism and promiscuity. It was a life-affirming scene that I would be part of on and off for more than ten years, and it seemed to be everywhere. At barely 16, my friends and I got our first taste of the addictive energy that came with the electronic dance music scene and most of us never looked back. It was an enthralling culture shock. I would club everywhere from Belfast, Dublin, and Glasgow, to London, Spain, and New York. Much like my other obsession, football, my adoration of this scene was yet another distracting, worldly modern-day idol that I would find very hard to shake off.

I would soon seek immediate gratification, earning money as soon as I could, helping me to escape my parental home and to live for the weekend. Now, it was clearly a time when I began to shift from Catholicism or Christianism, towards Capitalism. But, before I digress for a bit, let me be clear. People in Glasshouses must never throw stones. For as a Christian today, I am more than aware that it is not a sin, to have money, own a nice house, drive a nice car, wear nice clothes, or enjoy nice holidays. But what Jesus warns us in Mark 10:24 is, how hard it is for those who *trust* in riches to enter into the kingdom of God. For it is only wrong when we put our *trust* in money and materialism and put it first, because you can be the richest man in the world and still die and go to hell and not take a penny with you. Leaving your money for those who are still alive to fight over. It is also wrong when the love of money consumes us to such an extent that it distracts us from God and the eternal world to come. Therefore, by sharing the following observations throughout this chapter, I do so without judgement.

However, todays mammon-driven society is an influential world away from the era of dance music that I grew up with. Driven by both the controversial and the questionable world of celebrity and a modern culture propelled by the social media influencer, the prize on offer for today's young teens, is an enticing life of hedonistic and materialistic abandon, which appears to be on another stratosphere completely.

The Wider Dangers of Consumerism, Materialism, Individualism and Secularism

I have read of several multi-millionaires and even billionaire social media influencers, who I would not choose to be role models for anybody. There seems to be a very dangerous trend of excessive parties, girls, drugs, and money that, sadly, some young teenagers are blinded by. It deeply concerns me that these influencers can have such a profound impact on children and teenagers, by teaching them that the individual, material, and temporal is all that matters and that morals do not. This can lead to all sorts of trouble (emotional, mental, and spiritual) for the younger impressionable generation, one of whom may have been me if the internet had been around when I was that age.

Yet today there is growing evidence that a powerful billionaires' spending extends well beyond greed driven ownership of personal private jets, private yachts, islands, and exclusive properties for their pets. Let us consider the prodigious acceleration and convergence of NBIC. Nanotechnology, Biotechnology, Information Technology and cognitive science.

In the spirit of aggressive individualism and as if to highlight the danger of excessive wealth, there are those affluent enough to afford the necessary cybernetic augmentation 'improvements' to the human body and brain (that might one day enable those who dream of immortality to age less, suffer less and possibly die less). The ultimate overarching aim of such movements is to cheat death and extend life through the use of the aforementioned transhumanistic technologies.

Let us also consider their children. I once read that the first genetic manipulation of eighty-six embryos using biotechnological methods had already been carried out in China in 2016. The aspiration? To increase the IQ of a child before birth. The consensus on such mental enhancement was by selecting embryos after sequencing, *a country* could enhance its IQ by up to 60 points within decades. Of course, where there is NBIC for technological human enhancement there is also NBIC for human eradication. Take Down Syndrome, which is disappearing before our eyes. In UK 90%, France 97% and the US an estimated 75% of pregnancies with a prenatal diagnosis, are terminated with abortion, which is on demand and freely available for those harbouring desires for the a la carte genetic design of 'perfect' babies, which it is believed via NBIC will be (or already is) readily available.

Such technologies also now bring forth the reality of artificial wombs, making it possible to incubate future humans in vitro. In fact, biologist and philosopher Henri Atlan has posited that by 2030 as a year that the artificial uterus will become the norm, 'freeing women from the burden of bearing children'. Or to put it another way, technology and transhumanism is ready to "wipe out" traditional human reproduction and create a risk for the existence of the traditional family.

As doctor and entrepreneur Laurent Alexadre quotes, 'with every growing day societal equal rights for gay couples improve. Currently French gay men go to the USA or Asia where there is a whole market for invitro fertilization. They buy a bespoke egg and hire a womb for nine months before the parents come back with a baby and the authorities turn a blind eye after a bit of red tape to transfer the child's civil status.' 'In every case the child can only be biologically descended from one parent, which leads to an obvious source of understandable frustration for the other party left in the cold. However, NBIC is now going to make it feasible for gay partners to use the genes of both parents. A technique, developed by the Japanese inventor Shinya Namanaka who won the Nobel Prize in Medicine in 2012, involves manufacture of fibroblast cells found under the skin (please note scientific matters such as this are not my area of expertise).

In fact, it is already possible to make a mouse from two fathers, so transferring these techniques to humans is apparently only a matter of time, and pressure groups are campaigning for any delay in the research to be brief.' In fact, I read at the time of writing, a March 2022 article in the New York Times, which confirmed, that the prospect of women conceiving without men has moved a step closer after Chinese researchers produced a baby mouse from an unfertilised egg for the first time – with survival possible with only the mother's genetic information. Parthenogenesis, the ancient Greek term for a virgin birth, is used by scientists to describe a process where eggs spontaneously divide, without fertilisation by sperm, to form an embryo.

Much like humanism has been described as atheism rebranded, so too is there a school of thought that suggests transhumanism and eugenics could be considered in a similar vein. Where science and radical transhumanists are pressing to take control of all facets of life through genetic and scientific advances - from pre-birth, life and even post-death—and they do so with the seemingly bottomless, financial support of its 'Henchmen at GAFA'. That is, Google, Apple, Facebook, and Amazon. Indeed, with rapid advances in this biotechnological revolution with 'God like' advances in individuals own power and a would-be Jesus-like victory over death – who will want to remain a would-be obsolete human, fragile and sick when his neighbours are geniuses and more or less immortal through the use of human implantable biochips and cybernetic devices?

It was Dr Yuval Noah Harari, speaking at the World Economic Forum (WEF) and in line with the proposed Great Reset of 2030, who described humans as 'hackable animals'. He warned that 'God believing people who believed they once had a soul and free will' that this time "is now over". That through science we will have the ability to become... our own Gods. "We must never allow a good crisis to go to waste (Covid-19 Global Pandemic) for by implementing (implanting a chip or a mark in or on the hand) a new surveillance regime under one's skin, we develop the ability to collect biometric data to enable us to know them (humans) better than they might know themselves. By 'hacking organisms' to 're-engineer human beings', we can also control and create new life forms that are shaped by intelligent design…"

Such 'new world order' driven language, maybe deemed demeaning of God and diminishing of Christianity.

For those who are conspiracy minded, it is not implausible to suggest that such AI technologies could evaluate, track and control those who could conform to its use. Where they are, what they spend, what they search for online, where they worship and what they think. In essence we have already been doing this, analytically and algorithmically to a much lesser extent, through the use of our phones. Such technology will no longer be on us (we can leave phones at home), but it will be in us. However biblically speaking this opens up near endless possibilities for all kinds of new evil. That is the concern God raised at Babel when the people sought to reach heaven - "nothing that they propose to do will now be impossible for them."

Of course, I wasn't just singling out popular social media influencers when making my previous observations. For if one considers where the metaphorical saying people in glasshouses shouldn't throw stones came from? There are a number of options. The proverb appeared in Chaucer's Troilus and Criseyde, written in 1385. Later George Herbert modified it in this way: "Whose house is of glass must not throw stones at another." So, I speak without judgement.

But today, the world of celebrity and society in general, appears to have taken an overt, rampant, menacing turn. I read recently of an American based music artist who collaborated with a global company to release a 'bespoke' sports shoe marketed as "Satan's Shoes". As confirmed in a Guardian article, a company injected a drop of its employees' blood into the soles of 666 pairs of red-and-black trainers before selling out of the product in a minute. In a similar vein, a world-famous Skateboarder, was filmed online giving his blood to a company to be injected within the artwork on the base of his board. Is this ritualism?

The trainers added a pentagram 'charm' to the laces beside the words "Luke 10:18"—a reference to the Bible passage, "I saw Satan fall like lightning from heaven." Whilst nineteenth century occult groups such as The Golden Dawn, held that the 'point up' pentagram represented the rulership of spirit over physical elements the 'point down' pentagram, as highlighted on the "Satan trainers", represented the descent of the spirit into matter or a matter subsuming spirit. Such symbols are now universally synonymous with the sign of Baphomet, the Goat of Mendes or Satan. It is also the official copyright of the existing Church of Satan, which was formed by Anton LeVey in 1966. It is also the symbol used on the front cover of the 'bible' used by esoteric organisations such as, The Order of The Eastern Star.

Considering this, does the release of such products perhaps stray beyond the bounds of the consumeristic culture of hype or even detournement? Or, put simply, is the release of such products, marketed and advertised in such an overt and incongruous manner, blasphemy? Or is this merely further evidence of a secularisation of society and a seismic shift towards a consumeristic world promoting materialism and individualism? But note that such occurrences are not wholly unusual currently.

Take the erection of an eight-foot, one-ton bronze coated statue of Baphomet, developed by The Satanic Temple, in the state of Arkansa. In a Chicago Tribune article it highlighted the following, "The thing about members of the Satanic Temple: They don't (apparently) actually worship Satan. Or, at least, devil worship is not a requirement to join the organisation based in Salem, Massachusetts."

"The Satan of Modern Satanism is a metaphorical icon for *Enlightenment values*," the Temple's co-founder, Lucien Greaves, once wrote in an op-ed for The Washington Post. "I identify nontheistically with a Miltonic Satan that defies all subjugation, exalts scientific inquiry and promotes Humanistic, pluralistic values and freedom of conscience." At the time of writing, the Satanic Temple has taken it strides one step further having been permitted to host multiple after-school "Satan Club" meetings at a midwestern elementary school because, in the spirit of religious freedom, pluralism, equality and liberty, *any* religiously affiliated groups are allowed to hire out the school facility. But as the influence and force of godlessness grows in the world, can we expect to see an overt growth in this type of outlandish behavior? Can we expect to see the flaunting of graven images and the use of esoteric symbolism? It is as though our society has suddenly stepped through a ceremonial CERN-like portal and released all manner of demonic energy and dark matter, encouraging the worship of other Gods.

Although some might deem the aforementioned paragraphs and quotations as a tad sensational. My point is, that most of what I have highlighted is about as well known as the existence of the Georgia Guidestones. For the rise of such would-be diabolical, ritualistic occurrences, which would have been unthinkable ten years ago, are gradually becoming normalised and mainstream on our streets, in our schools and on our screens. This signifies a change in times and a seismic transformation at a global and a cultural level.

However, St Paul prepares us for the rise of such events in this world, when he talks about those who would be immune to such influences. For the secret power of lawlessness is already at work; but the one who now holds it back will continue to do so until he is taken out of the way. And then the lawless one will be revealed, whom the Lord Jesus will overthrow with the breath of his mouth and destroy by the splendour of his coming. The coming of the lawless one will be in accordance with how Satan works... and all the ways that wickedness deceives those who are perishing. They perish because they refused to love the truth and so be saved. For this reason, God sends them a powerful delusion so that they will believe the lie and so that all will be condemned who have not believed the truth but have delighted in wickedness. (2 Thessalonians 2).

Societal risks and challenges for Christians

Aligned with this, I encountered these challenging yet unforgettable words from Pastor Rick Warren, which highlighted the risk of such societal changes. "In today's society, materialism is idolised, immorality is glamourised, truth is minimised, sin is normalised, divorce is rationalised, and abortion is legalised. In TV and movies, crime is legitimised, drug use is minimised, comedy is vulgarised, sex is trivialised, the Bible is fictionalised, churches are satirised, God is marginalised, and Christians are demonised. The elderly are dehumanised, the sick are euthanised, the poor are victimised, the mentally ill are ostracised, immigrants are stigmatised, and children are tranquilised. In families around the world, our manners are uncivilised, speech is vulgarised, faith is secularised, and everything is commercialised. Unfortunately, Christians, you and I are often disorganised and demoralised, our faith is compartmentalised, and our witness is compromised. So, what do we need? We need to revitalise our worship, minimise our differences, mobilise our members, and evangelise the lost, and we need to re-energise our families."

There are many verses in scripture which condemn hedonism and the worldly pursuit of pleasure. In Ecclesiastes 2:1-11, Solomon openly tested a superficial life of hedonism and pleasure - "I said to myself, come now, I will test you with pleasure to find out what is good." But that also proved to be meaningless... And what does pleasure accomplish? I tried cheering myself with wine, and embracing folly... I wanted to see what was good for men to do under the heavens during the few days of their lives ... I amassed silver and gold for myself, and the treasure of kings and provinces. I acquired ... a harem as well— the delights of a man's heart... In all this my wisdom stayed with me. I denied myself nothing my eyes desired; I refused my heart no pleasure... Yet when I surveyed all that my hands had done and what I had toiled to achieve, everything was meaningless, a chasing after the wind; nothing was gained under the sun."

Solomon himself proclaimed that his hedonistic life lived for pleasure was meaningless and that all was vanity. There was no enduring, eternal sense of meaning to a life lived for such earthly pleasures. Yet setting aside what we learn from Solomon's vanity and vexation of mirth, sensual pleasure, riches, and pomp, or from what we discover from our own excessive worldly journeys, what's clear is that God is fully glorified in and of Himself and His glory is not diminished because of the disobedience of mankind (Malachi 3:6, Revelation 1:8).

Moreover, in Proverbs 4:14-15 it tells us to completely avoid any situation that might give rise to temptation that might invariably lead to sin and separation from God. It states, "Do not enter the path of the wicked, and do not walk in the way of evil. Avoid it, do not travel on it; turn away from it and pass on."

Furthermore, I stumbled across these wonderful words online, from a C. S. Lewis sermon entitled, "The Weight of Glory" June 8, 1942. "It would seem that Our Lord finds our desires not too strong, but too weak. We are half-hearted creatures, fooling about with drink and sex and ambition when infinite joy is offered us, like an ignorant child who wants to go on making mud pies in a slum because he cannot imagine what is meant by the offer of a holiday at the sea. We are far too easily pleased."

Of course, I do not write any of these words in a judgmental spirit, but it is by my personal experience and therefore in my humble opinion, that a mammon driven, secularized world dedicated to consumerism, individualism, and materialism, can only blind us to the truth. It can take us down many wrong paths and wide roads. It encourages a life lived for the self, which is a life not lived for Christ. It is a life where one can stray into many questionable ideologies. I once listened to an interview given by British theologian Dr Stephen Bullivant and author of Mass Exodus, who confirmed that up 75% of British under thirties today said they have no religion. The move away from Christianity is accelerating, whilst a move towards a British culture of paganism appears to be growing.

It can be argued that without God, many people will do as well in this life, as those people who have God in their life. For we only know what we know. Yet because God's Word can be deemed meaningless to an atheist or next to meaningless to an agnostic, for instance, then what exists for the unbeliever or the unsure, when faced with the prospect of one single, short lifespan? With no faith, where is the hope? It is for this reason that I, even at that point when I appeared to be most separated from God in my life, give praise that I was always a believer. I always believed. I may not have behaved in thought or word or deed as a believer should, but I always believed, and I give thanks and praise for that grace.

In Michael Novak's book, Belief and Unbelief he writes "I was born a Catholic, and many times that fact has prompted me to alternate between gratitude and despair: gratitude because I am quite sure that if I had not been born a Catholic, I would scarcely have found my way into a church. I have often felt despair because God came to be too easily, before I had a chance, entering my blood and bones through my mother's milk. It might have been easier to decide freely whether to believe or to disbelieve if I had been born an atheist... But there have always been contrary experiences and reflections that made it impossible for me to become an atheist conscientiously (because) there is no comfort in the heart, no oil upon the forehead or ointment on one's wounds. There is no vision of a heaven nor any haven of hope."

Conversely Aldous Huxley, in Ends and Means, admitted that a desire to avoid moral restraints was a motivation for disbelief, offering a 'liberation from a certain system of morality.' 'Belief in a divine being is accompanied by a sense of accountability to that being. So, to escape the condemnation of conscience, created by God, some simply deny the existence of God. But we can never claim that science either proves or disproves the existence of God.' What Solomon discovered was that the most learned of men, who die as a stranger to Christ, will perish equally with the most ignorant; and what good can commendations on earth do to the body in the grave, or the soul in hell?

Knowing this—do you and or members of your nuclear or extended family and friends currently live a hedonistic and an individualistic lifestyle? Do you live a life devoid of God, Jesus, Church, and scripture? Have you blindly stumbled upon other ideologies and encountered blasphemy or are you living an individualistically worldly life, with no thoughts of life after death? Have you found that you've climbed your own personal mountain only to have reached the top and discovered you have absolutely no further to go? Have you reached the pinnacle of career success or financial success and discovered that every element of this life is temporal? Regardless of what our chief vices might be, if we close our eyes and consult the secret tribunal of our souls, we might wish to ask ourselves this question. Can a life of frivolous ostentation enable us to find a way to truth?

For it is written, "Watch and pray, lest you fall into temptation. The spirit indeed is willing, but the flesh is weak." Matthew 26: 41.

CHAPTER 6:
THE APPLE DOESN'T FALL FAR

The Kibble Palace, Glasgow (1873)

"The first thing you notice is the absence of noise, a peaceful appreciated silence. You realise something has changed when you enter Kibble Palace – the gardens exude a romantic feel, as though nothing since the end of the 19ᵗʰ century seems to have changed. You can barely hear the sound of the traffic outside and the tropical heat under the gloomy Scottish sky transports you."

—The Garden Edit.com

LOCATED ON THE GREAT WESTERN ROAD in the heart of the 'self-confident' West End of Glasgow, The Kibble Palace comes with an enthralling past and is rightly regarded as one of Glasgow's proudest possessions. John Kibble has been described as many things such as a wealthy entrepreneur and an engineer, but he was also known to be a tad eccentric, a claim extenuated by the fact that he was the only man to have bicycled across Loch Lomond on floats, around the mid-1800s.

The palace was designed for Kibble by architects James Boucher and James Cousland and was constructed at his home at Coulport on the shores of Loch Lomond in the 1860s. By 1871 he agreed to deconstruct the glass palace and transport it on a barge from Loch Lomond, up the river Clyde, to Glasgow to be reconstructed in the Botanic Gardens. This delicate Victorian structure was extended with the introduction of a large 150ft diameter, circular dome before the newly completed ornate palace reopened in 1873. Once opened its interior was lit by 600 gas lamps, which could be coloured for theatrical effect.

A popular aspect of the Glasgow fabric, The Kibble Palace is loved by children, families, students, and visitors alike, but it has had a truly fascinating history, as a venue for events, concerts, flower shows and public meetings. One such event saw two famous politicians of the Victorian era, Benjamin Disraeli (1873) and William Ewart Gladstone (1879) ceremoniously installed as rectors of Glasgow University, in the Kibble Palace.

Another public meeting saw two North American evangelical Christian preachers, Moody, and Sankey, hold a religious revival meeting at which they preached the Word of the Lord from the back of a horse drawn carriage, to an estimated 6,000 people who were apparently shoe-horned into the palace, whilst another 15,000 to 30,000 had to stand and listen from outside of the conservatory.

When the aforementioned Moody and Sankey first came to Scotland in the 19th century, their 'mission was one of implicit faith and of unselfish zeal for the saving of sinners and of unsaved souls. A striking case of conversion was that of a notorious infidel, the chairman of a club of freethinkers. He declared his utter disbelief in the value of prayer and defied Mr. Moody to test its power on him. The evangelist accepted the challenge in faith and remembered him continually in his petitions until he heard of him finding Christ, months after.'

Ironically, The Kibble Palace and other such glass houses, is now an increasingly popular venue for non-religious, humanist wedding ceremonies. In the spirit of truth, I must admit that humanists and humanism were phrases that I did not have in my vocabulary, prior to commencement of this book. This non-religious, secular movement apparently looks to science and 'naturalism' to understand the universe and it would appear to be focused on individualism. Like atheism rebranded, it is evidence of a cultural shift and social change, which is presently transforming many perceptions within our society. I could not help but think that if any modern-day Moody and Sankey might be willing to, once again, convert today's free thinkers, then perhaps they might take to the Kibble Palace, to do so.

In 1878 a new set of glasshouses were constructed, separate from the Kibble Palace and these were constructed using teak, a popular choice of timber at the time, as opposed to steel. These were called the 'Main range' to differentiate them from 'The

Kibble'. Since the 1880s Kibble Palace has been primarily used to grow a large plethora of differing botanical species. In fact, much like the quality ingredients used to assemble a comforting haggis, this stunning Scottish- based glass house possesses a rare fern collection that comprises of Australian and New Zealand tree ferns, some of which were planted in the 1880s, still forming part of its national temperate plant collection today. In 1881 a loan was secured from the Corporation of the city of Glasgow to rebuild the main range of glass houses which had been moved from Loch Lomond but that was a fateful day in the Botanic Gardens history as the Royal Botanic Gardens were incapable of repaying the loan and so the Corporation took over the running of the Gardens on 1st April 1887.

In 2003 the Kibble Palace closed for the commencement of a significant restoration project, which saw the structure once again disassembled. Corroded and decaying metals, which were a major element of the proposed restoration works, were tagged, shipped off and returned, having been restored and made good. Go to any Victorian glass house around the world and you will discover that the risk of corrosion is a material characteristic when constructing any structure that uses cast or wrought iron metals.

Time to get all scientific for a moment. There are two main types of corrosion that occur to cast iron. Chemical corrosion and galvanic corrosion. I discovered this at a course in Stirling in Scotland, hosted by Historic Environment Scotland on Maintenance and Repair Techniques for Traditional Cast Iron, some months prior to my visit to Glasgow. Chemical corrosion occurs when iron oxidises i.e., the metal loses electrons to a non-metal substance such as oxygen. When cast iron is exposed to water and air for a prolonged period of time, the water lying on the metal surface acts as an electrolyte – a substance that enables the release of electrons from the iron. These released electrons then combine with the oxygen in the air - this is chemical corrosion. A method of reducing the risk of chemical corrosion is to ensure that Iron work is painted or coated, possibly specifying a marine grade paint, and reducing the risk of future maintenance, ensuring that the paintwork is not cracked or flaked. This will attempt to prevent moisture or air coming into direct contact with a metal surface, reducing the risk of chemical corrosion.

Galvanic corrosion (also known as bi-metallic corrosion or sacrificial corrosion) occurs when two dissimilar metals are placed in direct contact with one another in the presence of water – this is a form of electrochemical corrosion. In these circumstances, one metal will corrode sacrificially to another. Water, rain, moisture, condensation, all common place in Victorian conservatories, acts as an electrolyte, establishing an electrical current between two metals (forming what is effectively a battery acid). A 'less noble' metal such as cast iron or wrought iron will be attacked by a 'more noble' metal such as mild steel and will subsequently sacrifice itself and corrode and decay when affected by water ingress.

In glasshouses or Palm Houses, historically specified fixings such as nuts, and bolts are of mild steel. However, I'll let you into a little secret that I learned in Scotland that is neither scientific nor cost prohibitive. For the price of less than a ten pence piece, a simple plastic washer, positioned between the mild steel and the wrought or cast iron can greatly reduce the risk of corrosion occurring in this manner. A lesson learned via my colleagues in Stirling and Glasgow. Fellow Celt's, I salute you.

In Eric W Curtis 'The Story of Glasgow Botanical Gardens', he commented, 'the deterioration of the structure of the Kibble Palace had been causing concern for many years and considerable funding was needed for a complete restoration. After a successful funding bid and a Heritage Lottery Fund grant, a contract was put out to tender, and this was won by Shepley Engineering Limited. They were a firm with considerable relevant experience, having previously worked on the restoration of the Victorian glasshouses at Glasnevin in Dublin. The Kibble Palace was completely disassembled, and the elements were subsequently transported to Shepley's in England, where the contractor restored each element individually. The building was obviously closed to the public during the project, enabling all existing plants and four hundred tree ferns to be removed by hand and decanted to a nursery in Bella-Houston Park.'

As the project drew to a close, the central cupola and lantern, with new decorative finial were lowered by crane onto the reconstructed roof and the plants were suitably reinstated. The Kibble Palace project successfully completed before it reopened, appropriately on 2006 on 30th November, which is also St. Andrews Day.

When my visit to the beautiful Kibble had ended, I walked to a wonderfully named restaurant on Byres Road called Ubiquitous Chip, where I enjoyed a refined 'traditional' Scottish lunch of haggis, neaps and tatties with a whiskey sauce – modern Scotland on a plate.

I digress for a moment but to get to the Kibble, I took the subway from Buchanan Street to Hillhead, the station on Byres Rd in the heart of Glasgow's west end. It wasn't until I arrived and walked onto Byres Road that the place suddenly looked vaguely familiar, and the memories gradually came trickling back. In retrospect it transpired that I had dined at the aforementioned restaurant, some fifteen years before my latest visit, but I hadn't remembered. I used to spend a lot of time in Glasgow, but lively weekends left me with some very hazy memories. My then mate and I used to go to Glasgow a few times a year to enjoy blow-outs with his three brothers, all of whom studied in and subsequently permanently resided in Scotland.

Cut from a similar cloth back then, we all got on famously and always enjoyed being in each other's company. Travelling between Ireland and Scotland we would celebrate almost all key milestones together.

Yet, my memories of Scotland offer prime examples of the idols of hedonism and individualism that were prevalent my life at that time. They truly blinded me, but it wasn't long before they were joined by further new demons, in the form of consumerism and materialism. The common belief is that the definition of consumption rarely strays beyond the ingestion of stimulants that are legal or otherwise, but the truth is the idol of consumption has many ugly faces.

For instance, I have encountered many who purport to be followers of Jesus and who might well successfully appear to abstain today from consuming cigarettes and alcohol. Yet, I have witnessed that their alternative to cigarettes and alcohol might be binge-watching Netflix or an overt social media addiction. They might compulsively overeat refined sugars and saturated fats, by abusing food in a glutinous fashion. It may be regular frivolous consumption of impulse material purchases on the Internet, leading to the consumption of physical space within a household. Or the willful consumption of energy and power with relentless over-use of technological devices, appliances, or finite natural resources. And let's not overlook those who consume money by secretly gambling. It may be guys and girls addicted to the consumption of pornography, which has become a dangerous and very accessible vice for Christians and non-Christians alike. Consumption may merely impact a person's emotions, if they are physically consumed by envy, jealousy or spite filled covetousness. These are all examples of the far-reaching damage that can be caused by the infectious sin of consumption.

But as always, I say with love, 'people in glass houses'...

However, over the course of a decade, Glasgow was the Scottish city that I became very familiar with. It was a cool, happening city with a gritty edge and I loved anytime I spent there. On the other hand, Edinburgh, with its apparent superior air and its historical, tourist-driven nature, was by comparison a city that I was unfamiliar with. So, having found myself in Scotland for a work-related course in 2018, I factored in a prearranged morning visit, to the Royal Botanic Garden Edinburgh (RBGE). It was a beautifully mild morning when I arrived at Edinburgh's famous Princes Street. The sun was out, so I took a stroll along its wide public realm pathways, enjoying a glance at its world-famous Edinburgh Castle, which was located a short distance away on an elevated height. Following this, I promptly hailed a taxi, which took me to the salubrious sandstone bathed suburb at Inver Leith Row, which was about a mile or so outside of the city centre. Royal Botanic Garden Edinburgh (1858) was described In Glasshouse Greenhouse (2018) by India Hobson and Magnus Edmundson as "the first building (dating from 1858) and a rather grand looking stone Victorian affair comprising of tall arched windows and a curvilinear glass top, we head indoors. Inside, palms grow both tall and wide in equal measure, native to southern China and Australia but seemingly very happy here in Scotland, wrapped snug under a greenhouse blanket."

RBGE, like Glasnevin in Dublin has a splendid glasshouse collection, however for the purpose of this chapter I am going to focus primarily on its tremendous Temperate House. With construction completed in 1858, RBGEs Temperate House is regarded as one of the tallest traditional Palm House's in Britain, standing at an impressive height of 21.95 metres. Designed by Robert Matheson, the glasshouse was principally constructed of sandstone with a roof of curvilinear iron rafters and the end result was veritably palatial. The principal gardener at the time was a man called James McNab, who believed that the solid masonry prevented rapid cooling and provided shade for the successful cultivation of plants; he also argued that too much sunlight was not good for growing palms, hence the front of the glasshouse was made to face west.

Like almost all of the Palm Houses discussed in this book, the RBGE glasshouse range has undergone many transformations over the years. However, even though the Temperate House's powerfully imposing external envelope has remained relatively untouched – inside is where much of its changes have occurred. What I love about this breath-taking structure and what for me made it unique from many of the other glasshouses that I would visit through the UK, Ireland, and the world, was its imposing sandstone façade. In todays 'global-world', many of the glasshouse designs that I have witnessed have been analogous albeit in a beautiful way. Yet, if someone had blindfolded me and dropped me into RBGE, then once the blindfold was removed, I would have safely assumed that I was in Scotland, the moment I glanced at its commanding sandstone façade and its church-like window arches; and that for me added to its importance.

As I visually surveyed the Temperate Palm House, I inspected its glazing and metal work, which as you would imagine, highlighted slight evidence of ventilation issues that had caused minor corrosion and cracking, but I was impressed by its existing condition. Moreover, having gained privileged access onto its striking geometric rooftop, I was able to gaze down at its impressive collection of other glass houses, greenhouses, and fernery structures as well as its Tropical Palm House, which still houses a Sabal palm (Sabal burmudana) thought to date from circa 1790.

In Leonie Patterson's 'How the Garden Grew' she highlighted; The Sabal Palm photographed in the centre of the Tropical Palm house early in 1874. It is looking good despite its recent 'retubbing' and move from the Temperate House next door. Over fifty years prior to this it had been one of the plants transported from the gardens previous site on Leith Walk. It was eventually removed from its tub and planted into the ground of the Tropical Palm House at the beginning of the 20th century, and still proudly remains in place to this day. Whilst on the roof of the Temperate House, I was also in a privileged position to enjoy an unexpected, distant, eye level view of the illustrious Edinburgh Castle. It was a special experience that I would suggest very few Scotsmen or Scots-women will have ever enjoyed; and I very much appreciated that.

VERY EARLY ON IN LIFE I RECOGNISED that I was cut from a different cloth to my father. We physically didn't look the same. He was bulky and pale, whilst I was slight and swarthy. He was six foot four inches in height and at least fifteen stone in weight, which meant he towered above my modest, svelte five foot seven-inch frame. Physically he was very strong but behind the outward facade he could be one of the weakest men I knew. He was a people pleaser, who guffawed at things he didn't find funny. He was always the life and soul of the party when in full view, but behind closed doors he could be a completely different character.

It was not exceptional for him to dampen a Christmas period, a holiday, or a family event with one of his characteristic mood swings – usually about the cost of something or other. He was a blue-collar worker, whose rough hands and dirty fingernails were a testament to the physical nature of his tough life. There can be no question that he worked very hard. Manually grafting for eight hours a day, he could come home, and having barely eaten dinner, he might begin to paint the house, or chainsaw branches from our large oak tree, whatever needed doing. He used to encourage me to watch him carry out household DIY, like drilling holes in walls, erecting a fence or building furniture. But even then, I knew that wasn't something I was interested in. It wasn't for me, and as a teenager I used to say I would sooner pay someone to do that for me. I wasn't being aloof, effeminate, or lazy. But the mere notion that I would come home from work, to start working at home, wasn't something that ever appealed to me. True to my word, to this day, I have never owned a drill or a box of tools.

In the early days he always seemed to struggle to achieve any of society's success goals. This appeared to leave him bitter and with self-esteem issues, and I would suggest this negatively impacted upon his psyche, his marriage, and his household. But it would later transpire, there was something else deep and underlying that was the root cause of much of his darkness. Admittedly he had a difficult upbringing. Having been encouraged to leave school at fourteen with no educational qualifications, he worked to help his mother raise his three brothers and two sisters. His mother died when he was in his twenties, six years before I was born. He would later share with me openly about his very difficult relationship with his father, who although successful in his own way, had an ongoing battle with some personal demons. From what he would later share, aggression was prevalent throughout his upbringing and sadly, such an undercurrent was often present in my house as a child too. I can only surmise that this facet of his personality had cascaded down from his father. But times were changing, and that parenting style was becoming less acceptable. I didn't like to hear what he had shared with me about his father, because it deeply saddened me to hear what he went through. With that said, never once did my father ever attack me physically, and corporal punishment was never a thing in our world.

Sensational histrionics, were however, common place between my parents. They had a volatile relationship. But I recall one particular evening when things would come to a head and the awful truth that had been rotting the core of our family would be exposed. I was twenty-five at the time and had come home for the evening. My parents had separated again except this time, my father had moved out of our house. However, for some inane reason, he had come back to our home, a tad worse for wear. An awkward conversation quickly descended, as the tone changed when I confronted him about his attitude and his mental and emotional abuse of the family. Without getting into specific details, things intensified rapidly, and it was at this point I knew something was going to be spoken about that would change my life forever. It would be remiss of me to repeat exactly how the evening ended. But rest assured it had not ended well. For it wasn't until the next morning, when emotions had somewhat subsided, that my mother sat me down on my bed and said we needed to talk. It was at that point that I discovered that my whole life had been a complete lie.

She announced that the man I knew my whole life to be my father, actually wasn't my biological father at all. It transpired that my genetic father was born in Greece and, if alive, could well be residing in London. This revelation provided immediate answers to the majority of questions I had about the nature of their relationship; and the causation of the erraticism that I had witnessed throughout my family life. I was sickened. On and on she lamented and laboured but I was numb, truly disgusted. My *father* wasn't my father. My brother, who I had little in common with, was actually a half-brother. My extended family on one side, were not my extended *family* and my surname might not have been my surname. Worse still, I suspected that other extended family members knew well before I did, and somehow that made it even harder to accept. How could they have kept me in the dark for my whole life? I was devastated.

It was a cold but fresh Sunday morning and I needed to get away from the bad energy that existed in the household at that time. So, I went for a country walk, before stopping to sit on a traditional stone wall near a babbling river. It was really hard to think. As I watched swans and their signets glide by, I started going over things in my head. I recalled a few years earlier at approximately twenty years of age that I was experiencing random bouts of exhaustion. I was always feeling run down and was badly fatigued. So, I went to the doctor and then onto the hospital for a subsequent blood test. I really had no idea as to the causation. However, when I got my results, nothing prepared me for what the Doctor would confirm.

Thalassemia Beta is historically regarded as a Mediterranean blood disorder that had all of the aforementioned symptoms I was experiencing. After I had asked the doctor if he had mixed my results with someone else's; and after he confirmed that he had not; he stated, 'I think you better go home and have a chat with your parents'. I was perplexed, highly confused. Have a chat? About what? How was this remotely feasible? Was this medical negligence? These results *must* belong to someone else. The thing is when I told my parents they were vacant, agreeing that the results could have been a mistake. Focusing instead on the proposed remedy that was, to take iron tablets and increase my intake of iron by adding more red meat to my diet, which I duly did.

In the absence of any admission from anyone about anything, I gradually began to feel physically better, and my energy returned. I know it must be hard to believe, but I must have simply accepted it at that time, as some sort of administrative error, burying the experience deep in my subconscious, happy that I returned to fitness and to a normal life. However, it cannot be glossed over that this was one point in time when I could have and should have, known the truth.

CHAPTER 7:
ICONIC

The Great Exhibition Building - The Crystal Palace (1851)

"The Quantity of bodily industry which that Crystal Palace expresses is very great. The quantity of thought it expresses is, I suppose, a single and very admirable thought of Sir Joseph Paxton's, probably not a bit brighter than thousands of thoughts which pass through his active and intelligent brain every hour – that it might be possible to build a greenhouse larger than ever was built here. This thought, and some very ordinary algebra, are as much as all that glass can represent of human intellect."

—John Ruskin – 'The Stones of Venice' (1851-1853)

A FACEBOOK FRIEND, WHO ALSO happens to be a wonderful photographer of global architecture, posted an image one Saturday evening of an urbanistic high rise in Croydon that had been constructed in the 1970s. It looked to me less like a residential apartment block and crudely more like a tall stack of Millennium Falcon's. I usually like all of his posts. The structure in question was the Noble Lowndes Tower, also known as the Three penny Bit or Fifty Pence building. However, on this one occasion I posted "horrible design", at which point he politely responded that the building was "of its time" to which I replied, "I got that, but I still didn't like the design". A third party pitched in the next evening with the following light-hearted comment, "Croydon is not the place of iconic architecture!! But when one came off the train from

Victoria Station (very rarely) a few sheets to the wind…it was the landmark to get one home!!' The lady followed her post with a laughing emoji, and I responded in kind. Yet, I held back from what I truly wanted to say, not wanting to get 'too deep' on a Sunday evening. But what I could have posted was - 'On the contrary! Croydon (Sydenham Hill actually, which the London Borough of Croydon shares with Lambeth as part of their jurisdiction) was actually the birthplace of one of the most globally persuasive and iconic architectural landmarks that the Victorian curvilinear glasshouse world has ever seen!!'

To write a book about Victorian glasshouses and not acknowledge the influential Joseph Paxton would be inopportune, to say the least. Chatsworth House is a stately home in Derbyshire, England, that is located in the Derbyshire Dales 3.5 miles (5.6 km) north-east of Bakewell and 9 miles (14 km) west of Chesterfield. The seat of the Duke of Devonshire, it has been home to the Cavendish family since 1549. Joseph Paxton was the head gardener and engineer at Chatsworth House, and he would develop arguably the most magnificent of all English conservatories, the Great Conservatory (1836-1840).

It was Joseph Paxton's engineering that transformed the grounds at Chatsworth House. Wonderful feats of construction combined with clever landscape architecture, enabled Paxton to expand the Duke of Devonshire's extensive collection of conifers into a 40 acre or 160,000m2 arboretum. There were also towering rock formations and a gravity fed 296 feet tall Emperor Fountain and waterfalls, impressively installed.

However, the Great Conservatory at Chatsworth House, which was designed by architect Decimus Burton and took four years to construct, was arguably Paxton's greatest feat.

At 84m long, 37m wide and 19m high it was the world's largest glass house at that time, with the world's largest sheets of glass, each measuring an unprecedented 4ft in length.

A vast tropical bio-dome at c30,000 sq ft, it was located in the middle of the expansive Derbyshire estate. It was primarily designed to house William Cavendish, the 6th Duke of Devonshire's, elaborate collection of tropical plants that led Charles Darwin to remark how he believed he was 'in a tropical environment for real'. Yet, the conservatory was designed on such a majestic scale that it could also accommodate an impressive central pathway that allowed carriages to pass by each other comfortably, beneath its lofty glass ceiling. It was designed, of course, to house tall palms, rockeries, ponds, and aquatic plant life, and all of which would elicit eloquent odors for the pleasure of its many Victorian visitors.

Conservatories became popular in the 19th century providing shelter and an artificial climate enabling sensitive plants to flourish. Chatsworth required eight underground boilers and ten men to keep the fires fed and to keep the glass house suitably heated. However, during the First World War (1914-1918) there was an insufficient coal supply, so heating the conservatory became problematic. The upshot was that many of the plants subsequently died, and the conservatory gradually fell into disrepair. The proposed capital cost of any restoration project was cost prohibitive and the ongoing revenue costs attached to heating and maintenance of the structure meant that a tired Great Conservatory would be demolished in 1920.

Today, only the foundations of this incredible structure remain, but without the expense of a redevelopment project, visitors can enjoy the wonderment of modern technology, by donning headsets and taking a 3D virtual reality tour from inside the once, awe inspiring glasshouse structure.

Moving forward, The Crystal Palace was a modular, prefabricated, cast iron and plate glass structure originally built in Hyde Park, London, to house the Great Exhibition of 1851. The exhibition took place from 1st May to 15th October 1851, and more than 14,000 exhibitors from around the world gathered within its

990,000 square feet (92,000 m²) exhibition space to display examples of technology developed in the Industrial Revolution.

In John Hix's 'The Glasshouse', he had this to say of The Crystal Palace, 'The Great Exhibition building of 1851 has now become symbolic of an age of industrial and imperial expansion. It is a watershed construction, a pivotal building between a former period of experimentation and the later period of confident design and engineering.' Paxton suggested an arched roof on the lines of his conservatory at Chatsworth, which would take account of a group of elm trees which traversed the proposed existing site. Designed by Joseph Paxton, the iconic Great Exhibition building was 1,851 feet (564 m) long, with an interior height of 128 feet (39 m). It was three times the size of St Paul's Cathedral.'

It was constructed at a cost of £2m, which apparently equates to an eye watering £219m in today's language. The structure was subsequently disassembled and relocated to Sydenham Hill in South London. It stood there from June 1854 until its destruction by a 'great' fire in November 1936.

Apparently, a small office fire had started in a women's cloak room and given that one of the components of the building comprised of dry old timber flooring, the whole structure was engulfed in flames within a few hours. The glow was apparently visible from eight counties away. Up to 100,000 people came to witness the structure in flames and among the onlookers was Winston Churchill, who confirmed, 'this is the end of an age'.

The nearby residential area was renamed Crystal Palace after the landmark. Crystal Palace Football Club was subsequently founded at the site in 1905, and the team played at the Cup Final venue in their early years. In fact, if you look closely at Crystal Palace FCs club badge, it has an eagle partially obscuring The Great Exhibition building. Although never reconstructed and therefore no longer in existence, The Crystal Palace's ghost remains visible in many other glass house structures throughout the world, and I will touch on some of these examples, later in this book.

ON FRIDAY 16TH JUNE 2000 AT 11AM, the lobby of Belfast's infamous yet iconic Europa Hotel was to be the venue for my first ever meeting with my biological father. Until the moment we met I had little idea of who my father was and had no idea even what he looked like. I knew nothing about what he did for a living, and I knew nothing of his past. What I did know was that regardless of how he looked, his past or social status, I wanted to meet him.

It was the year 2000 and I had no access to a computer, and I certainly didn't yet own an Internet-enabled mobile phone. Though, even without the use of the Internet, tracking him down proved astonishingly easy. My mother knew his uncommon surname and with the aid of a phone book was able to work through the half a dozen names before calling the correct phone number of a contact in Athens, Greece. She introduced herself as an old friend who was looking to make contact and requested his contact details, which the polite guy on the other side of the line promptly and rather innocently issued. So, in June 2000, aided by my mother, I set about typing a short letter, which I posted to an address in London. Within a few days, on the 12th of June 2000, I received a standard yet encouraging response, which confirmed that he was indeed 'the man who knew my mother in 1972 and that he was most interested to hear what I had to say and would be happy to see me or call me to discuss the matter further.' In the first instance and as suggested in the letter, I called him, and for the first time in my twenty-six years on earth I spoke with my actual biological father. I can barely remember his accent although I recall it was a tad confused – a bit English and a bit foreign. It was a tense call with palpable nervousness on both sides of the line but nonetheless it was tinged with excitement and hope. We quickly arranged that he would fly from London to Belfast at the end of the week, at which point we could finally meet in person. With twenty-six years having elapsed, I would now be meeting my biological father, within less than one week of making contact.

I had always had an interest in fashion and always tried to be 'fashion forward', so when I saw a dark-grey haired, swarthy skinned, well-dressed man coming towards me, donned in cream chinos and a crisp white shirt, I could straight away see an overt aesthetic similarity. I know it will sound like inverted snobbery, but my first impression was that he looked like the type of man I would be proud to have as my father. When he drew near it became clear that there could be no doubt that he was my father, and I was his son. It is a cliché, but it was like looking in the mirror. The swarthy skin tone, the dark hair colour and our brown eyes complete with permanent- prominent bags under the eyes, which it transpired were a family trait. The eyes, I'll never forget his eyes because every time I look at my eyes in the mirror, I can see his eyes. In reality, I can see the same eyes in my own daughter and son today. We were the same. I stood up and as we shook hands and then hugged, he looked me in the eyes and said, 'you are my boy' and understandably both sets of brown eyes began to fill with tears. But as emotion tried its very best to take hold, we both simultaneously managed to keep-it- together and sat down.

Almost immediately, he pulled out his wallet and astonishingly he produced a black and white passport photograph of my mother, which she had given to him in 1972 and which he had obviously kept safe to that very day. I found this really surprising and very interesting to say the least because it was the year 2000 and he had been married since 1977. When he asked if my mother would be joining us, I replied 'No. To be honest, I thought it was better if she didn't attend this meeting'. This noticeably disappointed him.

When my mother was wholeheartedly trying to explain why this man had been kept a secret my whole life, she had said they loved each other, which I didn't believe at the time. But this revelation made me think a little differently. My mother had asked me if I wanted her to go to the meeting, but I didn't trust that she wouldn't take over the session. I sensed that it could turn into a teary cringe-fest or a poor-me-pity-party on her part. I wanted the meeting to be about he and I, but in retrospect and in some strange way, I think the meeting would have definitely benefitted from her having been there.

It is still one of the most emotionally draining days I have ever experienced. We spoke for a few hours about our lives, and I told him as much as I could remember but in reality, it was amazing how little I had to say because at that time I had yet to meaningfully achieve anything in life. I didn't want to come across cocky and didn't want the day to descend into a sad 'small-violin-session', but I tried to be as honest as possible. Sensing this he confirmed 'don't worry we have many years to make up for lost time'. He asked if I believed in God and when I confirmed that I very much did, he stated that he 'wasn't yet sure what to believe'.

It is difficult to recall our conversation in detail but from what I can remember his journey was a fascinating one. He left Agios Nikolaos in 1971 and travelled to London, arriving with literally no money and barely able to speak English. Moving forward, there was one night he went to a London casino with a friend, where the friend won 'big money'. The friend apparently lent him enough money for him to start up a little shoe business, which he gradually built up from strength to strength, resulting in him owning a successful string of shops and a portfolio of units across London including Oxford Street, Pimlico, Paddington, and Camden. Unfortunately, his friend wasn't so business savvy. He would squander his money and would apparently become jealous of my father's success, resulting in them drifting apart.

He went on to marry a French lady and together they would have two children; one boy and one girl enjoying a multicultural life based in London. When I asked him what he thought his family's reaction would be to this revelation, he responded that 'his wife is an intelligent woman who would understand and his daughter would be very excited by it, whilst the son, maybe less so initially', laughing as he said it. He stated I had 'family in Greece and London' and there was talk of meeting them all, moving forward. He confirmed how he would often work between London and the US (even offering me a job in London that summer if I wanted) and boasted about how he enjoyed travelling regularly to Dubai. He wasn't a big drinker but would occasionally have wine with dinner and enjoyed champagne when celebrating.

After a couple of hours, we went for lunch at a spacious eatery called TATU on the Lisburn Road in Belfast. As he was a guest in my city, I insisted on buying my dad lunch. I can't recall what he ordered but I had goat's cheese and a dressed beetroot salad. Although it looked fresh and delicious, I could barely manage a morsel, as I didn't have much of an appetite. I guess a part of me found the experience energy zapping, and the unorthodox nature of the occasion must have got the better of me.

It was his first time in Belfast, so after lunch we took a taxi back to the city centre. It was a mild day, but the sun didn't come out. We walked about together; and I recall him complimenting the layout of the city. He was asking me about the cost of commercial units, commenting particularly on the impressiveness of Belfast City Hall, as the city's focal point. During our walk he took a phone call. It was his daughter (my half-sister). The conversation went like this – 'Where are you?' - 'Belfast' he replied. 'Belfast!? – What are you doing there?' 'If I told you, you would never believe me – I'll speak with you when I get home…no-no, I will speak with you when I get home.'

It was around 3pm as I walked him to the black taxi rank that faces the entrance to Belfast City Hall. We hugged again and he said, 'OK, I obviously have some things to discuss when I get back to London, I will be in contact very soon.' As he stepped into the taxi, I said 'wait' and I reached into my pocket and handed him a slightly creased white envelope. He looked at me quizzically but opened it there and then. Ironically, two days later it would be Father's Day. I had bought him a Father's Day card and signed it 'Happy Father's Day times 26, Love M'. His eyes started to glaze a little, at which point he too reached into his pocket and handed me a white envelope. It was bulging and spongy and straight away I knew it was full of cash. I immediately said

'No – you don't have to do that' but he replied, 'It's for you, now go and enjoy yourself and I'll be in touch.'

I stood and watched as his taxi drove off down Chichester Street and into the distance. It was a surreal event that left me feeling physically, mentally and emotionally exhausted, not to mention a little wistful. Yet, I was also very excited about what our future might hold, and I couldn't wait to meet my half-sister and half- brother.

However, little did I know that Friday the 16th of June 2000 would be the first and only time in my life that I would ever see my biological father. After our meeting I waited in anticipation and excitement for a follow up communication. But the longer it took to receive a call or a letter, the more I sensed that things were perhaps not going to go, as I was led to believe they would. It would be some six weeks later, before I would receive a formal letter from my father. The wording was standard and controlled and although it included a few compliments as an apparent after-thought, it transpired his overarching wish was that all contact between he and I should *cease* from that day on. To be honest it was completely unexpected, and unbelievably harsh.

Having met him, I had apparently 'gotten answers to my questions. That I had a biological father and that he was alive. But, put simply, too much time had passed, and he couldn't love me like he did his other two children.' Initially, I was perplexed because this letter absolutely flew in the face of what we had discussed in person. The tone was completely different. It was as if he didn't write the letter at all. I obviously wrote back to him seeking an explanation, asking that he fill in the blanks and elaborate on what had caused this dramatic change of heart. When he didn't write back, I tried calling him and when he eventually took the call, he ensured it was very rushed. Whilst I found his tone both forthright and assertive, overall, I found him disrespectful.

To this day I have never received an explanation as to why things suddenly took a turn. What or who caused him to say one thing in Belfast and do another in London. What were the perceptions? What were they afraid of? The situation was unhealthy and because of the open-ended nature of proceedings, it made it challenging for me to achieve closure. It left me to surmise and second guess, what people who I didn't know, might be thinking? Did my half-brother and half-sister in London even know that I existed at all? Once again, I didn't get the truth but was given yet more lies.

After a short period of time, I decided to try to respect his wishes by drawing a line. What else could I do? Beg for an answer? Grovel for him to perform another U-turn? By moving on, I believed that it might enable me to get on with my own life. This was, as you would imagine, easier said than done. For although I tried desperately to bury the matter away, deep in my sub-conscious and get on with life, the disappointment would occasionally manifest itself after a few drinks, in the form of heartfelt tears in front of friends. What an unsatisfactory ending to the promise of something so wonderful. What a mess. When I look back at that time, now that I am a father myself, I fully understand what he tried to say in his letter about not getting to watch me grow up. I totally 'get that'. Yet, I also know wholeheartedly that I would never have ended things the way he chose to. In fact, I can say with great confidence that I would have embraced the matter with backbone, integrity, and love. It is not as though I came with any personal baggage at that time or any risk. Yet, when push came to shove, I knew it was merely yet another direct disappointment that I had no option but to tolerate. The matter was, yet again, completely out of my control and I had, put simply, to accept it.

'Our Father who art in heaven hallowed be thy name…' in prayer and scripture we find constant reminders and reassurance about what it is to be a father and what it is to be loved by one. In 2 Corinthians 3:2-3 it states, who we are and how we live (as father's) is like a "letter from God" knowing full well that how our children see us behaving is like a letter that our children see and read every day. In my case, I didn't know my biological father but on the one occasion I did meet him, he confirmed that he was unsure about his belief system and in that respect, he, and the man who I was led to believe was my father my whole life, were cut from a similar cloth.

Knowing this, I can say with confidence that it is unlikely that either father ever spent time speaking with or praying to God for me. In 1 Chronicles 29: 19, King David prayed for his son, Solomon. Children who know without any doubt that their dads pray for them every day can take confidence in the fact that they are loved and secure. God answers prayer and it is he who can supply all our needs. In 1 Thessalonians 5:16-18, we are urged to pray without ceasing. Consider how much time Jesus took out for prayer? If Jesus felt the need to pray, I would suggest that we need to take time to pray and to receive prayer, wouldn't you?

Knowing this, children could take confidence in the fact that their father is a man of faith and therefore they too can be young people of faith and hope. That their father, who prays for them and reads scripture and is perhaps active in his parish and navigates life in the right spirit, is not only a hearer and a sayer of God's word, but he is also a doer of God's word. That their father admits and confirms that although he is an earthly father, there exists a loving heavenly father who loves them with unconditional love.

Although the man who I was led to believe was my father often devoted time to my favourite sporting pastimes (and I enjoyed that), my upbringing was bereft of the type of heart-to-heart conversations that might convey insightful, much needed worldly or spiritual knowledge and wisdom, the type within reach in Scripture for example. In Deuteronomy 6:6-7 it imparts, 'these commandments that I give you today are to be on your hearts. Impress them upon your children.' In retrospect it is clear to me now that I was not being 'trained up in how I should go' (Proverbs 22:6).

There was no question, my *father* was a very hardworking man. He worked hard alongside my mother to provide some sort of a foundation because my upbringing wasn't completely foundationless. However, the foundations constructed by my parents were not conducive to a stable life or a smooth future. As a father he was everything then that I am not now. He was the type of man who loved hunting, fishing, and poking a stick in fire in the interests of being manly. He was often belligerent, which is something historically that I am not. This was perhaps because he never led the family with an eternal vision in devotion to God. He wasn't known to pray, didn't attend church, he didn't read God's Word and he wasn't a God-fearing man. Therefore, I would suggest that it is not unreasonable to consider that he may never have operated in the correct spirit. In Proverbs 14:26 it states that "Whoever fears the Lord has a secure fortress, and for their children it will be a refuge."

Looking back, although life is relative, the environment I grew up in was far from a sanctuary. It seemed as though my parents less removed blockages from my pathway and more placed obstacles in my way. Whether those obstacles were placed through resentment, bitterness, confusion, or a lack of knowledge, it is not for me to say what emotions were driving their decision-making processes. What I can say is, as a father myself I have learned lessons from their mistakes, and the mistakes of many other parents for that matter.

Now, please be assured that I am not using this book as a subtle opportunity to kick back at my parents with low blows or jibes, for that would fly in the face of my overarching purpose. For I grew to see my parents as two people who endured very difficult upbringings, which brought about their own unresolved traumas that manifested itself in their erraticism. For example, my mother, for all of her flaws, is a beautiful person, and a very affectionate, caring and loving mother who was protective and biased in the extreme. Yet I believe her belief system, upbringing and subsequent traumas shaped and affected the way she thought and lived. Not to mention the stranglehold the Catholic Church had on Catholic families in Ireland, at that time.

However, although none of us are perfect, I knew the second that I would become a father that I would teach my children the importance of appreciating time, of time management and of making the very best use of time. That time is not only to be used for the accumulation of temporal goods that we cannot bring with us; but it may be used wisely to make reparation for our sins. I would teach my children how best to avoid life's obstacles and pitfalls and how best to discern who it is that places those pitfalls in the way.

I would teach how to traverse a blind world full of broken spirits and minds crippled by damaging envy, jealousy, anger, egos and lies. I would impart how to appreciate all creation and above all else, the creator of that beautiful creation. How to pray properly, giving thanks and praise for what we have in life and how to develop a precious personal relationship with God the Father, Son, and Holy Spirit. How to develop their faith and an understanding of God's grace, as unmerited reward.

I would teach of the importance of church attendance, of being part of the body of a church and belonging to and serving within a church family. How to live life in the right spirit, by concerning oneself with more than money or material gain. How to walk in the spirit of truth and how to live an honest, integrity driven life. How to help care for those in need and above all how to love our neighbours as ourselves – in thought, word, and deed. And all of the aforementioned can come when we open our hearts to the living and active spiritual power that can come from reading, explaining and studying God's Word with our children. Practicing what is being preached by backing it up with a lifestyle, which makes Christ the unseen guest at every meal and the silent listener to every conversation.

In Catholic link.org I read, in a world with so much physical and spiritual fatherlessness, many of us find ourselves confused today about who we are and what we're here for. As the holy and inspired word of God, the Bible helps us to answer the deepest longings of our hearts. It teaches us that we were created in God's image (Gen. 1:27), and He loves us so much that no matter what we do, we can never escape His presence (Ps. 139:9-10). The Word of God teaches us that our identity does not rest on our social status, family situation, wealth, physical health, or accomplishments. Rather, we are first and foremost defined by the Father's love for us. He is the one who gives us our identity and reveals to us the meaning of our lives.

This project is not an opportunity to fire toxic darts in the direction of anyone who has shattered any part of my journey. It is a public testimony and an opportunity for me to share my life experiences, thoughts, and perceptions in a respectful and a constructive way. Therefore, I can confirm, first-hand, that by immersing myself in scripture and seeking God, that it became clear that even the very best fathers in the world will inevitably mess up. There will be occasions when they will make poor decisions, when they will fail to be accountable or when they would not be entirely kind or fair to their families.

As Christians, we have to remember that only God is perfect, and he will never make the same mistakes that our earthly fathers did or do. Keeping the line distinct between our earthly fathers and Heavenly Father helps us view God with the reverence and understanding He truly deserves. Some of us had wonderful fathers but none of us had perfect fathers. Yet some of us may have dealt with fathers or father-figures who failed us badly. Some may have been absent or indifferent, while others may have been downright abusive and harsh. Still, we must try our utmost to never judge but to forgive. People in glass houses…

'Our human fathers will (and have) inevitably fallen short of perfection. We and I as fathers (and mothers for that matter) will and do fall short of perfection. But God is the benchmark of everything that the perfect Father should be. He is our protector, provider, healer, creator, sustainer, corrector, and comforter. The biblical image of God as both King and Father is no coincidence. God concurrently fulfills the role of omnipotent, omnipresent God who handles everything in the universe, but He is also the caring Father who has time to listen to each of His children at any given second. It's an incomprehensible thought, yet a priceless one. Our relationship with our Heavenly Father will always outshine even the best relationship with an earthly father.'

For it is written in Ephesians 4:6 that we have One God and Father of all, who is over all and through all and in all.

CHAPTER 8:
SHENANIGANS

Coombe Cliff Conservatory (1894)

"Dear Ken, this is the Irishman that doesn't blow up buildings, rather the reverse. A simple yes or no would be the best, at this stage is it on or off, I would love to know. From the Irishman who is trying to save English buildings."

—Spike Milligan (1983)

I T WAS A GLORIOUSLY WARM EARLY MORNING in May when I stepped out at Monument tube station to walk to London's much maligned Walkie Talkie Building. This exploration would be the first of three London-based visits I had scheduled for that day. The Walkie Talkie is a bit like the Eiffel Tower to some of the Parisians or the Victor Emmanuel II monument to some of the Romans, in terms of the manner in which this 'marmite' structure has divided opinion amongst Londoners. However, to be unambiguously clear, much like The Shard and The Swiss Tower, I am a major fan of this contemporary sky-scraping landmark.

Located on the 43rd floor of the Walkie Talkie Building is The Sky Garden, which was opened in 2015. It is an emerald jungle situated above an urban jungle. Entirely clad in twenty-foot high floor to ceiling glazing, it is a foliage-filled modern-day glass house structure in the sky, offering leafy lush landscapes but at a heavenly height. Moreover, by being at such a height, the Sky Garden obviously boasts tremendous panoramic views over many of London's most famous sights, such as The Shard, The Gherkin, St

Paul's Cathedral, Tower Bridge and, of course, the river Thames. This, as Londoners would say, makes any visitor 'double lucky'.

It was barely 8.30am when I arrived, so I immediately purchased a black Americano at the coffee bar and took a seat to drink in the sensational views. There had been some serious thought given to the end-use of this multi-functional event space because as well as offering food and drinks by day, I discovered that it also afforded early birds an opportunity to relax, with sunrise yoga sessions. Conversely, at night, it became a bar-come-night club, where clubbers could energetically dance to house-music into the late hours. I loved this find. I loved its innovation and its energy. I love that the designers borrowed heavily from their Victorian counterparts, but they did so by turning everything on its head. In fact, without implying this structure is some modern 'Tower of Babel', I would suggest that God-fearing Victorians would have also loved hanging out in this contemporary, tranquil Garden of Eden in the sky, with the good Lord within apparent touching distance.

With the Sky Garden there is no need to build higher glasshouses to accommodate taller Palms at ground level because with this garden, the sky was already the limit. Besides, it already accommodated some beautiful palms. Moreover, as rare as a two-hundred-year-old Sabal Palm, access to this experience was completely free of charge for the general public and that is truly something to behold in London today. After I drank the remainder of my black Americano, which I enjoyed sat beside the foliage, it was time to make my way to my next destination.

Often attending for work and or pleasure purposes, London is a destination that I had become very familiar with over the last number of decades. However, the only previous time I was in *South* London, was to attend a football match at Selhurst Park, the home of Crystal Palace FC, to watch Arsenal cruise to a comfortable 2-0 away win. Unbeknown to me at that time, Crystal Palace was also the name of an area in South London, called after The Crystal Palace, which was a great glass exhibition building, constructed in 1851. Unfortunately, this ground-breaking structure would be destroyed by a fire in 1936 and would never be reconstructed. However, on this occasion I would be visiting a stunning glasshouse structure not far away, in Croydon. The following words borrow very heavily from an insightful report kindly shared by a Director of Horniman Museum, Kirsten Walker.

'It would be some years later in 1894 before the Coombe Cliff Conservatory was built by Frederick John Horniman on the side of his father John's house in Croydon in South London, 6 months after his father died. John Horniman had amassed considerable wealth as a tea merchant; his company undertook to supply unadulterated tea in sealed packets and this reassurance led to his tea being drunk widely across the UK. He was an active liberal MP, a traveller and a philanthropist. Frederick shared many of his father's interests, he was a tea merchant and a Liberal MP, he travelled widely and collected art and artefacts from around the world. He was inspired by the Great Exhibition and wanted to bring the world to the people. So in 1891 he opened up his home in Forest Hill so that people could come and see his collections. In 1898 he had a purpose-built museum built on the site of his house in Forest Hill.

The Coombe Cliff conservatory castings were made by the Glasgow firm of MacFarlane's. For a prolonged period, Scotland was a world leader in architectural cast ironwork and at its heart was the Saracen Foundry of Walter MacFarlane and Co. The company was well known for its decorative cast iron and was awarded an international prize at the 1862 exhibition.

It has impressive dimensions, being 56 ft long, 22 ft wide and 20 ft high, with a projecting porch and a tall octagonal lantern over the central area, supported by slender cast iron columns. The whole structure was supported on a rendered brick plinth. The cast-iron work-panels, friezes, roof spandrels within, and the fish scales, terminals and crestings, all show the wealth of pattern available from MacFarlane's. The decoration is ornate, but it lightens the effect of the structure and gives it an airy appearance belying the weight of the materials from which it is made.'

In June 1972, the conservatory was rightly included in the list of buildings of special architectural or historical interest for Croydon. And by 1983 various groups became involved with finding a solution to secure the future of the conservatory. Local architects and conservationists put forward a plan for Croydon to re-erect it in Town Hall gardens and use it as a restaurant. Even celebrity Spike Milligan waded in, writing three letters to Ken Livingstone regarding the conservatory: "Dear Ken, this is the Irishman that doesn't blow up buildings, rather the reverse. A simple yes or no would be the best, at this stage is it on or off, I would love to know." The conservatory was installed on its current location in 1989 by English Heritage and they have carried out various refurbishments since then.

With many of the conservatories erected during the 19th century having gone, Coombe Cliff conservatory proudly remains today as a popular venue for events and activities including cutting edge performance art, dancing, concerts, weddings and parties and other such revenue generating solutions, throughout each year. In fact, at the time of writing one of my favourite contemporary jazz artists, Ashley Henry, held a summertime jazz gig in this precious venue. A worthy restoration project, it makes a splendid enhancement to the visual environment of Forest Hill and preserves for posterity this elegant structure, which is a unique part of the nation's heritage. I highly recommend a visit if you ever find yourself in South London.

My final scheduled visit enabled me to visually inspect a plethora of existing glass house structures located in upmarket Chelsea, at the Chelsea Physic Garden (1902). Word to the wise, if you are ever taking a tube to Gloucester Street tube station, try not to take it the week of the Chelsea Garden show. Shoe-horned in amongst the throngs of beautifully colourful elderly patrons, I witnessed pastel-like hydrangea coloured blue and pink rinses, the type of which I haven't seen, since the halcyon days when 'Mrs. Slocombe' graced our television screens in 'Are You Being Served'. Having walked briskly from Gloucester Street tube station, I made my way past the thriving Chelsea Flower show entrance and then past the subsequent Chelsea Pensioners building, before arriving at the impressive brick walls of the Chelsea Physic Garden.

My first impression was that the Garden's location felt special and secret. The main public entrance to Chelsea Physic Garden is through an early 18th century tall iron gate with side pieces and stone-capped brick piers (listed grade II), set in the brick boundary wall which runs along the length of Swan Walk. It was a lush leafy environment where bird song was prevalent. The Gardens were neatly nestled behind high brick walls with iron railings and were positioned close to the river Thames. The ideal Thames location is apparently no accident, as back in 1673 the Worshipful Society of Apothecaries chose their Chelsea village site for its proximity to the river to make the most of its warm air currents.

The site is also blessed with a south facing aspect and good quality warm light soil, having previously been the site of a market garden. The river access allowed plants arriving from around the world to be introduced to the British Isles via the Garden, allowing the Garden to make a big impact from early on. Yet, with over a century of constant use, the Victorian glasshouses had clearly become fragile leaving them in need of significant restoration, to preserve them for years to come. Apparently, the gardens boasted the first heated greenhouse in England, but it has long since been demolished. The array of teak framed glass houses, all of which were operational and stacked with botany, were complimented by a beautiful shop and eatery with outdoor seating that enabled its patrons to soak in the private tranquility and the rear elevations of some of the eye-wateringly expensive Chelsea real estate, which overlooked the gardens.

Whilst there, I was encouraged to take a walk along a short gravel path which leads west to the Cool Fernery. It was here that I encountered a 'Wardian case', which had been made according to the design developed by Nathanial Bagshaw Ward for a collection of ferns and bog plants. The 'Wardian Case', which describes a sealed glass case popular in the second half of the 19th century, is used for transporting living plants from abroad. After the restoration, the Cool Fernery was replanted with a selection of ferns, the majority being native varieties or cultivars, first described and popularised by Thomas Moore, curator between 1848 and 1887.

To the east is the area now used to illustrate the work of Philip Miller. The remainder of the north-west quadrant to the east of Philip Miller's Garden is taken up with the level formal lawn. The historical walk continues north-west to the west gate (not in use, 1999). Some 5m to the south-east of the gate, the path divides and a branch runs north-east along the south front of the new (1987) Research and Education Building, then past the principal buildings and a 20th century range of glasshouses.

FROM A VERY EARLY AGE, I would suggest that I was conditioned to objectify women. We were coming out of the age of the Carry-On films and other such seventies capers, which granted, were of that time. I recall those occasions when my young uncles would crane their necks to innocently wolf-whistle 'Carry-On style' after attractive girls on the street. Walking through alleyways, my young friends and I would occasionally stumble upon discarded 'erotic' magazines. Or on one occasion my primary school friends and I even encountered a very creepy guy hiding out in the bushes of our football playing fields, reading such smut. How do we know? Because he invited us all to join him! The advent of channel 4's Red Triangle movies in the mid-nineteen eighties, meant I, like many other children, might on occasion be unintentionally exposed to graphic sex on terrestrial TV. In terms of newspapers there were only 'red tops' in our household, so glancing at topless "Page Three Stunners" was practically a daily occurrence.

Moving forward, and having entered my early teenage years, I recall a one-off occasion when a number of my school friends and I crowded into a musty local video store, in school uniform I hasten to add, to awkwardly procure an adult movie from 'beneath the counter'. We must have cumbersomely milled around for up to half an hour, giggling and whispering, before a reluctant spokesman was shoved towards the till area to commence excruciating negotiations. Only then would the guy behind the counter put us out of our misery by recommending a movie. So, with parents out working the curtains were pulled, and a darkened family living room became a temporary pop-up venue for an awkward, cringey experience.

At school, desire levels would be through the roof. In the company of some attractive female classmates, boys would invariably rush to get to class first, thus ensuring we had prime views of the girls who directly sat opposite us. I recall how crude, Scottish comedian Billy Connolly described, during one of his stand-up shows, how he and his male classmates in Glasgow, would quietly will their female counterparts, most of whom wore short skirts, to cross their legs, in the hope of witnessing a flash of white underwear that would cause all sorts of excitement and hilarity during their after-class discussions. In reality, these shenanigans were no different, to how the immature motley crew in my class behaved. In fact, we developed our very own, innovative ways of objectifying girls in our classroom. One such example extended to a handful of us boys creating a weekly "football game" that enabled us to score our female classmates based entirely on how they looked from head to toe. We did this by disguising on paper, Abigail as Arsenal, Tara as Tottenham and Lisa as Liverpool, for example, before scoring each physical category (also disguised on paper) out of five and adding the totals. Although there was a lot more to the game than that, what was even more unbearable at that time, was how gut wrenching it was for me, to willfully enable Tottenham Hotspur to beat Arsenal on paper on a regular basis.

Now for the more repressed or prudish reader, one might suggest that I am unnecessarily labouring the point here. But trust me when I say that I am not irrationally fixating on this item, because *teenage boys finding teenage girls attractive* is hardly front-page news. In reality though, my point is, opportunities to objectify women came at us from numerous angles. But this, it seems, was all part and parcel of being a teenager and, moving forward, a twenty something at that time. I was surrounded by so many deviant like-minds, as extended family, friends, colleagues, and acquaintances, remained all for the most part, blinded by similar interests. Either part of the same youth culture and doing (or aspiring to do) exactly the same things at a sub-cultural level. Objectification was another accepted worldly norm, which cut both ways, by the way. Although with instantaneous access to all of the aforementioned nonsense on the internet and phones these days, I would suggest that the risk of objectification and the pressures for young teenagers, must be even more intense – if that were possible.

With absolutely all that said, if I knew then what I know now and given a choice, I can confirm for the record, that I would have given *anything*, and would give up everything I had experienced, to have met a childhood sweetheart. Someone I would have fallen in love with and subsequently travelled through life with.

However, at twenty-one years of age I had started to meaningfully date a girl. During that time, I was floating between banal retail and office jobs, whilst she was studying at university in a city called Derry. To get a flavour of Northern Ireland's bizarreness, you only need mention the name Derry. Today, in 2023 people will, of course, be quick to mention the popular TV show 'Derry Girls' (which I have yet to watch actually) but it was also the venue of the infamous Bloody Sunday murders (this book is not the forum for that particular topic). Catholics would refer to it as 'Derry City' or 'Free Derry'. On the other hand, ardent Protestants would refer to it as 'Londonderry', with a strong emphasis on the London of course. Whilst those preferring to sit on the fence to appear balanced, would refer to it in a neutral fashion as 'Stroke City', the 'Maiden City' or the 'Capital of the North-West' or, more recently, 'Legenderry'. Preposterous stuff, you'll agree.

Either way, she would study there for four years and during that time I would travel up and down as often as I could to see her. With a student population of more than ten thousand, it was a lively enough spot, and I became very familiar with the place. Four years would come and go really quickly but as her time at university drew to a close, I had decided at that time that I, too needed to go to university if I wanted to progress in life. I was in my early twenties.

I had applied to and been accepted into Herriot Watt in Edinburgh to study Planning and Development. But my *father* had quickly poured cold water on that proposal, confirming that he would not be paying towards the travel cost, relocation, or accommodation. Therefore, knowing Derry as I did and with it being located an hour and forty minutes away from Belfast and being reasonably affordable, I decided it was better the devil you know. I got accepted into university where I would spend four years there, studying the Built Environment.

I would work and study hard enough to successfully graduate, but overall, it was a fun filled experience that afforded me some wonderful opportunities. This included a year's fully paid university placement that enabled me to live and work in Dublin. It would be one of the greatest, carefree years of my worldly existence. Enjoying life to the extreme maximum, I thrived in an atmosphere that was anything but intense. With a decent circle of friends, we would socialise with 'gold card' access into some of the capital's choice venues. This meant we often didn't have to queue and got free drinks upon arrival. This included The Viper Rooms on the Quays, which was apparently, part-owned back then, by Huey Morgan from the American band, the Fun Lovin Criminals. We would hang out in the famous Horseshoe Bar in the Shelbourne Hotel or enjoy evening drinks in Bono's Clarence hotel. Or, more often, we could be found frequenting the lively establishments of Temple Bar, Dame Street and Grafton Street. Moreover, with Lansdowne Road stadium only ten minutes-walk from our house, we were able to attend almost all Ireland soccer matches that year. The opportunities for fun were relentless, and there was always something to do, once work had ended.

I lived with three friendly girls, in a 'modern-ish' three-storey townhouse, not far from Lansdowne Road. They were all lovely in their own way. I met new people, some of whom I am still friends with to this day. I also had a wonderful boss who took me under his wing. He was a brilliant, upbeat, charismatic character and was a spectacular communicator. He was really influential and always willing to provide advice and guidance in matters of work and life. He was forty-four at the time and married, but he was socially energetic and always operated with a glass half full outlook. I always look back at that time with much fondness, in what is still surely one of the world's most wonderful cities. And with it being practically 'on my doorstep', I still travel up and down on occasion to watch Ireland play International football matches at the Aviva Stadium.

Having completed my work placement, I returned to university at Derry for my final year. It would, of course, have all of the normal coursework and exam stresses but very much on the plus side, it would also include a university subsidised two-week trip to Hong Kong, to study housing. Based in the BP International Hotel in Kowloon, it would be a truly memorable experience for any number of reasons. I recall taking a bullet train from Hong Kong to Shenzhen, which was one of the most rapidly developing Chinese cities in 2001. As we stepped off the train, I could see in the distance a few Chinese guys fidgeting and writhing about on a concrete pedestrian footbridge. I could see colours on the bridge, all reds, and purples. I assumed they were zany artists or something but as we approached the bridge, I noticed some of them had missing limbs. They were rocking back and forth and some were just bashing their gashed-open heads off the concrete bridge. The purple and red were not paint and they were not artists, it was their blood. According to one of our lecturers, it was likely that with no governmental help, that these people were left to exist alone in poor health and in abject poverty, and their extreme behaviour was a desperate reaction to this.

We were encouraged by our Chinese guides to quickly slalom through that scene and off the bloody bridge. We were scheduled to travel to some newly constructed high specification residential apartments, all of which it transpired were being acquired by foreign investors. The units were interior-designed, turn-key, modern, spacious, and airy. The quality of these properties was in stark contrast to the Hong Kong Housing Authorities rather depressing social housing units that we visited the day before, where families of up to five had to live in shifts, to exist within a single room, measuring at approximately four meters squared.

Such dark and depressing living spaces, they comprised only of a bunk bed facing a cabinet with a very small portable TV positioned on it. Behind a curtain to the left of the cabinet was a WC and protruding above the WC was a shower head. To the left of this and behind a small wall was a two-ring cooker on top of a small fridge and opposite that was the external door. That was it. One parent and an older child might work a night shift, whilst the other parent would work during the day, ensuring people always had a bed to sleep in whilst the children were at school, and that someone was always there to look after the children, when they returned from school.

It was an amazing fun filled trip full of many wonderful memories. One such memory was me learning to use chop sticks. Which I did by eating peanuts from a bowl over the course of an hour, whilst sat in a Hong Kong bar. But culturally and educationally it was a real eye opener. It was my first sight of robust bamboo scaffolding, which was something else entirely. It was so warm and humid. I recall standing at Hong Kong harbour waiting to board the Star Ferry and visibly noticing the pollution in the sky as I looked out across the choppy blue waters towards Hong Kong Island. In fact, the pollution levels were so high that when we returned to our hotel in Kowloon that night, I would blow my nose and the white tissue would be black. Moreover, the mercury levels in the water were apparently so high that the recommendation was that you should not eat seafood more than once a week, if at all. Although, such a threat didn't stop me trying jellyfish for the first and only time. For the record, I found it to be bland and gelatinous, as you might imagine.

Something else that sticks out in my mind was a conversation I had with a lady whilst standing looking out of an expansive hotel window from the seventeenth floor. Hong Kong is so high density. They say if there's a small plot of green in Hong Kong that they simply build on it – and as far upwards as is reasonably practicable. I recall being amazed at the vast array of high-rise structures, which lit up the humid charcoal Hong Kong night sky. However, the lady in question was less enthused. 'At the end of the day, those buildings are nothing more than bricks, glazing and steel. They are superfluous', she replied. On the one hand, she was correct. Yet she was also over simplifying things a tad because there is an inherent beauty in architecturally designed structures and there is always an over-arching purpose. Perceptions.

Sometimes in life we have to stop and take a look around and give thanks and praise for what we have and what we have been blessed with. A number of weeks after leaving Hong Kong, the SARS epidemic kicked in and of course some twenty years later Hong Kong has now become blighted by Belfast-esque civil unrest. Although Capitalism and the West are not without flaws, I also considered how claustrophobic and restrictive it must be to live life in a communist, socialist society run by an oppressive, authoritarian state. China, Cuba, Russia, Vietnam, the list goes on. Where Marxism, pluralism and godlessness is preached, with Christianity and the traditional family frowned upon.

Needless to say, during our combined eight years of university, we were a committed couple, and having successfully dated for almost nine years, I decided that it was time to take the leap and propose. But my decision to do so would only happen *after* my first encounter with death and grief. It would also be the beginning of a crazy five-year culmination of unforeseen events, that would unexpectedly send my steady world, spiraling out of control.

CHAPTER 9:
POOR VISIBILITY

Sefton Park, Palm House (1896)

When you walk through a storm, hold your head up high, and don't be afraid of the dark…

—Gerry and the Pacemakers

FIRSTLY, EVEN AS AN ARDENT FOLLOWER OF ARSENAL, you would be forgiven for thinking that I'd have difficulty including the above lyrics within this book. However, from a Christian perspective, the poignancy of the words cannot be glossed over. I believe in many ways those words encompass the challenging storms and dark times that the city of Liverpool and its wonderful people have endured. The storms I have endured. The personal storms that you the reader have endured.

I had only ever been to Liverpool on a few fleeting occasions, remarkably to watch Arsenal win premier league matches at Anfield, on two separate occasions. However, on this occasion I was on a summer break with my wife and daughter that enabled me to see and enjoy the actual city itself. Our time included sailing on a ferry across the Mersey, which was a pleasant way to travel on a warm summers day. Liverpool is celebrated as being the home of sixties pop band The Beatles but on this occasion my plans were focused on something a little less cliched.

Located on the fringe of Toxteth is a Grade II listed, three-tier dome, conservatory palm house, designed and built by MacKenzie and Moncur of Edinburgh (noted for their design and build of the Temperate House in Kew) which opened in 1896. Liverpool

137

millionaire Henry Yates Thompson (the great nephew of the founder of Princes Park) gifted £10,000 to the city to fund the construction. It was designed in the tradition of Joseph Paxton's glass houses and was stocked originally with a rich collection of exotic plants. Today you can enjoy upwards of twenty different types of palms.

During the Liverpool Blitz of May 1941, a bomb fell nearby and shattered the glass. It was re-glazed in 1950 at a cost of £6,163 with costs covered by War Restoration funds. A period of decline and deterioration culminated in its closure in the 1980s on grounds of safety. In June 1992, a public meeting was held highlighting the dereliction and calling for restoration. A petition was presented to the City Council by what had become the "Save the Palm House" campaign. A public fund-raising campaign was established, with a "sponsor a pane" programme generating over £35,000. This led directly to the conversion of Save the Palm House into a registered charity (Friends of Sefton Park Palm House). The Palm House was partially repaired and reopened in 1993.

The eight 'corners' of the Palm House are marked by statues by the French sculptor Léon-Joseph Chavalliaud. These include explorers Captain Cook, Christopher Columbus alongside, Peter Pan, and Charles Darwin to name but a few. The Dome-shaped Victorian palm house with lush flora is now a popular location for staging weddings, music and charitable or corporate events.

Another popular glasshouse located in the city of Liverpool can be found at Stanley Park. Named after Lord Stanley of Preston, it is located in a 110-acre park and was designed by Edward Kemp. It was opened on 14th May 1870 by the Mayor of Liverpool, Joseph Hubback.

The Isla Gladstone Conservatory (1899) is one of Liverpool's most iconic venues, showcasing Victorian architecture dating back to 1870. It has been fully restored and modernised into a distinctive events space, whilst retaining its heritage charm. A Grade II listed building built by Mackenzie & Moncur of Edinburgh, it is set within its own private grounds and is nestled within a beautiful, picturesque scene that also includes a stunning Victorian band stand. All of which makes it a popular location for wedding receptions. The conservatory, which is flooded with natural light, also provides a spectacular venue for internal corporate events, with its grounds also a popular venue for an outdoor cinema.

The good people of Liverpool are often regarded as being religious about football and Stanley Park is literally central to that perception. Located between the home grounds of rival Merseyside football clubs Everton and Liverpool, I enjoyed my walk across this famous expansive green space, even though on this occasion I had just stood in the away end at Anfield to witness Arsenal lose by three goals to one, albeit in the warmth of a glorious August evening. Stanley Park also has an Evangelical church located on one corner in between the two football stadiums. It is named "Stanley Park Church" and is over 100 years old.

IN THE FEW YEARS AFTER THE TRUTH had finally been set free concerning the existence of my biological father, the weight that had caused so much lasting damage throughout my parents' relationship appeared to have lifted somewhat from their shoulders. They were already in their fifties and had to a certain degree mellowed by comparison. The relationship between my *father* and I would also slowly improve a little, but a few short years later he was diagnosed with an aggressive malignant melanoma. Detected in June 2002, he died by November 2002, as the once six-foot four-inch man-mountain with shovels for hands, physically shriveled away to a pitiful shadow of himself. In the run up to his death, he had asked me for forgiveness for all he had said and done—and I said that I forgave him.

I had finished university and had straight away got a job, but it wasn't an ideal situation. I had to do a round trip of fifty miles per day to get there and the physical office was poky, dated and grim. Each night I would drive from the bleak office to my mother's house to help her look after my dying *father*. My boss at that time was, put simply, a bully who made life very difficult for me, from day one. From the word go, I noticed that he seemed to enjoy belittling people. He never explained things well to anyone, which created confusion and stress in the office. He knew all about my *father's* illness but was never supportive. I will never forget asking to leave the office an hour early one day. My *father* was in his last days and had gone downhill rapidly. I had received a call to come home but my boss refused to let me go stating there was still work to be done. I tried to reason with him about my *father's* state but will never forget his shocking spite-filled response - "I couldn't give a f**k about your *dad's* cancer – there is *still* work to be done". I was incandescent with rage, as he looked back at me with a wry smile. It was as if he was goading me. He knew I was exhausted and fragile, but although he was clearly provoking me, and although I was furious, I just about managed not to overreact in the way he perhaps thought I would. Shocked by his words and white hot with anger, I stormed out of his office, got my coat, and exited his cramped, tired building. I wouldn't be around to prove or disprove it, but I believe to this day that his hatred stemmed from religious bigotry.

It was a wintery Thursday evening in November 2002 when I left that office for the last time. Driving home in very poor visibility, my window wipers were on full speed, for most of my dark motorway journey back to Belfast, as the rain came sheeting down. My decision not to return to the office on the Monday was well timed, as my *father* received his last rites and passed away on the Tuesday night.

I was stood sardined into a small bedroom surrounded by a host of nuclear and extended family members. I had never been in this situation before and had zero experience of it. The atmosphere was tense, and I was understandably upset at what I was witnessing. The doctor and the parish priest had both come and gone. It was a strange period of time because no matter how prepared I thought I was in the run up to that point, when death finally came calling, it was actually a truly shocking moment.

The steady build-up of the 'death rattle' seemed to go on for eons, but when his breathing suddenly stopped there was a couple of seconds of eerie silence, before I and others let out these short bursts of collective crazy wails. It was an uncontrollable sound, which came from somewhere deep inside me. It wasn't a shout or a cry, it was a sound I hadn't made before, but I immediately forced my way through the crowded room and into a bedroom next door to be sick.

Christmas and New Year were depressing, but they would come and go, and I would get another job within a couple of months. This time-off gave me an opportunity to reflect. With grief there must be no judgment because in my experience, it is something unique to each person. No one person grieves like another. People generally don't understand grief and I was one of those people. Given everything I had experienced only years before, I even judged my own grief. But the sheer fact I was affected by grief triggers (such as hearing a song or seeing a movie on tv) to the extent that I was at that time, shows there must have been some love in the relationship between my *father* and me.

That New Year's Eve, my girlfriend and I were on a train on our way to Glasgow for Hogmanay, with her sister and her partner. We found ourselves sitting beside a number of university students who were also in their mid to late twenties. We all got chatting. They were a decent bunch, who were playing card games and having a laugh when suddenly one of them produced a large bottle of Scotch Whiskey from his bag. He then rummaged around for a glass before producing a small black plastic cup, the sort you might find on top of a flask. Transpired it wasn't a cup at all but the lid from his bottle of Lynx Africa deodorant. Now, I generally steered clear of spirits, and I already knew that I didn't like the taste of whiskey, least of all whiskey with a 'classy bouquet' of Lynx Africa! But it was that festive time of year, and we were up for having the craic, on our way to Glasgow for New Year's Eve and Hogmanay. We were all in high spirits, so within no time we were partaking in the shots of whiskey from the innovative tumbler. By the time we arrived at a bitterly cold Glasgow Central Station we were feeling more than jolly. We headed to my sister in law's tasteful but compact apartment for dinner but after a few more libations, I reached into my inner jacket pocket and produced my palm-of-the -hand -sized, tiny black phone book. Against the advice of those around me, I telephoned my biological father and left a short, whining message about love and rejection, before crawling to bed. It was a one-off call, as far as I can remember, but to reduce the risk of me making the same mistake again, I soon discarded that little black book and everything in it, for good.

Nonetheless, three months after my *father* had passed away and armed with a diamond ring, I took my girlfriend to New York where I had planned to propose on top of the Empire State Building. We had been dating almost nine years. It was our first time in New York City (NYC), so I booked us into the famous Waldorf Astoria Hotel. Some say the hotel was getting tired by then, but I fully disagree. I thought it was beautiful and full of historic charm. Our room was warm and traditional in style, complete with lavish carpet, a green leather writing bureau and marble sunken bath. There was no TripAdvisor back then, but it was just what I envisaged it would be. However, I can say with confidence that I was very much unprepared for the extreme nature of the NYC weather. I knew it would be cold, very cold in fact, but New York in February is unbearably *freezing*! In effect, it was minus sixteen on the ground and minus twenty-three on top of the Empire State Building, when we visited it that very night.

As we stepped out onto the illustrious observatory deck the icy winds ensured visibility was incredibly poor. I had a navy and red woolen hat and a green, padded snorkel coat, which had a grey and off-white fur rim around the front of the hood. I pulled my hood up over the hat and zipped it right up, leaving a little tunnel to peer through. As I peered out through the furry gap in the hood, I produced a diamond ring and offered a muffled proposal, as my teeth chattered loudly. I could barely get the words out it was so cold. After she very quickly said yes, we hurried back inside to stand amongst the King Kong memorabilia and get some much-needed warmth. It certainly wasn't as romantic as it ought to have been, but it was a memorable experience, nonetheless.

Having proposed in New York in February, we decided that we would get married in Italy that October. Neither of us were interested in a traditional stay-at-home church wedding, so we opted to get married on the world-renowned Amalfi Coast. The San Pietro chapel is a tiny Catholic-Church, idyllically suspended between sea and sky on a picturesque mountain top in the salubrious and luxurious Italian village of Positano. It was paradise. I would be decked from head to toe, fully suited and booted in Paul Smith. When I say head to toe, I mean it, down to socks, boxer shorts, belt, tie, cuff links and shoes. All purchased from The Bureau in Belfast. She would also have an expensive dress and a second designer outfit to change into that evening for the party. Now, you would be forgiven for thinking that I am being self-congratulatory here but let me assure you that I am not. For looking back, the occasion seemed primarily focused on outward, consumerism, individualism, and materialism. Nonetheless, we would subsequently travel onward to spend time in Rome, and it would be a truly memorable experience.

Prior to Italy, my wife's father had lent us the money for the deposit on our first house together. We bought a four-bedroom, new build turnkey property located in a desirable suburban postcode, which we bought off the plans. It was an exciting time. Throughout that first year of marriage, we would travel to Dublin, Glasgow, London, Rome (again) and to Tunisia. Life appeared perfect. I say appeared perfect because in reality it was never perfect, for bubbling beneath the surface there had always been an underlying issue.

Now, this book is definitely not the forum for hurting or offending anyone; or retrospectively raising perceived injustices or reopening old wounds. For the past is in the past.

I wanted to write about *my* life experiences in a respectful and constructive manner. But let me just admit that for one reason or another, I entered this phase in my life with an incessant restlessness and an inner rebelliousness.

It was during our first year of marriage that I started a new job in a high rise office. I was in a professional arena, which was where I aspired to be. It was a relentlessly busy environment where it's safe to say that the pay was not commensurate with the role and responsibility. Still, it would be an eventful place to work. Throughout my working life, I would often date girls from the office or shops I worked in. Proximity was always a good way to meet girls, but I was now married. I had stopped accepting invitations for after-work drinks on a Friday evening, preferring to go home to unwind instead. However, on this one occasion I accepted a direct invitation to attend a party, from a girl who frequented a coffee shop that I used daily. She was a vivacious English girl, with fiery red hair, who I regularly bumped into when I went for coffee. She was clearly confident and clever, and she would often dally around my table when I sat for refreshments. We got on very well in an acquaintance capacity but given that I was also still a bit shallow, I happily accepted her invitation.

On the evening in question, there was a decent mix of revelers in attendance. After some food we all headed to a packed nightclub where we danced and partied. It was loud and hot, and I recall commenting how warm and sweaty the place was. It was at this point that the girl from the coffee shop slipped her hand up my tee-shirt, touched my back and whispered in my ear, 'Why are you married, damn it?' I laughed it off and we danced and drank some more. As our crowd dwindled a bit, a few of us walked downstairs and exited the premises, at which point she looked back at me and said again, 'damn it.' We were with another female acquaintance at this point and as it was still barely eleven pm, I hailed a cab and suggested we all get in it. She lived loosely in my direction, so I travelled with them to her house first. The intention was to drop the girls off and for me to go on home, but as they stepped out of the taxi and as it was still 'quite early' they both persuaded me to join them, which I readily did.

She would be flying to Rome a couple of days later to embark upon a new career in the Eternal City, and there was a likelihood that I would never, ever see her again. That evening would inevitably and predictably present me with a golden opportunity, for what would later be crudely described by a then-friend as, the 'perfect crime'.

Yet, what could have been the 'perfect crime' would in reality become a springboard for the most bizarre chain of chaotic life-events. That would, put simply, drag me to hell and back.

CHAPTER 10:
SHADOWY

Enid Haupt, New York (1902)

"I look out the window and I see the lights and the skyline and the people on the street rushing around looking for action, love, and the world's greatest chocolate chip cookie…"

—Nora Ephron, author and filmmaker. Taken from her autobiographical novel 'Heartburn' (1983)

THE ENID A. HAUPT CONSERVATORY is a greenhouse located at the New York Botanical Garden (NYBG) in the Bronx, New York, United States. Named in 1978 after the publisher and philanthropist of the same name, the conservatory was designed by Lord & Burnham Co. in the Italian Renaissance style. Its major design features were heavily influenced by the Palm House at the Royal Botanic Gardens at Kew, and Joseph Paxton's Crystal Palace.

In their book 'Glasshouse-Greenhouse', Hobson and Edmondson write, 'Originally established, in 1891, the Botanical Garden had quite a romantic start in life, as the idea was heavily influenced by a honeymoon trip to the Botanic Gardens in Kew, which Nathaniel Britton and his wife Elizabeth, very much enjoyed. The couple who were both botanists, were particularly inspired by Kew's ornamental Palm House and Paxton's sensational Crystal Palace and brought their experiences of both grand glasshouses back to New York with them.' This influence is recognisable with its Victorian inspired curved metal and copious amounts of glazing.

'Groundbreaking' took place on January 3, 1899, and construction was completed in 1902 at a cost of $177,000. The building was constructed by John R. Sheehan under contract for the New York City Department of Parks and Recreation. Since the original construction, major renovations took place in 1935, 1950, 1978, and 1993. By the 1970s, the building was in a state of extreme disrepair and had to be either substantially rebuilt or torn down. Enid

Annenberg Haupt saved the conservatory from demolition with a $5 million contribution for renovation and a $5 million endowment for maintenance of the building. A subsequent renovation, which started in 1978, restored the conservatory closer to its original design, which had been compromised during the 1935 and 1950 renovations. Due to her contributions, the Conservatory was named the Enid A. Haupt Conservatory in 1978.

The 1993 renovation replaced the inner workings of the conservatory. At this time, the mechanical systems to control temperature, humidity, and ventilation were upgraded to computerised systems. The exhibits were also redesigned. The conservatory serves as a focal point of the park and a centre for education. It is a New York City designated landmark.

According to John Hix in his wonderful book, 'The Glasshouse', the United States public gardens were being endowed by wealthy families that had enjoyed prosperity and low taxes for many years. The New York Botanical Garden Conservatory in 1900-1902, the Bronx New York, is representative of many glasshouses built in major cities. The New York Botanical Garden came into being largely as a result of the vision and tireless energy of Nathaniel Lord Britton, Professor of Botany at Columbia University, who enthused to the Torrey Botanical Club about his recent visit to Kew Gardens, in 1888. Among forty-eight public spirited citizens listed in the Act of Incorporation, fully subscribed in 1895, were John D Rockefeller, JP Morgan, Andrew Carnegie, and Cornelius Vanderbilt.

WHO KNEW THAT THE CITY OF ROME would have such a part to play in my life? Before the girl from the coffee shop flew to Roma, she had left me with an email address and mobile phone number, and we immediately opened up a channel of communication. She always excited me with tales of her Italian adventures, and this made it impossible for me to get her out of my head. Often, when I eventually got to sleep, I would wake up to find texts from her the next morning. There was something uncontrollable yearning inside me because within a number of weeks, I had booked a flight to Rome. I don't believe she thought it was something that could ever happen. However, I very quickly set about scheming. I devised a plan that would be as slippery as the wet and wintery cobbled streets that surrounded the Pantheon. For by the start of December, I would be boarding a plane and flying to Rome to meet her. Looking back, I was delirious, and my sorry behaviour was despicable.

"So here it is Merry Christmas, everybody's having fun. Look to the future now, it's only just begun..."

Christmas decorations were already up, and Christmas music was being played at full tilt, as I killed time in the overpriced shops in a bustling Dublin airport. Sitting alone on the airport's cold metal seats having a spiced festive latte, I felt more than a little nervous. Actually, I felt as though I was cloaked in an overwhelming darkness. I had this dark cloud looming over me. It was a feeling that would travel with me throughout that trip and beyond. But I believed I was already too far down the line to turn back.

Having boarded the plane at Dublin, I was immediately joined by a stunning blonde Danish woman who would sit beside me for the duration of the flight. In for a penny in for a pound, we got chatting and as the conversation flowed like warm mulled wine, we dallied and laughed until the festive flight had landed. When I disembarked from the plane, the girl from the coffee shop was there to greet me outside Leonardo Da Vinci International airport. Slowly walking towards me with her silky red hair and a dark green coat and set against what must have been Roma's first snow that winter, this scene only added to the ardor.

However, the one poignant moment from that trip that stayed with me was the afternoon we briefly visited an art museum together. I nonchalantly perused the art, as one does, but it wasn't long before I stumbled upon an unsettling image. It was an oil painting of two shrouded faces, one male one female. Even though both identities were concealed by two shadowy cloths, both parties were still locked in a kiss. The painting was ironically called 'The Lovers' by Rene Magritte 1928. There was a dishonourable darkness to it, which made me feel uneasy because it was as though the girl from the coffee shop and I were the couple in the painting, shamefully disguised behind those charcoal-veils.

I always had an arm's length interest in art and, moving forward, I would infrequently paint on canvas. Steering clear of the soft hues and undulating lines born of brushing in watercolour, I would prefer instead to use acrylic or oil in a more colourful, impactful fashion. Yet, I would sometimes revert from using brushes, attempting instead an impasto style by gradually building-up thick layers of paint with a palette knife. The work would often quickly become a thick mess and would usually end up destroyed.

Unknowingly at that time and by embarking upon this 'romantic fling', my life would become an impasto-mess, as I uncontrollably turned sin into an art form. What started off as a darkish palette made up of some sinful primary colour wheel, had quickly descended into a veritable tertiary wheel of errant shadowy blacks, dim greys and dusky charcoals. And in a short time, this would transform my steady existence, into some visceral hellscape.

Following my return to Belfast, the girl from the coffee shop and I would continue our clandestine communications in the run up to Christmas. And as I rapidly constructed a frosty glass wall between my wife and I, like the crumbling Roman Forum, it appeared that our relationship now sat in ruins. Backboneless, I admitted nothing of course, but she suspected that my trip to Rome had been the catalyst for our rapid downward spiral. That said, having been in each-other's lives for almost a decade, we agreed to spend some time apart to reflect on what we wanted to do next.

After she had packed a bag, she went off to spend some time with family and friends for New Year. I spent New Year's Eve and New Year's Day alone. However, the next day I decided to pack a bag of my own before jetting off to Rome for the second time in a month. Like the slimy and scandalous Silvio Berlusconi's lust for the forbidden. So too had I, an insatiable appetite for more time spent in the Eternal City.

When I arrived, I found Rome to be extremely cold. However, once greeted by the girl from the coffee shop, we immediately embarked upon our short walk along the dirty streets from the Roma Termini, towards her apartment near the Via Nationale. When we arrived, we opened a large old, external wooden door before entering the residence. Walking across a gorgeous parquet floor, we slipped into a living space that was already dimly lit and atmospheric. An uncorked bold, deep, old-world red was breathing on the table, beside two large wine glasses, and the room was already aglow with romantic candlelight.

What started as a drunken one-night stand and had progressed to a 'romantic fling'; had quickly developed into a fully blown 'star-crossed love affair'. I felt as if I was truly living in a Hollywood movie. It is, of course, ironic that Hollywood today is regarded by many as a modern-day, Nimrod-driven Babylon, and the 'devil's playground'.

For I was already in a spiritual dance with the devil, only I hadn't realised it at that time.

When I left Rome, I was badly confused and like busy rush hour traffic round the Roma Repubblica fountain, I was in a dreadful spin. I wasn't focusing on work, and I wasn't motivated at home. It was as though I had been possessed by something else that was now driving my thought and decision-making processes entirely. I wasn't my true self in any capacity at that time.

Moreover, given that my *father* had died at fifty-four, it made me consider the finite nature of life and I didn't want to waste a precious second of my time on earth. I believed there was a high risk that ten years down the line I could find myself in exactly the same position that I found myself in now at 30, and I wanted to avoid that risk. I had met this girl from the coffee shop and the possibility of a leftfield move to Rome now beckoned. The excitement and the possibilities absolutely blew my mind to smithereens.

CHAPTER 11:
SHEEP

The Birmingham Botanical Gardens Tropical House (1852)

"In the conservatory or Palm House the collection of tree ferns drew special praise from all commentators. 'On fine days the superb foliage of the tree ferns is most beautifully illuminated by sunbeams' 'nothing can be more beautiful than the tree ferns at Edgbaston"

—An Oasis of Delight – The History of the Birmingham Botanical Gardens, Ballard. P

IT WAS A CHILLY, LATE NOVEMBER when I found myself in Birmingham, England for the very first time. I had been invited to interview aspiring chartered surveyors, at Aston Villa FC's historic home ground at Villa Park. With a stunning Victorian façade, it might well be one of the most beautiful premier league stadiums. However, the afternoon before the interviews, I ensured that I time-managed in enough time to pay a visit to the Birmingham Botanical Gardens.

The Horticultural Society, which manages the Birmingham Botanical Gardens, was founded in 1829 with an initial subscription capital of £2,000. The site selected was 'Holly Bank Farm', farmed purely for recreation by a successful fire insurance broker on 18 acres of leased land on Lord Calthorpe's Estate. The Gardens were designed by J.C. Loudon, a Scotsman who was a leading garden planner, horticultural journalist, and publisher.

Apart from the glasshouses, the general layout is much the same today as Loudon's 1830 plan. Planning and construction took 3 years and the gardens opened to Society members on the 11th of June 1832.

The glasshouses have always been a major attraction, and the collection comprises of a tropical, sub-tropical, Mediterranean, Arid and Alpine houses. The Tropical House was built in 1852 to house the famous tropical water lily, Victoria amazonica; the Subtropical House in 1871 and the present range of Terrace Glasshouses replaced the original conservatory and lean-to houses in 1884.

Throughout their history, the Gardens have been important as a centre for social functions in the city, for flower shows, political meetings, festivals of drama and music, wedding receptions, but especially as a place to take children on day trips. Sunday concerts in the bandstand, built in 1873, remain perennially popular.

The most recent addition of zoological interest is an aviary constructed in 1995, housing a varied collection of birds in four separate flights. This was a sensitively considered addition to the gardens and is wonderfully appropriate. From a distance the aviary is cleverly designed to look like many of the domed conservatories I had previously explored throughout the UK, and it therefore blended beautifully.

It was a crisp but fresh day, so once I finished my visit, I returned to my city centre hotel room for some heat and to write some notes and flick through the images of the conservatories that I had taken on my phone. That evening, after I went for a bite to eat, I went for my first ever walk around Birmingham city centre and I liked it. Christmas was round the corner, there was a lively atmosphere and unlike the birds in the aviary, its cheery, festive Christmas market was in full flight. That said, I noticed a lot of people were heading into a historical looking Anglican church that was located in the city centre, so I thought I'd pay a visit to admire the baroque architecture and above all else, make some time for prayer.

As I made my way to the entrance, a man was standing outside the doorway reading a sign. As I approached the guy I said, 'good evening, I was looking to view inside the structure is it OK to go in, or is there a service about to start?' At which point he stared at me vacantly for a few seconds before responding with a nod and a quiet 'yes'. I thought his response a tad peculiar, but I proceeded over the threshold and into the church, at which point I was warmly greeted by three pleasant people, one of whom was a lady who approached me holding a pamphlet.

'Good evening' I said. 'I was walking by and noticed you were open and wanted to view inside your beautiful structure.' At which point she smiled and replied 'yes, no problem at all, our service is starting in ten minutes, you are more than welcome to join us if you wish', at which point she handed me the aforementioned pamphlet. The pamphlet was for a memorial service for the Birmingham Pub bombings. Now, this is related to a pub bombing that was allegedly carried out by a paramilitary group in 1974, but the event still resonates with the people of Birmingham some forty-five years later.

This, perhaps, explained the standoffish reaction of the guy at the door who probably didn't expect to hear my accent at that particular church on this precise occasion but when he did, I can only assume he was momentarily taken aback. I would have been a one-year-old at the time of the bombings. I wasn't part of the event nor were my family or any friends but yet when people from outside of Ireland speak of such episodes, my friends and I agree that we are sometimes made to feel as if we were in some way directly involved or responsible. Those few seconds outside the church resounded with me because trust me, growing up in Belfast I had first-hand primary experience of witnessing bombs going off.

I digress for a moment but recall clearly, one occasion in 1990 when I was working for a retail company in Belfast city centre. Things were still pretty feisty in Belfast back then, as my colleagues and I used to have to check the pockets of coats, jackets, and suits for incendiary devices every night before we finished our part time job. However, on this one occasion I recall there was a bomb that had been planted on a city bus that had been parked on Donegall Square East, left of city hall as you look at it. It was a particularly loud bomb, because once detonated it shook our shop floor violently enough for a few of us to stumble and lose our balance. I also remember the windows reverberating like crazy with the power of the blast, somehow remaining intact.

Needless to say, the shop was quickly evacuated and with Donegall Square East cordoned off by the RUC, we were hastily guided right, past the front of Belfast City Hall, round Donegall Square West, up Bedford Street and onto the Dublin Road, towards the Botanic area. However, as we headed towards the giant electronic advertising hoarding on Bradbury place, we were quickly stopped in our tracks. Straight ahead, in the middle of the road, was another abandoned red and white city bus that apparently had another bomb on board.

Within a couple of brief minutes, we realised there was no 'apparently' about it because as the second bomb blast detonated, it sent the city bus flying twelve feet into the air before it crashed back down to the tarmac. The alarming thing was that although there were 'Oohs and Aahs' and even a bit of nervous excitement, most of us, even at seventeen years of age, were so de-sensitised to the whole 'Troubles' thing that we quickly moved along without any real fear. As we continued negotiating cordons, the noise, smoke, and dust, we were ushered up past the burning bus and towards Queens University before we were guided into the peace and tranquility of Botanic Gardens and past its Victorian glass Palm House. It just stood there calmly glistening, surrounded by the warm wind blowing through the rustling trees and surrounded by birdsong. It was as if it was beautifully composed beneath the blue summer sky, untarnished and blissfully unaware of the chaos that was ongoing half a mile away. From here we were able to head in the direction of the Ormeau embankment, as general public of all ages traversed our way home on foot, in time for tea.

In terms of that beautiful existing church in Birmingham, it transpired it was called St Phillips and the structure was much older than I originally anticipated. Having been constructed in 1715, it was a Grade 1 listed structure and given more time, I will one day gladly revisit it.

IT WAS A BITTER JANUARY, but I was bombarded by warm calls from in-laws and friends asking what was happening and what they could do to help us patch things up? I had no intentions of patching anything up. But by the time March came round this decision would come back to haunt me, as any aspiration I had to relocate to Rome was gone in a flash. The girl from the coffee shop had been calling me frequently and was very upset about events that were unfolding in the Italian capital and she wanted to come home. The omens weren't good. I tried to convince her to stay there, but she wasn't having it, so she moved home.

My stable life as I knew it, was about to become anything but, and any opportunity to consider any of the red flags that I may have raised in my mind, would soon be gone. For the matter would be unexpectedly taken out of my hands.

Having known my wife, and my in-laws for more than ten years, I had grown very close to all of them but now, having created such strong bonds, our relationships were about to go up in smoke, like the aforementioned city buses that had been blown to smithereens in Bradbury Place, as news of the betrayal leaked out. Looking back, none of those people deserved the hurt that they must have felt, and I have to say at the time, I truly didn't grasp the enormity of what I was doing. I was deep in the middle of a very thick, dark forest and I couldn't see the wood for the trees. Looking back, I was completely immature and self-centred, and had no comprehension of the far-reaching hurt and the irreparable damage my individualism would cause. None.

I can only imagine how they must have felt because in retrospect, if I was in their shoes, I would have been devastated too. Yet, in my naivety, I actually thought everyone would understand things from my perspective. I believed that they would want to talk it out, but in reality, I was absolutely blind and completely off-course. From that point on I would be black balled, ostracised and judged by people who were close to me; but also, strangely from some who were not. I never got the opportunity to seek their forgiveness for any hurt that I caused. With ranks quickly closed like a Roman testudo, no one would communicate on any level and that lack of closure made things especially challenging.

It would be the commencement of a period of abandonment, as the demons of hedonism and individualism took control.

I had found myself inextricably drawn towards this flesh driven situation and I was incapable of resisting sin at that time. Looking back, it was definitely a period when I was tripping along unfamiliar roads, without a map. And, as the very latest man to fall in love or lust, so too would I fall from grace.

As time quickly moved on, the more I got to know the girl from the coffee shop, the more I believed that she was opposite to what I first thought she was. Sure, it is fair to say that she was wonderful at everything she did. But unfortunately, I felt I was being lied to and this gave rise to feelings of insecurity and inadequacy; and such unanticipated negative traits were not at all good for my well-being. In my life, I had of course become very used to being lied to at this stage, but this was rich coming from me. Who was I to judge? People in glass houses…

Yes, I'd been driven by a tornado of carnality, but there was no open communication, and we simply didn't have a shared vision or a deeper reality when the surface was scratched. We were working off two differing frequencies and this led quickly to what I can only describe as an unhealthy dynamic. Upon reflection I was starting to see that a man truly does reap what he sows – "The one who sows to please his sinful nature, from that nature will reap destruction..." (Galatians 6:8).

With my soul not at rights, I began to flag during that period. I felt as though I was slowly sinking into quicksand, without a foothold. But on one particular evening, I felt especially deflated. I badly needed fresh air. Residing in a penthouse apartment, I fully opened the floor-to-ceiling gun powder grey aluminum doors and stood out on the balcony. In doing so, I immediately gripped the black powder coated, steel railing tightly. The darkness that had followed me from Dublin Airport enveloped me, as I stared out at the black night sky and then down at the velvet tarmac below. One of my favourite movies of all time, is the wonderful Margin Call. In it a cocky, sharp suited stockbroker called Will Emerson, is standing smoking with two young colleagues, whilst looking down from the rooftop of his New York office block. He advised the following, "you know, the feeling that people experience when they stand on the edge like this? It isn't the fear of falling, it's the fear that they might jump."

Although my negative thought processes may have momentarily run riot that night, early the next morning and in the cold light of day, I began to reflect more rationally on the mess. The stark reality was that I would *never* consider doing the unthinkable for anyone. *Never.* Yet, the culmination of everything and particularly the events leading up to that evening, had certainly led me to revel in a sorry state of self-pity.

Despite a higher than 43% divorce rate, which was highlighted in UK divorce office for national statistics, people continue to happily demonise the (often very messy) process that leads to it. In 1736 Benjamin Franklin wrote, "Don't throw stones at your neighbours, if your own windows are glass." For although I am not suggesting that I deserved a 'pat on the back'. In the run up to that evening, I had been on the receiving end of judgmental attacks in writing, had been vitriolically confronted in person on a night out, and I had been belittled by people, who thought nothing of using their words like envenomed arrows. Through *my* actions, my world had taken a turn. For having worked hard and having taken time to get to where I previously was, my personal descent was rapid, as my soul melted like that 'romantic' first snow in Rome.

Gabor Mate once stated, 'trauma is not the bad things that happen to you but what happens inside of you, as a result of those bad things that happen to you'. Either way, trust is the basis of any relationship but given how the girl from the coffee shop and I first got together, trust was something that she and I could never have, as we called time on a frenetic period.

I had now crept over the threshold from my twenties and into my thirties. Having previously spent a couple of decades flying relatively stealth like beneath the radar, I had by contrast spent the last two or more intense years living my life in a gold-fish bowl. I no longer had a private life. It seemed everyone, whether family, friends, or colleagues, knew my personal business. There is a wonderful saying that goes, 'an invitation to use the staircase, is not an invitation to slide down the banister!' For as much as I had been open and honest with whomever I had spoken with, I had in reality provided many disingenuous gossips and slandering fools (Proverbs 10:18) with plenty of calumnious coffee table chit chat. So, I was very much ready to revert to living a quiet, private life again.

I was emotionally exhausted by it all and I recall leaving my office one warm summer's day at 4pm, feeling dead on my feet. So much so that I walked around to the front of city hall, folded up my navy, single breasted, double vented suit jacket, like a pillow, and lay my head down on the grass. As I looked up to the pale blue sky, I began to immediately fall asleep in the sunshine. I was far from ready for my 'pipe and slippers' but I was truly ready to sit under my vine and my fig tree, with no one to trouble me anymore. I was ready for peace. (Micah 4:5)

As Pastor Rick Warren once wrote, "You never know God is all you need until God is all you have."

For it was at this time that I started to meaningfully pray to God for his help. I also started to make more time for church on a Sunday, which was something I hadn't done in quite a while. Moreover, during the week I had begun to spend every lunch break alternating between two city centre chapels, praying with a renewed emphasis to God for as long as I could, before returning to the stress of the office. It was in church that I could seek solace, confess my sins and be honest with God. The Gospel according to Matthew 7:7 states, 'Ask and it will be given to you; seek and you will find; knock the door and it will be opened to you'. It was a time that I sought the Lord, and I was praying for His direction.

Historically when I prayed, it was usually discoloured with selfish ambition or in 'negotiation' with God. I really didn't get it. Nevertheless, I now prayed for peace and for a release from the constant chaos that was tormenting me. I was also praying for someone special to come into my life. Having been married, albeit very briefly, I knew that ultimately that was where I wanted to be. In a union. I knew that living an individualistic lifestyle was not to be my purpose in life. For as written in 1 Corinthians 13: 11, When I was a child, I talked like a child, I thought like a child, I reasoned like a child. When I became a man, I put the ways of childhood behind me.

I wanted to be married and I wanted to settle down. So, I prayed to the Lord, complete with my exact specifications for the type of woman I wanted to meet. Most surprisingly of all, I prayed for someone Christian. This was a first for me but here I was praying for someone Christian. What was peculiar about this was, as a Cradle Catholic from Belfast, the word Christian wasn't something I regularly used. The reason being it was a word that often-evoked connotations of members of the many non-Catholic Christian denominations that existed. It evoked images of 'hardcore' biblebelter types standing in city centres untidily bellowing scripture through megaphones or badgering unreceptive members of the public to take tracts – and this was a sector that I knew zero about. I wanted someone Christian but someone with whom I might also want a family in the future when the time was right.

Yet, little did I know at the time, but a change of heart was already on its way, along with a change of mind, spirit, culture, and lifestyle because the Lord had already brought that very person I needed into my life. He had already known what I needed before I had even prayed about it. In fact, I had already met her, and we had already been in communication. My life as I knew it was already slowly turning like a damaged battleship returning from war. I was in the process of being restored and transformed but being so self-obsessed, I hadn't seen it coming. For I was about to witness an immediate answer to prayer that would see my life take an unanticipated but much welcomed, transformation.

I was about to be given an unmerited opportunity to draw a thick black indelible line under all of the mess I had experienced. I had been a lost sheep. Now let me assure you that I do not suffer from some excessive form of scrupulosity. For I am giving this testimony in the spirit of helpfulness. But whether I was responsible for creating the mess or not, it was a passage of time and an experience that could as of this moment, be left behind. When I met with my biological father in the Europa Hotel, he gave me this sage advice. "The past is in the past we cannot go backwards we can only go forwards. We must have no regrets, and there must be no lies, only truth." Indeed. Although in my opinion, it seemed he never heeded his own advice.

However, I was about to discover the true meaning of what it is to actually know Jesus and therefore, to truly know who I was. For when we know Jesus, we quickly realise that he loves us and that he has a plan for our lives, giving us a real purpose and meaning. Once I understood this, I never again tried to think or become what another human being or construct thought I ought to be. Never again would I allow any human being control of my life, nor would I provide them with the opportunity to contribute towards my commodious self-destruction. As Leonard Ravenhill once stated, a man who is intimate with God is not intimidated by man. A power I would soon discover.

Throughout Scripture, you will find sheep mentioned hundreds of times, more than any other animal. In the Gospel's according to Matthew 18:12-14 and Luke 15:3-7, we read of the parable of the lost sheep. It tells of a Good Shepherd who leaves his flock of ninety-nine sheep so that he may find the one sheep, which is lost. It is the first member of a trilogy of parables about redemption, that Jesus tells after the Pharisees and religious leaders accuse him of welcoming and eating with sinners. The two parables of redemption that follow, the Lost Coin and the particularly relevant, Prodigal Son, are also found in Luke's Gospel.

That said, I once stumbled upon a powerful online article that confirmed that when sheep get their heads caught in briars, it can be a painful experience. In fact, they can get trapped and die trying to get untangled from the unforeseen situation that they find themselves in. Whilst tangled there are horrid flies who torment the sheep by laying eggs in their nostrils, which turn to worms and drive the sheep to bang their heads off rocks, sometimes to death. Their ears and eyes are also susceptible to the torment of insect infestation. However, if found in time, and to reduce or eradicate the risk of damage or death, the shepherd anoints the sheep's head with oil. The oil then forms a barrier of protection against the irritation that tries to destroy the sheep, and only then can peace gradually be found. Only then is the sheep saved.

In a very similar vein, I once read of a sheep who was discovered hiding out in caves in New Zealand for six years. "Of course, during this time his fleece grew thick without anyone having shorn it. When he was finally found and shorn, his fleece weighed an amazing sixty pounds. Most sheep have a fleece weighing just under ten pounds, with the exception usually reaching fifteen pounds, maximum." So, for six years, the sheep carried six times the regular weight of his fleece, simply because he was away from his shepherd. In John 10 Jesus compares Himself to a shepherd, and His followers are His sheep. The sheep in New Zealand is much like a person who knows Jesus Christ but has strayed from his flock. Therefore, if we avoid Christ's constant presence in our lives, then I would suggest there is a high risk that we are going to accumulate the extra weight of this world—a weight we don't have to bear. When the sheep was found, a professional sheep shearer took care of its fleece in twenty-eight minutes. Its sixty-pound fleece was finally removed and reused to make suits for twenty men. 'All it took was the sheep to come home to his shepherd.'

For only he can lift the burdens we carry - if we only stop hiding from him. He can shave off our 'fleece'— that is, those self-imposed burdens brought about by wandering away from God, and like the excess wool used to make twenty suits, so too can we share the former weight of our experiences, to help benefit and provide great optimism to many others in desperate need.

In Matthew 11:28-30 it states, "Come to Me, all you who are weary and burdened, and I will give you rest. Take My yoke upon you and learn from Me, for I am gentle and humble in heart, and you will find rest for your souls. For My yoke is easy and my burden is light." In this deeply comforting and instructive verse, the Lord Jesus Christ is of course addressing all of us. That is, a global multitude that man can scarcely number, and it describes the desperate need of millions of people, in every part of the world.

Both sheep analogies perfectly describe the torment that I have experienced in my life. Often, metaphorically speaking, beating my head against a stone wall, heavily weighed down by my self-imposed errors of judgement or from my naïve decision making. For having contributed greatly to my own mess during this time, I dearly longed for peace and tranquility. It seemed no matter what I tried that I couldn't get untangled from the thorny briars or be shorn of my tribulations.

Taking matters into my own hands hadn't worked because the peace, stability, and security that I longed to achieve, never seemed to come. I could never find a suitable solution to the problem. I couldn't manage the risks or the changes in my life that I was encountering. Put simply, I finally realised, and I had to accept, that I couldn't do it on my own anymore and this latest series of crisis had in reality become a catalyst, that led me to recognise the need for a spiritual change. That said, it was a time, without doubt, that something was pulling me in a direction and encouraging me to make that change, and grow closer to God.

Knowing this, I recommend you ask yourself some salient questions. Have you led a sinful life or encountered dark times? Have you ever encountered anxiety, chaos, depression, embarrassment, or stress in your lifetime? Have you encountered worrisome, sinful thoughts that invade your mind to such an extent that you become sleep and rest deprived? Have you ever allowed people and situations to occupy your headspace to such an extent that negative thought processes have run riot? Have you ever, even for the merest moment, felt completely overwhelmed? Are you labouring and heavy laden?

If the answer is yes, then ask yourself these questions. Have you ever sought calmness, peace, and serenity of mind? Have you ever prayed to the Lord to seek direction and ask him to anoint your head with oil? I did. It was a time when I realised that there are instances in life that you cannot control, and some things you simply cannot change. My recommendation? Three words make up the sum and substance of the invitation which He offers you today. 'Come unto me...and I will give you rest.' Rest of spirit, rest of soul and rest of conscience. Come in faith, as someone feeling his or her own sin and as someone convicted by that sin.

Sin defiled, come to Christ and take up His offer and let Him work things out for you, for we no longer have to be sheep for the slaughter.

Like a drowning man's desperate grasp on the safe hand, held out to help him, it was a time when I learned that I could lay all of my sins and worries at the foot of the cross, and leave them there, once and for all. It was a time when I started to trust that God sees all and hears all and that I could let Him work things out for me. It was a time when my sorrowful ailing was about to lead to an unanticipated triumphal recovery via an ascending surge toward the light. I sought the Lord and he found me; and he shepherded me home.

In the Gospel according to John 10:7-11 it states, Jesus therefore said unto them again, "Verily, verily, I say unto you, I am the door of the sheep. All that came before me are thieves and robbers: but the sheep did not hear them. I am the door; by me if any man enters in, he shall be saved, and shall go in and go out, and shall find pasture. The thief cometh not, but that he may steal, and kill, and destroy: I came that they may have life, and may have it abundantly. I am the good shepherd: the good shepherd layeth down his life for his sheep."

CHAPTER 12:
RESTORATION AND TRANSFORMATION

Missouri Botanical Gardens (1915)

---

*"Therefore, if anyone is in Christ, he is a new creation.
The old has passed away; behold, the new has come".*

—2 Corinthians 5:17

BIBLICAL GARDENS ARE CULTIVATED collections of those plants that are named in the Bible. They are a type of theme garden that botanical gardens, public parks, and private gardeners maintain. They are grown in many parts of the world, with examples including the Seinan Gakuin University Biblical Botanical Garden in Fukoka, Japan, and the Missouri Botanical Garden in St. Louis, Missouri, in the United States. The is even a microcosmic version situated 'locally' at The Ark, which is a beautiful, outdoor Christian venture, located not far from the Mountains of Mourne in Newcastle, County Down.

A list of plants in the Bible includes species of plants mentioned in the Jewish and Christian scriptures. Other plants with associations to the themes and subjects of the Bible are sometimes also included, especially in areas with different climates. Additionally, some gardens exhibit objects in order to illustrate Biblical stories, verses or to demonstrate how people lived in Biblical times.

There are a number of noteworthy biblical gardens in the world but one such garden is The Rodef Shalom Biblical Botanical Garden (0.3 acres). Located in Pittsburgh, and open and free to the public since 1987 from June through September. It was founded by Rabbi Walter Jacob and his wife and horticulturalist, Irene Jacob. It now displays more than 100 plants once grown in ancient Israel, including cedars, dates, figs, olives, and pomegranates. All are labelled with biblical verses, or their biblical name. The garden also includes a waterfall, desert, and a representation of the Jordan River from the Sea of Galilee to the Dead Sea. It produces a new show on ancient Near Eastern horticulture each summer. The garden is on the grounds of the Rodef Shalom Congregation, which houses Western Pennsylvania's oldest Jewish congregation, dating back to the 1840s.

Also, at the time of writing, Missouri Botanical Gardens was undergoing a major transformation, in the form of a $100m dollar sustainability driven, centrepiece construction project. This new build project was designed to enhance the botanical gardens but also compliment all of the existing, surrounding assets, facilities, and environs. Structures such as, the historical Emerson Floral Conservatory and the Orthwein Conservatory Garden, which were the first conservatory and display hall constructed on the garden grounds since 1915.

There was also a proposal to renovate and restore the longstanding Shoenberg Temperate House, as a permanent display space for the Garden's expansive arid collection. The Shoenberg Temperate House was dedicated in March 1990 after almost two years of construction. This building replaced the 1913 Mediterranean House on a site just north of the famous Climatron® geodesic dome conservatory. The new facility was given by the Trustees of the Shoenberg Foundation, Inc.

The Shoenberg Temperate House is glazed with the same low-emissivity, energy-efficient glass used in the Climatron, and its southward roof slope allows maximum penetration of solar rays. A computerized climate control system aims to maintain the Temperate House at temperatures between 40 and 90 degrees. Moreover, the Linnean House Conservatory, which was restored to its origins as a historic orangery, houses fragrant and vibrant fruit trees.

Yet throughout this book, and when one visits many of the world's prominent and less prominent glass houses, it is clear that many plant species played a role in early civilisations and their presence during that time was recorded in ancient documents, such as the Bible.

On the Missouri Botanical Gardens website, they highlight that this ancient book mentions about 110 plant species within its pages, many of which grow in an area of the world where the continents of Europe, Asia and Africa converge. It's an area of unique geological structures with diverse climate, plants, and animal life. It's also a land of snow-capped mountains, fertile river valleys, and extensive dry deserts with oases, where a great variety of plants are found. See in the reference section, a wonderful biblical plant list found in Missouri Botanical Gardens.

IT TRANSPIRED PROXIMITY WAS to play its part, one more time. My early thirties had crept up on me, yet I had been engaging with a beautiful younger woman, who worked in my office. We slowly started chatting and over the course of a couple of months our friendship blossomed. I took her for lunch here and we went for a drive there. I could tell she was uncomfortable with the outward nonsense that came from being seen in a gleaming, posy black soft top sports car, but that made her all the more endearing to me. Attention seeking was not for her. There were no airs or graces with this girl. She was humble, gentle, and softly spoken and I loved being in her company. There was something very different and special about her and she made me feel totally at ease. I would openly share all of my experiences with her, but she would never judge or mock. So, without committing, our friendship developed slowly over the initial summer months before I would officially ask her out.

She had a flawless, singular, natural beauty, like no one I had ever met before. She was peaceful, serene, and calm, with a shyness akin to a photograph of Lady Di. She had a warm persona that enabled her to walk around seemingly protected by this impenetrable force field. For instance, when I witnessed people in the office speak to her in the wrong tone or with attitude, it seemed to bounce off her, never fazing her in the slightest. She seemed to exist in a tranquil bubble of calm, and I desperately wanted to know how she achieved this. I very quickly discovered that she was a Christian. She described herself as a follower of Jesus who had given her heart to The King at the age of eleven. She often had a small bible in her bag that was encased in a little silver tin with a rugged cross emblazoned on it. I noticed her bible had fluorescent highlighter marks throughout it, where she had stroked through verses she had read when taking study notes. I thought this was fascinating. I suddenly realised that as a Catholic I actually didn't own a bible and in fact I couldn't remember the last time I consulted one; or had even been encouraged to do so. Knowing this, it wasn't long before she quickly surprised me with my own New International Version (NIV). It was a tremendously thoughtful gift, not to mention a very useful one and I would start referring to it immediately.

Although, it is fair to say from the very moment I opened my bible, that I discovered quickly that I badly needed to get right with God. What was immediately clear was that I had been a very lukewarm Christian. I had been apathetic. In Revelation 3:15 we are warned 'because you are lukewarm—neither hot nor cold—I am about to spit you out of my mouth'. Secondly, at that time and by my very limited understanding, I had always believed I was a Christian, no, hear me out! I was baptised and believed in Christ, therefore I too must be a Christian, right?

However, without batting an eyelid she smiled and politely confirmed that I was not a Christian, before softly starting to explain things. 'You have to give your heart to Jesus,' she proclaimed. 'You have to have a personal relationship with Jesus'. 'You have to confess your sins and repent.' Now I had zero idea what she meant by some of this language. I was a Catholic, I was baptised, I went through the sacraments, I prayed and went to mass occasionally—so what else was I supposed to be doing? Well, it turns out there was a lot I had yet to discover and a whole lot more that I was supposed to be doing.

I can say with confidence that this period of time was the meaningful commencement of my spiritual growth. The seeds that had been planted in me by my mother, had either been replanted or had now been watered. In 1 Peter 2:2 he recommends that we be like 'new-born babies, craving pure spiritual milk, so that by it we may grow up in our salvation'; and from milk we progress to solid foods and on to picking up a knife and fork and eating full meals. This analogy perfectly describes spiritual growth. However, the wiser and more spiritually mature we become the more treacherous and subtler life's choices are, for spiritual growth leads to opposition. The devil is no fool.

As our relationship deepened that year, we travelled to Amsterdam, London and Paris and within seven months of dating, she and I would be engaged. I had already called and subsequently met with her father to ask for his blessing, which he duly gave albeit with a caveat or three. One of those caveats was that we must have God and Jesus at the centre of our marriage, household, and future family. Although he wouldn't have understood it at that time, this was something I was already *very* on board with.

I digress for a moment but as much as my good lady would only *ever* describe herself as Christian, some of her family and friends were from an historic protestant persuasion. There were certain people who crossed my path at that time who had clearly been conditioned by some anti-papal ideologies, and I encountered some deeply peculiar perceptions, which I was, simply, flabbergasted by.

Either way, it was April and I had booked us a table for dinner at Vertigo 42, the tallest champagne bar in London where the panoramic views of London from the top of the tower were immense. Moreover, having meticulously researched, I had specifically booked a table for 7pm so that I could 'get down on one knee' at exactly 7.22pm, which was the precise time the sun was scheduled to set over London that evening. Of course, being Christian my good lady had never taken alcohol, so the Champagne bar side of things didn't resonate with her at all. So, after we had dined, we went straight back to our hotel, where we marked the occasion at her request, by celebrating with cake.

Although my intentions aspired to be memorable and romantic for all the right reasons, she later admitted she would have been just as happy with a simple proposal walking through a leafy local park. That comment encapsulated her and still does. She, unlike me, remains unchanged to this day.

I wanted to move heaven and earth to make the occasion special but to her it would have been just as special without the pomp, ceremony, and pretention. She wasn't at all materialistic or consumeristic and had no time for ostentation. She was the definition of beautiful humility. She didn't buy into any of that insecure worldly nonsense that I had been conditioned to believe was necessary and because of this, I thought she was wonderful. So unique and exceptional and unlike anyone I had ever met to this very day—even many of those who purport to be Christian.

When she returned home from London to break the news, there was a family engagement party and we set about arranging and preparing for a traditional church wedding in her local Church of Ireland church. It was a crisp and fresh early afternoon in late December, when we tied the knot and enjoyed our beautiful pre-Christmas wedding. Soon after, we honeymooned in Miami and took a wonderful Caribbean cruise before travelling home to embark upon our new life together.

As Proverbs 12:4 states, 'a wife of noble character is her husband's crown and as highlighted in Proverbs 31:10-12, A wife of noble character who can find? She is worth far more than rubies. Her husband has full confidence in her and lacks nothing of value. She brings him good, not harm, all the days of her life.' These words remain true and can be applied to my wife every day.

Conversely, as the Venerable Fulton J Sheen stated, 'When a man loves a woman, he has to become worthy of her. The higher her virtue, the more noble her character, the more devoted she is to truth, justice, goodness, the more a man has to aspire to be worthy of her.' From the moment she came into my life, inspired by the Holy

Spirit, she helped me become the very best version of myself and my life has become unfathomably better, ever since. Her kindness to me and her understanding was and is to this day, beyond expression.

Yet, it became unambiguously clear to me at that time, that I was bankrupt. Morally and spiritually bankrupt. And Jesus was calling me, in the first instance, to declare my bankruptcy having clearly accrued an unaffordable amount of bad spiritual debt. In Micah 7:18 it states, "Who is a God like you, pardoning iniquity and passing over transgressions." I was having a change of mind. Through reading scripture, through prayer and by the power of the Holy Spirit, I quickly developed an awareness that the Lord that I have always had faith in, is a Lord who is rich in mercy and forgiveness. He is a Lord of second chances. He had answered my prayers and I wasn't about to pass up this golden second chance, to live a purpose driven life, in line with God's plan for me. From a scriptural perspective the Apostle James says, "We all stumble in many ways. If anyone is never at fault in what he says, he is a perfect man, able to keep his whole body in check... ' He also states that 'the tongue for such a visibly small part of the body, it makes such great boasts and yet the merest spark from a tongue can set off an unstoppable forest fire.' It was clear to me that many of the people I encountered at that time had an innate inability to bridle their tongues. Preferring instead to bite like fiery serpents, by using their spite filled words like poisoned arrows to attack. They veritably thrived on gossip, and I have discovered over the years with people I have crossed paths with, that a significant proportion of them, sadly, cannot resist discussing the business of others. And I found that not only surprising, but disappointing, considering many claimed to be Christian... people in glass houses.

It was through God's Word and his Grace that I first developed an understanding of forgiveness, that it was wrong to criticise others if I first refused to criticise myself. For if we first turned the spotlight onto ourselves, we would never feel compelled to turn it onto anyone else. Having an awareness of the true state of our minds and souls and our need for pardon, is a key element to forgiveness... people in glass houses. Unfortunately, many of us are blind, ignorant of the true condition of our souls. But like Jesus, those of us who are willing to be hardest on ourselves, are also those who might be kindest to others.

I suppose by touching on this subject, I am only stressing the pharisaic tendency of increasing numbers of Christians or non-believers alike to be moralistic and self-righteous. Such judgmental behaviour is not Godly, but it is becoming more common. Moreover, by way of a false measure of people, didn't the Pharisees place emphasis on their righteous rule keeping and condemn others who didn't adhere to the same rules? Pharisees believed they were righteous on the inside because they kept the rules of men on the outside. Surely that's not how it works? Didn't Jesus say they (the Pharisees) were like white-washed tombs, which on the outside appeared beautiful, but on the inside, they were full of dead men's bones and all uncleanliness. Such uncleanliness can easily be aligned with dangerous traits such as ruthless judgementalism and sanctimonious self-righteousness – wouldn't you agree?

Either way, my wife and I moved into a lovely small house, in a quiet and a very private, leafy suburb on the outskirts of Belfast City Centre, where we resided very happily for several years. The property in question was located minutes away from my old south Belfast stomping ground, and so we set about finding a church that my wife would be happy to attend.

It was during this time that I still attended Mass on a Saturday evening (my wife attended with me) but we also decided to explore a couple of 'non-Catholic Christian' churches in Belfast. However, after a short while we settled on an Anglican church, located in South Belfast, which my wife and I felt comfortable in.

You may recall from an earlier chapter, but ironically this was the church on which a mortar bomb landed without detonating, some twenty years earlier. It was that exact church. It would be, of course, my first time inside the church. But, once inside this historic building, there was a pleasant family atmosphere and from the outset, we were quickly made to feel welcome. Structurally, the church was similar to a Catholic church and there were also several sacramental and creedal similarities to the Catholic Church. In fact, it was during this time that I discovered that both churches were deuterocanonical.

I started to take up invitations to attend men's Christian breakfast mornings on a Saturday, where after a gut-busting cooked breakfast, guest speakers would share their personal, life changing testimonies. I began to attend Christian music gigs, listening to powerful artists such as We Are Messengers, Rend Collective and Phil Wickham. I would also attend large-scale Christian events such as Remission and New Wine, where event-spaces full of people would sing, pray, praise and worship. It was another opportunity to listen to powerful testimonies.

I recall standing at one such event, in a dark warehouse, looking forward with everyone else towards a stage, listening to a band playing through a seriously loud sound system. There were also large projection screens and lighting. The audience faces were flushed and rosy cheeked and as they looked to the heavens smiling, hands in the air and eyes closed, some in apparent ecstasy. It was just like being in a rave – except flipped. Instead of listening to a DJ playing techno (technological dance music) we were listening to a band blast out music with a Christian message. Instead of the projection screens having acid faces or trippy fractals, they projected images of a beautiful, bloodied, and battered face of Jesus. Instead of being high on simulants, these people were high on life; having been in-filled by the Holy Spirit.

I would learn of impactful evangelists, preachers, and theologians such as Billy Graham, Jeff Cavins, Father Mike Schmiz, Scott Hann, Bobby, and Jackie Angel and many, many others. It was a whole world I didn't know existed. What was remarkable was that these events were not always driven by clergy but often by laity. It was at this time that I was quickly developing a deeper understanding of God's Word. I was invited to stand at the lectern on a Sunday to read liturgy at church, which I duly did. Moreover, I began listening in private on my headphones, to scores of inspirational testimonies given on-line at differing churches, by people who had previously turned their lives around and repented of their sins.

Although only one method of evangelising, these people impressed me greatly with their explicit personal truths and their graphic honesty, as they set about publicly proclaiming the power of the Gospel and its undeniable influence. Now, I once spoke with an ardent Pentecostal acquaintance, who in a superior fashion, described my wife and I's life choice at that time, as a bit of an 'oddity'. Well, it may well have differed from the stereotypical and established 'Northern Irish' social norm, that we attended each other's churches. But my perception was always this. What would Jesus do? Did I have to proselytise my wife by converting her into becoming a member of my preferred church; or vice versa?

Regardless of the fact that I had been brought up in an unorthodox part of the world. In an oppressive society, blighted by inequality and unfairness, where unscriptural, idolatrous flag flying was oft prevalent – I was still capable of looking beyond all that nonsense. And I have my mother to thank for that outlook. I had attended an integrated school, dated protestant girls, and had many good protestant friends. So, the supposed differences never overly worried me – irrespective of what other's perceptions were of my background.

All I knew was that I was praying like never before, except this time my prayer was not tarnished with personal ambition. I also developed an insatiable hunger to learn more about God and Jesus and I rapidly drew closer to Him through His Word. And it was during this time that God's Word brought about for me a realism of finitude and the reality of death.

I listened to a wonderful sermon from one of my local parish-priests, who described two friends speaking about life. One friend said to the other, "what will you do after you leave school?" To which the other friend replied, "I'll go to university to study". "And what then?" To which the friend replied, "I'll embark upon a successful career in engineering." "And what then?" "I'll find a wonderful woman and I'll marry her." "And what then?" "We'll have beautiful children and watch them grow?" "And what then?" "I'll hopefully retire early and enjoy time with my wife." "And what then?" "I'll likely get old and sick." "And what then?" "Well, I guess I might die." "And what then...?"

In the book of James 4:14, the Apostle James states, 'Why, you do not even know what will happen tomorrow! What is your life? You are a morning mist that appears for a little while and then vanishes.' When the penny finally drops that we are not infinite and that our time on earth is finite, we can develop a wonderful spiritual awareness, of the 'supreme reality of God'. Right now, we are all in this world but ultimately, we are not of it, merely passing through. We are going to die. No ifs, ands, buts or maybes, death awaits us all. But what awaits us after death?

In Scott Hahn's book, 'Hope to Die', he proclaims - Again and again, the author of Hebrews drives home the point: Abraham knew. Isaac knew. Jacob knew. Joseph knew. The faithful Israelites knew. They knew there was more to life than this life—that there was a "better country." They knew that God had something better prepared for them—a "heavenly" homeland. They knew that their story wasn't over when their life was over— that their bodies, somehow, someway, were destined to be a part of that story, and so it mattered where and how those bodies were buried. When the day came to go to the "city" God had "prepared for them," they wanted to walk into that city together, as a family. By highlighting death, I am not suggesting we travel through life in a morose spirit, looking to meet the grim reaper halfway. For life is to be lived and enjoyed to the full, but in the right spirit!

I recall attending a funeral with my wife, at which the forthright Presbyterian minister set about warning everyone in attendance, that this very day was coming to us all and that we must repent and not consider offering the Lord the 'dregs' of our lives, as he put it. There was no 'softly-softly catchy monkey' with this guy. His impactful preaching truly resonated with me. As much as some of my old habits were dying hard, I knew what needed to be done. I had truly sought the Lord and he called me in my mid-thirties. I had encountered his saving grace and I now needed to know what ministry he had in store for me. Trust me when I declare that I still to this day give thanks and praise for that impactful sermon.

I started to give thanks and praise to the Lord every day for this awareness and for the golden opportunity that enabled me to get right with Him. I prayed for forgiveness and that the Lord might inspire others to forgive me and for me to *genuinely* forgive them. These prayers were as much for their benefits as they were for mine. Let us consider the parable of the unmerciful servant (Matthew 18:21-35) who was forgiven a debt of ten thousand talents by his master but who immediately went out and choked his colleague who owed him a mere one hundred pence. The debt the master forgave was apparently 1,250,000 times greater than the debt owed by the colleague. Such a great disproportion aligns with how much greater man sins against God are, when compared to the sins of our fellow men against us.

In Tony Cooke's 'The Grace DNA of God' he states, 'it is extremely important to understand that none of us are going to make it to heaven because we have been law abiding citizens. Heaven is not for good people, perfect people, or religious people. Heaven is for people who have been forgiven. And forgiveness is available because of what Jesus has done on the cross at Calvary. "Lord, forgive them for they know not what they do." Once we know that Christ died for us, even though we deserve hell and judgement, we begin to understand that the price for our sins has been paid by Jesus as a ransom, on the cross.

Like all of those differing cultures who stood angrily beneath the cross at Calvary that day, willing Jesus's body to be ripped to shreds, it was only through my complete ignorance of the extent of Jesus's act of love that day and an inability to see the far-reaching consequences of my sinful behaviour, that I behaved in the manner I once did. It was Fulton J Sheen who eloquently stated, 'with the first words from the cross, "Father, forgive them for they know not what they do", the greatest sinner may now be saved; the blackest sin may now be blotted out... the unforgivable may now be forgiven... for if they (those stood at the foot of the cross; and you and I today) did know what they were doing as they fastened Love to a tree, and still went on doing it, they would never be saved. If there were full consciousness of the evil (acts perpetrated), perfect deliberation, perfect understanding of our acts, there would be no room for forgiveness. That is why there is no room for redemption for fallen angels. They knew what they were doing. We do not. We are very ignorant of others and ignorant of ourselves and it is only that Divine ignorance, which saves us from being damned on judgement day.'

I knew that key to my conversion was the ability to truly forgive others. We must forgive all who have wronged us and pray that those we have wronged have forgiven us too. Forgiveness is something we all must do. With forgiveness, there is freedom. Although we may choose to sever ties in some situations (each situation is different), we must forgive. Because when *God forgives, God forgets.*

Moreover, it was Fulton J Sheen who confirmed, "Gathering the nucleus of His Church around Him, He said to His Apostles, "Whose sins you shall forgive they are forgiven." Somewhere in the world today then, the successors of the Apostles have the power to forgive. It is not for us to ask: But how can a man forgive sins? – for man cannot forgive sins. But God can forgive sins through man, for is not that the way God forgave His executioners on the cross…" That said, during the unprecedented global pandemic when confession was unavailable for those who availed of it, is it not true that one could also go straight to God for forgiveness, from the comfort of their own homes?

With that said, are you in need of forgiveness? Do you need to forgive? And are *you* in need of confession and repentance? Once again, in relation to the thematical A- Z of sin - have you or anyone you know ever been guilty of the following sins which are highlighted in scripture: Adultery, bullying, conceitedness, divisions, envy, false witness, gluttony, hypocrisy, idolatry, judgementalism, knowing to do good but not doing it, lust, malice, neglect of scripture, outbursts of rage, pride, questionable lifestyle choices, reviling, sorcery, thievery, unbelief, violence, wickedness… I'd suggest the answer can only be yes to some or many of these items for us all.

The Gospel is the power of Jesus Christ and only He has the power to save every single believer. How many of you believe the gospel is the power of God? I believe it is. I read His book and it changed my life; and no longer did I continue living, or even aspire to live, in rebellion to God.

CHAPTER 13:
WE ARE ALL PIGS

Glass Green House, Curitiba, Brazil (1991)

The Botanical Garden of Curitiba (Jardim Botânico de Curitiba), in the middle of the city, provides a tranquil respite for locals and visitors alike. Designed in the style of French royal gardens, the park's crown jewel is the 4,844-square-foot *(450-square-meter)* art nouveau, metal and glass greenhouse that sits against the Curitiba skyline.'

—www.viator.com/Curitiba-attractions/Curitiba-Botanical-Garden-Jardim-Botanico/d23058-a21785)

I T WAS DURING MY EXTENSIVE DESK-BASED RESEARCH, that I discovered this stunning example of 'Victorian' glass house architecture. About 6 hours from São Paulo is the city of Curitiba, the capital of Paraná. The Botanical Garden of Curitiba is a modern- day version of Victorian glasshouse construction, having been constructed in 1991. The Botanical Garden, also known as Jardim Botânico Fanchette Rischbiete, is designed to resemble a French royal garden, such as the one at Versailles, and features waterfalls and fountains, nestled among neatly manicured hedges and angular stone walking paths.

However, this impressive structure, which was designed by architect Abraão Assad, was also inspired by the Crystal Palace in London.

I came upon these wonder words online. "The soaring glass structure is visible from the main entrance, and is situated to catch the rising and setting Sun. Even though it is not nearly as large as the Crystal Palace, the greenhouse is impossible to miss!

The building consists of a metal and glass structure, with three separate silos. The white metalwork serves as a decorative frame for the glass in the greenhouse, creating vibrant geometric patterns." Although this is one glasshouse that I have yet to visit in person, by viewing its images on-line I see great value in it as a project. Although clearly pastiche, the design, materials and construction methods used in 1991 would have barely differed from the methods used when The Crystal Palace was constructed in 1851. Once again, the far-reaching influence of Victorian design and construction and of The Crystal Palace in particular, is absolutely undeniable. The main greenhouse is 458 square metres. This wonderful building shows up in the background of the garden. It looks magnificent and resembles a huge crystal.

In the Westbury's pick website, it informs us that 'the extensive Botanical Garden of Curitiba is home to many tropical plants from around the world, along with cascading waterfalls, fountains, and pools. Additional plants and floral displays can be found inside the main greenhouse where 24 flower beds—fenced off with ornamental and seasonal blooms – are split between six geometric garden areas. Each area is illuminated with Republican-style chandeliers which give the building a wonderful glow long after the sun goes down'. Moreover, in highlighting the structures multi-functionality, it states it is located behind the greenhouse is the Museum of Franz Krajcberg —a Polish Brazilian, devoted to environmental conservation—another stunning example of glazed architecture, the space offers an auditorium, multimedia classrooms, and exhibitions.

Another factor which gives this glasshouse its iconic status is the thematic lighting displays hosted throughout the year when the building glows with colorful lighting to symbolize awareness days or seasonal events and holidays. The curvaceous building offers an important hub for environmental education and conservation and has become an iconic symbol in the southern region of Brazil.

Although I have yet to visit this stunning structure, I visualise it less as pastiche but more as a respectful and sensitive modern-day nod to those many original prominent Victorian structures of a much senior vintage, that exist globally. It is a personal aim that I one day inspect and explore this structure in person to consider its design, materials and the method of construction used at this location; I would further contemplate on the duration of the construction project and the success of its end use, its cyclical maintenance procedures and its anticipated lifecycle. Not to mention its popularity and diverse end uses. Fascinating.

IN THE PREVIOUS CHAPTER, I DECLARED that when God forgives, He forgets. This truth is continuously repeated in scripture. For instance, according to the Psalmist, God has removed our sin from us as far as the east is from the west (Psalm 103:12). Moreover, in Jeremiah 31:34, the prophet proclaimed that when the Messiah came, God would forgive all our inequity and remember our sin no more. Therefore, people in glass houses must never throw stones.

For much like the gloriously diverse array of humble glasshouses, impressive conservatories or magnificent palm houses that exist within our society, so too are we human beings just like existing, visible, emerging, living and breathing People in Glasshouses (PIGs). Well, what I mean is, we can be as robust or as fragile, or as simplistic or as complex as a Glasshouse. We can be as cold or as warm, or as versatile or as inflexible as a Glasshouse.

We can be as curvy or as slender, or as aesthetically pleasing or as unattractive as a Glasshouse. We can be as practical or as impractical, or as innovative or as unoriginal as a Glasshouse. We can be as open and as transparent, or as closed or as screened off, as a Glasshouse. We can be as white-washed and protected; or as exposed and as corroded as a Glasshouse. We can be as current and trendy or as historic and conservative, as a Glasshouse.

Yet, although you might not have realised it until this moment, you and I, *we* are all People in Glass House's (PIGs). All different and yet all the same, we are all cracked by conditioning, history and perceptions; and tarnished by the differing degrees of sinfulness, that we *all* struggle with daily to overcome. Sure, whilst some of us can be compared to the lowliest potting shed and others to the most grandiose conservatory, each of us is as capable as the other, of developing defective cracks and corrosion or of falling into a

189

state of disrepair at any given time.

In fact, I would go one step further in suggesting that with free will, we are all people in defective Glass Houses.

Buckled and bent by time and sin; each of us can be battle-weary, fatigued and damaged, by dents, darkness, dirt and double mindedness, as a result of our access to freewill and our sinful natures. We are all PIGs who, undeserving of God's grace, deserve nothing more, than to be driven into the lake to drown like the impure swine demonically possessed by Legion (in Mark 5: 1-20).

And yet, *without* the right protection in place, *I* have discovered that sin and temptation are to the soul what water is to an iron filled glasshouse - a significant risk. Sin and disobedience are a risk that can cause the type of acidic damage that might overload the spirit. They are a risk that might bring to the fore at any time, the type of existing latent defects that lurk buried within a frazzled mind. That said, with the appropriate level of protection in place - spiritual risk and the risk of sinful behaviour occurring, the type that might separate us from God, can be managed effectively. For like a 19th century Wardian case, designed to protect foreign plants from exposure and death during long sea voyages. So too is God and his Word, the ultimate method of protection for our life-long journeys. For if Satan and his demons were condensation, steaming up a glasshouse and obscuring our view of what is good and right, then God and His Word are the pure ventilation, which breathes fresh air into the glass house demisting and demystifying, what it is we have become blind to. Therefore, as people in Glass Houses (PIGs) we must never, *ever*, throw stones.

One of the over-arching aims of this book, was to highlight the risk of judgementalism and hypocrisy in life, and to confirm that there is no ink-like sinfulness to which we are addicted that cannot be blotted out by Christ. I aimed to encourage us to not judge the life choices of others… People in Glass Houses. For it is my firm belief and according to scripture, that in time we will all be judged and called to account, for our sinfulness whilst in this world. We will be judged for our negligence, our weakness, for what we do and by what we fail to do.

In Matthew 7:1-5 it warns us, "Do not judge, or you too will be judged. For in the same way you judge others, you will be judged, and with the measure you use, it will be measured to you. "Why do you look at the speck of sawdust in your brother's eye and pay no attention to the plank in your own eye? How can you say to your brother, "Let me take the speck out of your eye, when all the time there is a plank in your own eye? You hypocrite first take the plank out of your own eye, and then you will see clearly to remove the speck from your brother's eye."

In my personal experience, of course, we can rebuke each other in the spirit of righteousness but we must never burn each other up or tear each other down. We must use our words only in the spirit of edification, to embolden each other and encourage each other on our expedition. We must not judge for it is not for us to do, but we must forgive each other for those inequities and transgressions that often come about as part of our journeys. For the acid of bitterness only serves to damage the container in which it is stored, not those the bitterness is supposed to be directed at. CS Lewis once stated, 'Forgiveness is a beautiful idea – until you have something to forgive'. I have things to forgive but yet that makes me no different to any other character that ever existed. Moreover, I once read that forgiveness is a great gift, but it's a penultimate gift, intended to prepare us for something still greater.

That said, we can forgive people for what they do to us, but it doesn't mean we have to have those people in our lives. For if those people who have harmed us continue to do so, and do not truly change their ways, and if our propensity to sin is increased by being around those people, then as scripture says, we should shake the dust off our feet and move on.

If there is even a risk that sinful feelings of anger, bitterness, envy, lust or profanity could return, then we should 'flee' and avoid such risks, at all costs. Preaching ultimately only to receptive listeners.

In Matthew 6:15 he states, "We can forgive others because God forgave us and for the same reason it is our duty to forgive others." Moreover, in St Paul's letter to the Ephesians (4:31-32) he proclaims, 'Let all bitterness and wrath and clamor and anger and slander be put away from you, with all malice, and be kind to one another, tender-hearted, forgiving one another, as Christ forgave you'. Furthermore, Pope Francis confirmed that 'a person who only thinks only about building walls and not building bridges, is not Christian'. For it was from the cross that Jesus, not only forgive the repentant criminal on the cross beside him, but also, forgave those who had not yet repented; or perhaps never would.

By forgiving others, I am stating unambiguously that I am in no position to judge that person. For as a person in a glass house, I too am a sinner who is also in need of forgiveness for my iniquities, sinfulness and transgressions. In John 8:7 Jesus proclaimed, 'Let he who is without sin cast the first stone'. The outcome in that Chapter was that everyone involved went away because no one was faultless. The caveat was that the sinful woman in question, instantly left and turned her back on the life of sin that had caused her to be in the predicament in the first place. I was that person.

Also, take the aggressive persecutor of Christians, Saul of Tarsus, who was blinded by God's light on the road to Damascus. He was changed to such an extent, that he was to become supernaturally transformed into becoming the Apostle Paul. Through God's Word, I was aware of the possibility that such a radical transformation was also open to me too. And if it is also open to me then it is also open to you too.

Because the opportunity for us to become apostles, disciples and saints exists as a reality, even though a saint is just a sinner who keeps on trying (St. Jose Maria Escriva). Is it not therefore, demonstrably possible that the sinner of this hour might be the saint of the next?

According to theologian John McArthur, 'in Christ's day the world was filled with intellectuals and influential people. There were celebrated philosophers in Athens and unsurpassed scholars in Alexandria, the most powerful political leaders of the world in Rome and some of the most meticulous Rabbis of all time in and around Jerusalem. Christ by passed them all and called simple crude, unknown, uneducated fishermen from Galilee to be his disciples' and they turned the world upside down with their bold preaching. No, he went for the ordinary people, like you and me.

Whether through naivety, inexperience, hubris, youthful exuberance or simply by being a misguided fool,

I can say with confidence that I have made mistakes, errors of judgement and was guilty at times of poor decision making. Yet that makes me no different to any other human being, biblical or otherwise, that existed throughout the history of time. But why do we gravitate towards sin?

Evagrius of Pontus was a fourth century spiritual guide to monks based in the Egyptian desert. In his book, Talking Back, Evagrius was encouraged by a monk named Loukios to compose for him a treatise that would explain the tactics and the intense conflict which spawn from demons that try to undermine the monastic life, creating a struggle for virtue, for purity of heart and thus for salvation.

Opposition from demons, whether through anxieties, circumstances or temptation to sin, or through demons assailing a monk into abandoning the aesthetic life, was a physical and a spiritual struggle for Evagrius and for the Evagrian monks. Evagrius presented a primary strategy for such assaults. By speaking relevant passages from the Bible as testimonies from Holy Scripture, one might successfully contradict, or as Evagrius put it, "cut off" and resist demonic suggestion. He collected some 498 biblical passages that he believed should be addressed during specific demonic conflicts and in particular the eight primary demons that he claimed continuously attacked the monks – gluttony, fornication, love of money, sadness, anger, listlessness, vainglory and pride. All certainly sound familiar to me - do such demons sound familiar to you? I suggest with confidence that we are all aware that these are areas of temptation, that are not specific to those living a monastic lifestyle. These are damaging temptations that can and do, cause us _all_ to fall down, with great regularity.

Such writing and recommendation aligned with the words of the Apostle Paul in Ephesians 6:10-17, by helping to warn us of the risk of spiritual warfare. 'Finally, be strong in the Lord and in his mighty power. Put on the full armour of God, so that you can take your stand against the devil's schemes. For our struggle is not against flesh and blood, but against the rulers, against the authorities, against the powers of this dark world and against the spiritual forces of evil in the heavenly realms. Therefore, put on the full armor of God, so that when the day of evil comes, you may be able to stand your ground, and after you have done everything, to stand firm then do so with the belt of truth buckled around your waist, with the breastplate of righteousness in place, and with your feet fitted with the readiness that comes from the gospel of peace. In addition to all this, take up the shield of faith, with which you can extinguish all the flaming arrows of the evil one. Take the helmet of salvation and the sword of the Spirit, which is the word of God.'

By His Word, God specifies the armour that He wants us to use. He calls it "the armour of God." Surely, He knows what is best for us. What does this God-prescribed armor include? Loins girded about with truth (to protect us from licentious lust and fornication);

the breastplate of righteousness (to protect our hearts), feet shod with the preparation of the gospel of peace, the shield of faith (authentic genuine faith in our Lord Jesus Christ), the helmet of salvation (to protect our minds), and the sword of the Spirit, which is the Word of God (6:14-17). This is God's plan for making us ready to do battle with the wicked one and his servants. He urges us to lead by example in our lives by 'putting on' (6:11) and 'taking up' (6:13) this armour, not giving thought and consideration to its possible use.

The Apostle Paul teaches us some powerful Christian principles throughout the book of Ephesians, but he closes with this "final" section on the battle that wages behind the scenes—spiritual warfare. God takes the Devil seriously and so His Word equips us to withstand regular attacks from the enemy. The church and her people need to stand firm in the truth of God's Word and be alert to the risk of attacks. Paul first reminds us of the risk of such attacks from the evil one, who desires to steal a "part" of our soul in each small conflict against us. The Lord has given us wonderful "spiritual armor" with which we can withstand powerful attacks from the evil one and live out God's purposes in this world. For in Corinthians 2:11 we are warned that we are not to be ignorant of Satan's devices.

According to Evagrius and from a scriptural perspective, he recognised Biblical King David as a warrior against demons, whose reputation rested on his reputed authorship of the Book of Psalms. Many of the Psalms were directed against his speakers, persecutors and enemies and on his successful warfare against the Philistines, whom Evagrius equated to Demons. Evagrius referred to the entire context of the monastic life, which the Holy Spirit also taught David through the Psalms, and thus places verbal refutation of the demons at the core of monastic struggle against vice and for virtue. Jesus, who hailed from King David's bloodline, oft used biblical verses to respond to the temptations of Satan, and these can be found in the Gospels of Matthew (4:1-11) and Luke (4:1-13).

Evagrius saw Jesus's use of Scripture, as gifts of the Saviour handed down to Christians, in their struggles against Satan and his demons, and against sin and temptation.

In the book of 2 Samuel 11, King David knowingly, willfully committed adultery by sleeping with Bathsheba the wife of Uriah the Hittite. Moreover, to make Bathsheba his own he arranged for Uriah's death. In Samuel 12 the Lord had sent Nathan to rebuke David for his sin, but David confessed of his sin and was forgiven although he would not go indirectly unpunished, and his actions would still have far reaching implications.

The Old Testament is clear about the risk associated with adultery. In Exodus 20:14 it states 'You shall not commit adultery. Moreover, in Proverbs 6:32 it is written, 'That a man who commits adultery lacks judgment; whoever does so destroys himself.' Whilst in Hebrews 13:4 it states, 'Let marriage be held in honour by all, and let the marriage bed be kept undefiled, for God will judge fornicators and adulterers.'

In the New Testament Jesus extended the definition of adultery to include sexual relations between a married man and a woman other than his wife (Mark 10:11-12; Luke 16:18). This is also understood in 1 Corinthian 6: 15-16 and 1 Corinthians 7:2.

However, Scripture is also unambiguously clear that adultery can also come in the form of non-sexual relations because Jesus said, "You have heard that it was said, 'Do not commit adultery.' But I tell you that anyone who looks at a woman lustfully has already committed adultery with her in his heart. (NIV Matthew5: 27-28) In other words, if any married individual has had impure thoughts about another person, married or otherwise, without even lustfully acting in a carnal manner on those thoughts, then Biblically speaking, in their heads and their hearts they too have committed adultery.

Scripturally speaking, adultery also extends to 'spiritual adultery'. In James 4:4 it states, 'You adulterous people, don't you know that friendship with the world means enmity against God? Therefore, anyone who chooses to be a friend of the world becomes an enemy of God.' This is further emphasised in Ephesians 2 – 'As for you, you were dead in your transgressions and sins, in which you used to live when you followed the ways of this world and of the ruler of the kingdom of the air, the spirit who is now at work in those who are disobedient. All of us also lived among them at one time, gratifying the cravings of our flesh and following its desires and thoughts. Like the rest, we were by nature deserving of wrath.' But because of his great love for us, God, who is rich in mercy, made us alive with Christ even when we were dead in transgressions—it is by grace you have been saved.

Now, before I confessed, repented and had my conversion, the language of the cross would have been illogical to me as someone who wasn't on his way to salvation, but to those of us who are on the way, we see it as God's power to save. That is why, when you place all of life's problems at the foot of the cross and entrust your life into Jesus hands, do His will, and you believe, trust in and live by His infallible Word, then clarity on life's matters quickly becomes apparent.

Within many reformed Churches a sin is a sin, but with me being a cradle Catholic and having a preference for the bells and smells of a magisterium driven church, the Catholic Church promotes a classification of sins, such as mortal or venial sins. In my experience, like a ten-pin bowling ball that powerfully knocks down all ten pins with one strike, so too can one mortal sin shatter the majority of all ten commandments.

Look at my earlier example as a case in point. When I was living an individualistically worldly life. I deliberately described my primary sin as an exhilarating 'one-night stand', or a 'romantic fling' or a 'star-crossed love affair.' In reality, I was living for the self and justifying my actions by doing so. When the stark reality was, biblically speaking, that I was committing the mortal sin of adultery. By doing so, I was also simultaneously doing my best to shatter all ten commandments, the many hundreds of biblical commands and decrees, and the seven deadly sins into the bargain. In fact, little did I know then, but getting out of the taxi and crossing over the threshold that first night, was tantamount to me straying through the Arch of Palmyra and into the ungodly world of Nimrod or Baal. Satan, the 'light bearer', 'the morning star' and the God of this world, is devious. So, we need to call our sin what the bible calls it and not dilute it with worldly phraseology. In Michael Novak's Belief and Unbelief, he stated, "Men cannot listen long to the language of a foreign age, nor can even the man of faith endure a life divided between two cultural worlds: he will give up one or the other."

During my conversion, it was a period of time when the Holy Spirit really rested on me, ensuring my whole outlook changed. Sure, I was physically fit, climbing mountains for charity and riding my road bike on journeys exceeding one hundred miles but it was during this time that I also became very spiritually fit. Like a Tour De France peloton rapidly eats up tarmac I would get on my spiritual bike by hungrily devouring God's Word morning, noon and night. I would listen to Christian music, readings and preaching in my car on the way to and coming home from work. Once in work, I would sit at my desk and read a verse of scripture from my daily bible reading guide before my working day commenced. I would then switch on my computer and to gain access to the system, my password would be a chosen bible verse. Christ be on my mind, on my lips and in my heart.

At the weekend, I could read scripture from the lectern at my wife's church and be a Minister of the Word reading liturgy at my own church. I knew I had developed a passion for some form of ministry, but I didn't know what, where or how. So, I would pray to the Lord for guidance, direction and help, that I might discern my God-given ministerial passions, spiritual gifts or talents. I began to place all queries that I had solely at the foot of the cross. I felt a powerful calling to do good works for the Lord and to walk in the spirit of apostleship and discipleship, but I didn't know what it was that he wanted me to do. In fact, I was becoming so dedicated to living a scriptural life, that it was all I could do one evening, to not leave a fleece or blanket out in the garden overnight, to see if the Lord would answer my prayer and give me much needed direction the very next morning (Judges 6:37). But the Lord works in mysterious ways.

For a start, I recall one day staring out through my kitchen window at my back garden. My lawn needed cutting. The very next day, a few doors up from my house, I spotted a random guy mowing my neighbour's front lawn. So, I approached him. Turned out very quickly that he was the son in law of my elderly neighbour, but he thought nothing of bringing his mower down to my house and immediately agreed to cut my lawn. Within minutes we got talking about God. At this point he announced that he was actually an aspiring evangelist who it transpired had lived round the corner from me for a couple of years, only we hadn't realised. He confirmed that he was starting a bible study class in his home, one night a week, that very week. I went on to attend his midweek bible study for more than two years. I grew spiritually during this time, became friends with relative like-minds and learned a lot in the process.

It was also during this time that unthinkably, I considered exploring ordination via my wife's church. Now, for me it was one thing attending church with my wife and enjoying impactful preaching. And I enjoyed proclaiming God's Word and listening to God's Word being methodically dissected on a Sunday morning. But this insatiable drive was something else entirely. For to even consider being part of any church other than the 'one true church' would have been improbable, given the history of Ireland's past. But I was learning about God from as many directions as I could at that time, so I felt it worth bearing in mind, without completely dismissing the notion out of hand.

I prayed extremely hard about this leftfield consideration. I prayed that the Lord blessed me with discernment, so that I may discern if such an option was viable or realistic, or if it was indeed God who was leading me in this direction. Yet again, pretty quickly the signs began to come. To begin, the wonderful influential Minister, who was also an impactful preacher, kindly gave me the opportunity to read scripture at his church and to lead a couple of church services with him. He was a decent man, and it was a positive experience. However, one morning a parishioner mentioned encouragingly and light-heartedly before a service began, that I would already be off to a wonderful start with the parishioners due to my shirt selection. I had randomly selected a red, white and blue checked shirt. His humorous comment, although a tad strange, was a harmless, throwaway comment, on the face of it. Quietly though, it resonated with *me*, because the colour of my shirt should have had nothing at all whatsoever to do with God, Jesus, God's Word or this House of God.

After that, when I spoke with a knowledgeable acquaintance about the possibility of exploring ordination in Dublin, I was rather surprised when I was told, that I would have to 're-baptise' - if I were to discern a calling to work within this given church. Having previously spoken with a number of people about this item, this wasn't my initial understanding, and I found the apparent proposal highly questionable. But I continued to pray for direction and to deal with the item respectfully.

Then, in my everyday role, as a surveyor, I was randomly approached to inspect the inside of an Orange Hall, that required some minor works. This in and of itself, was fine. It would be my first time in such a structure. Unbelievably, it was geographically located less than a mile from the church in question but within minutes of accessing the building, I had noticed a large colourful material banner that was fully unfurled and sat open against an internal wall on full display. On the banner, was a painting of the church in question and it was at this point that I knew, that this was not the right path for *me*. Were these three consistent signs impeccably timed answers to prayer? Were they coherent evidence of spiritual experiences that transcend the normal realm of the objective world? Or were they, put simply, continuous chance coincidences? I would suggest to you that the timing was "too coincidental" to be chance coincidences.

It was undoubtedly a time when The Lord was calling me to something more. And although I pushed doors in a number of different contexts, the truth is there was something that prevented me from walking fully over the threshold. What my reservations were, I cannot say. But in the absence of any flashing neon directional signage, perhaps I had initially misunderstood God's call, but I discerned that this wasn't where I was called to be.

The rapid chain of events was then fully rubberstamped when I attended a summertime Christian event, with my wife and in laws. Participating in classes by day and listening intently to testimonies and becoming familiar with some of the praise and worship music by night. It turned out to be a great week of learning scripture and of fellowship, and I grew spiritually and drew even closer to God because of it.

But on the last night I decided that I would take things a step further by getting off my seat to join one of the small queues and head towards two team members for prayer, to confess my sins and to repent.

I didn't see it as being that much different from what I would do in the Catholic church with a priest, but when I tried to speak, I got very nervous and remember getting really tongue-tied. As I tried to confess my sins, it was like something was stopping me from getting the words out with any distinction. One representative started sensationally claiming that Satan was blocking my speech, whilst the other got busy pressing his thumb against the base of my skull, as my mouth slurred like a washing machine. I eventually got some words out and at the end of the experience I was warm and clammy and a bit dazed. That said, I have to say I felt lighter when I left the auditorium.

It was a beautiful, bright late summer's night, as we strolled home to our accommodation. I was experiencing waves of peace and a calmness that felt strangely wonderful. I slept well that night, but the next morning as we packed up to go home, an excitable acquaintance, who had also been in attendance the night before, eagerly thumped our apartment door. No sooner had the door opened, when he enthusiastically shoved a blue pamphlet into my hand inviting me to "Convert from Catholicism to Protestantism today!" I looked at it quizzically before responding politely but accordingly. But whilst his perspectivism may have been misinterpreted by wanton subjectivity, perhaps my perceptions had unknowingly become too openminded, relaxed, modern and liberal. But in all civility, his perception and my understanding of the previous night's events were clearly worlds apart. It made me think of the words of the poet Thomas Bracken who once wrote: 'Poor souls with stunted vision, oft measure giants by their own narrow gauge'.

CHAPTER 14:
HIDDEN IN PLAIN SIGHT

Fota House and Gardens, Co. Cork (c1840)

I T WAS BACK IN 2016 THAT MY good lady and I took a weekend break in the 'Rebel County' in County Cork. And it was on this trip that we first became aware of the tranquil beauty of Fota House and its Victorian Working Garden. Fota House is located just outside the city of Cork, near to Cork Harbour. Fota Gardens consists of a structured arboretum, walled garden and terraces. The gardens include rare and exotic shrubs and trees, along with an extensive rose garden. The layout and structure of the arboretum and gardens date largely from the tenure of the Smith-Barry family, who recognised the significance of Fota's sheltered location and warm soil — "Fota" is derived from the Irish "Fód te" meaning warm soil. The changeable conditions are appropriate for the growing and cultivation of certain trees and exotic plants. This stunning 19th century property in Cork, Ireland, had been abandoned almost 40 years ago and had deteriorated to a virtual ruin.

Fota Gardens includes a beautiful orchard, pit houses and working glasshouses. Dating to the late Victorian period, this wonderful horticultural Victorian Working Garden comprises of three stand-alone glasshouses, pit houses and a bothy building, which were all fully restored since the Irish Heritage Trust took responsibility for Fota in 2007. The Victorian Working Garden is a beautifully restored space, lying to the back of the property. Since its restoration in 2012, our team have been sharing the beauty of the Victorian glasshouses, bothy buildings and a wide variety of interesting and unusual botany for visitors. The glasshouses were given paramount importance to the project as they embodied the Edwardian horticultural heritage. It was here that the Smith-Barry family started planting the most exotic species of trees as far back as the 1840's.

The Glasshouses of Fota House were restored to their former glory with the use of Accoya wood. Accoya wood was selected as the material of choice for the restoration due to its renowned durability and stability in all weathers. I enjoyed a detailed case study which confirmed that restoration works included the reinstatement of as much of the glasshouses' original historic feel, and to do so, it was essential to save as much of the initial construction as possible. The restoration project of the three glasshouses was in fact more of a challenge than it initially seemed. It required much patience and attention to detail as every element of the construction needed to be carefully documented before being dismantled. Moreover, every element which could be, had to be reused, making it a meticulous and lengthy process, but the results proved to be well worth the wait.

Accoya was also the obvious material for the parts that could not be reused. Not only for its aesthetic appeal but for the exceptional durability it possesses. Accoya wood has created a visually beautiful construction that will last for decades. The conservation architect John O'Connell and his team oversaw the project, which apart from the glasshouses, included four Edwardian hothouses. "Even before we started working on the project, we knew that it would be quite a challenge. This time it was more about reviving the old feel and making sure that we maintain as much of the old structure as possible. There was a lot of pressure, but it was a great experience to be part of such a historical project", said John.

The combination of the extraordinary work of the architects, construction specialists and highly skilled joiners along with the use of white coated Accoya wood, has converted the aged and derelict building into wonderful glasshouses that recapture their previous essence.

WHAT GRADUALLY BECAME CLEAR TO ME at that time was, that I may have unknowingly swayed over the years, in the spirit of tolerance. For if one were to suggest that one add a drop of collectivism and relativism to a sprinkling of indifferentism (the notion that one set of axiomatic beliefs are, relatively speaking, collectively as good as any other), with some pinches of traditional liberalism and modernism; then one might suggest that you have a recipe for ecumenism? For wouldn't such 'progressive' gentler, kinder notions be particularly appealing, if you had been fighting with your close neighbour for thirty years? Often preferring to promote unity by finding compromise in reasonable discourse, in what we as followers of Jesus have in common. Setting aside historic differences, enabling us to co-exist and respectfully 'get on'. Is that so bad? Well, on the face of it, no. That said, Proverbs 18: 13 warns us, that 'he who judges a matter before he knows it is folly, and shame onto him.' Therefore, one must always be cautious to ensure that one does not unintentionally stray away from scripture and love, and into the realms of arrant religious pluralism, or the 'progressive' principles of humanism or pantheistic naturalism (that human nature and human reason are supreme and that there are no truths revealed by God that men are bound to believe). For by unwittingly stumbling towards esotericism, or any 'irregular' oath bound secret societies, or 'illuminated' fraternal movements, which one might deem symbolically, ceremonially or ritualistically linked. One might at worst, be charged with blasphemy or being injurious to the church of Christ. Moreover, one must discern if anyone who claims to have 'seen the light', has perhaps only done so from beneath an historic banner of 'enlightenment' or having been inadvertently blinded or conversely illuminated by the differing degrees of light that might unexpectedly lead one to the 'light-bearer' and not to the true Light of the world, Jesus. Perceptions. In reality, there is so much corruption, inversion, manipulation, perversion and subversion in the world. Christianity, Catholicism and Protestantism alike, it seems, has many diverse enemies who, under a cloak of probity and respectability, can create confusion at any moment. Because that is what I would suggest can historically go on in the world of NI religion and politics. A lot of 'gaslighting'. That is, a lot of pretences. What I mean is, there can be a lot of pretending. Pretending to not understand what we see or what we hear. When the reality is we understand full well, what we see and what we hear. We know fine rightly.

But we will never please everyone in this life. For there are undoubtedly those reading some of what I have written, and probably judged me as one, operating in the 'spirit of error', or by 'the doctrines of devils? However, returning to my original point, following all of the aforementioned experiences, including the kind offer to convert to becoming a 'reformed' catholic, I had prayed to the Lord for discernment and within several weeks those three unexpected occurrences had happened, and I very suddenly realised that I had been sat in the middle of an historic game and I simply hadn't known *any* of the rules. Sure, I unexpectedly found myself in unforeseen circles where I had briefly tried to fit in and to a much lesser extent, learn about some of its existing values. But whilst there, I was unable to wholly identify with the movement, particularly after I gained sufficient awareness about it; and historic developments came to light. Also, scratch the surface and the overarching perception amongst several of the people I met at that time was, that unless I was proselytised into becoming a member of *any* of the existing, bewildering array of non-Catholic Christian denominations—then I would never *truly* have been regarded as a Christian, in *their* eyes.

Although never overwhelmed by this frequency, which on occasion came at me as some jarring, prodding discourse level, I encountered some pushy people, who pushed so hard they successfully pushed me right back to where I felt most at home.

It later made me think of a quote from Saint's John Fisher and Thomas More: 'Men for All Seasons'—how being faithful to one's conscience often goes against the majority and is therefore costly. Being faithful to one's conscience is a matter of eternal significance, for it determines whether we end up in heaven or hell. When moral pressure was applied to Thomas to sign the oath of supremacy recognizing King Henry as head of the Church of England, one of his colleagues urged him to sign the oath as he and others had done for the reason of "fellowship." To this pressure, Thomas replied: "And when we die and you are sent to heaven for being faithful to your conscience and I am sent to hell for not being faithful to mine, will you join me in hell, for fellowship?"

But with all that said. I must be unambiguously clear, and please note, that there is no criticism here. For It is my hope that this chapter, like all of the chapters in this book are taken in the spirit with which they are written, a Christian spirit, and the spirit of love. This is not a book about esotericism or occultism or alternative ideologies any more than it is a book about Catholicism or Protestantism. It is a book about perceptions, paradigm shifts and changes, that I have encountered throughout my lifecycle. It is about changing perceptions and the management of change. It is a book that offers a chapter which touches on conditioning, cultures, history and perceptions. It is also about a confused world and the risk associated with judgementalism, negativity and prejudice. Therefore, I do not, and I am not entitled to judge anyone because of their culture, their perceptions, principles, and belief systems or what they might be conditioned to believe. Any more than they might judge what I have been conditioned to believe, my values, principles, or my preferred belief system. I am merely sharing what my true faith is. And I fully understand that can be different for everyone. To put it another way, in Romans 2: 3 the Apostle Paul draws our attention to the weak position of those judging: They are guilty of committing the same sins, or ones just as bad as those they are judging! People in glass houses...

Moreover, my words in this chapter are not some sweeping generalisation, designed to offend or be controversial—absolutely far from it. That would be me moving towards an area that I have been trying to suggest that we should all, as Christians, be increasingly trying to move away from! It would be hypocritical and judgmental in the extreme, of me to sweepingly generalise. Furthermore, it is my understanding that anyone who uses their beliefs to mobilise judgement of another person (from a cultural perspective for example) isn't really operating with spirituality, morality, or ethics in mind. In fact, they are perhaps disregarding, the underwriting sense of oneness, love, peace and reconciliation central in Christ's message. But as I said at the outset of this work and repetitiously stated throughout it, there are many constructs, ideologies, movements, and perceptions out there and I am merely attempting to respectfully share in a constructive manner, personal observations and personal experiences, but in a balanced way.

With absolutely all that said, I consulted the Book of James, and in doing so, I have noted that he repetitiously warns us *all* of the risk of doublemindedness. For instance, in (1:8) it states that 'He is a double-minded man, unstable in all his ways.' Whilst in (4:8) he urges us to, 'Draw near to God, and he will draw near to you. Cleanse your hands, you sinners, and purify your hearts, you double-minded.' While in Psalm 119:113 the psalmist states, I hate those who are double minded, but I love Your law.

Put simply as a cradle Catholic I have, and always have had, a preference for the bells and smells and ceremony that comes from worshipping God and Jesus in a Magisterium driven church. It is what I know and what I am familiar with. Does that mean I am a perfect Catholic or that I agree with every arcane rule, doctrine, or dogma? In short, certainly not.

Yet, I prefer to believe that the availability of God's providence, saving designs and goodness can extend to *all* humanity. 'It was Pope Benedict XVI (2005) who stated in Dues Caritas Est, n.1 that 'being a Christian is not the result of an ethical choice or a lofty idea, but the encounter with a person (Jesus Christ) which gives life a new horizon and a definitive direction. Then in 2012 Pope Francis stated during an interview with the Argentinian director of YWAM (Youth with a Mission) that, 'You can dress up like a Christian, you can use make up like a Christian, you can speak Christian jargon, but if you haven't met with a person, you aren't a Christian. If you haven't had an encounter with Jesus Christ, you aren't a Christian.'

Although the double minded perceptions of hypocritical believers (from all backgrounds) might confuse me at times, I cannot and will not ever judge any of my authentically Christian brothers and sisters, for without that beautiful journey around the fascinating world of the 'separated brethren', I may not have enhanced my knowledge, wisdom, and discernment to the extent that I have today. Without some of that passionate and impactful preaching, which I admired and appreciated, and without having been directed to the wonderfully addictive video archive of Billy Graham classics, including his short documentary-movie, The Cross, I may not have understood that I was saved. I may not have had that encounter with the Holy Spirit and may not have developed that precious, personal relationship with Jesus.

Above all, without my wife buying me a Bible, I may not have immersed myself in God's Word and may not have developed spiritually. I may not have been inspired to write these words or understood the power of a testimony and gotten off that treacherous wide road. I may not have gotten dedicatedly switched back onto being a fully active 'member of the body' in my own church and within my own parish. So, my overarching, intuitive perception of the majority of those who I encountered during that part of my journey was that they were certainly authentic Christians who operated only in the spirit of discipleship; clearly tasked with sharing the Good News and bringing people to Christ. I give thanks and praise to all my Christian brothers and sisters regardless of their perceptions, customs, cultural heritage, backgrounds, or belief systems.

There is no getting around it, our historic disagreements will continue to remain deep seated, particularly 'whilst the minefield of all kinds of emotional, unresolved issues emerging right across the political and religious spectrum remains'. However, when considering such debates, I hope I have managed to somewhat establish those areas where our positions converge, and that is fundamental. In my experience the importance of reasoned discussion that is well argued and respectful of the differing points of view and the conviction that differing ways in which we worship the same God is neither good nor bad per se. But it is how we use God's Word, how God's grace builds on nature, how we pray and how we attempt to authentically do what Jesus would do, is what truly matters. If we in NI can look together at life beyond the restrictive confines of localism, nationalism or even globalism - to eternal-ism, then I believe we too might find *authentic* inclusivity palatable. By encouraging efforts to *genuinely* promote interfaith and *sincerely* engage in intercultural dialogue, we might, without hypocrisy, heresy or horrendous hermeneutics, advance to a culture of reconciliation among religions; in pursuit of a vision of ... peace, security, and prosperity (1 Thessalonians 5:3).

However, setting aside the very thorny, hot potato of religiosity, what became very clear to me at that time was this. It was God who took me on that eye-opening, educational journey. It didn't happen randomly by chance. It was meant to happen. Via that journey God spoke to me and encouraged me to write these words. He helped me get beneath the plastic veneer of my worldly existence, gently circumventing worldly belief systems and religiosity, and at the same time he liberated me from a fruitless lifecycle - opening my eyes to the would-be risk of following man made, esoteric, worldly or paganistic constructs.

This book is a Holy Spirit driven project. After the Holy spirit had rested on me, he kept revealing to me that I had a powerful testimony that many people needed to hear and that it needed to be shared with the world. There were many occasions, when I would awake in the middle of the night and be unable to get back to sleep. There was nothing wrong, other than I continuously started to prepare a testimony in mind that I could one day share with those who might benefit from hearing it. Without the power of the Holy spirit driving me, I may never have had the confidence to 'go out into the world' to share my life experiences. But the old me is dead and has been for quite some-time now. I have long since removed my filthy rags and donned pristine new white garments, regardless of how often Satan tempts me and tries to convince me otherwise.

The truth is the last ten years or so, was a period when I was truly open to accepting a call. It would be a call that would test my life as I knew it and one that would drag me out of my comfort zone, that is for sure. But it would be a call that would enable me to live a better, more virtuous existence. It was a time when I was prepared to listen, to be persuaded to set aside my own partial or insufficient ideas and ways of handling matters. It was a time when I was comfortable to dispose of my usual, old habits and to see life through a different lens, and to live a different life but in a more constructive way.

There is an adage which states, if you want to walk on water then you must get out of the boat. In Matthew 14:29 Peter acted in faith by answering Jesus's call by getting out of the boat and walking across crashing waves to meet him. I wanted to do the same. That said, when Peter sank because of his momentary lack of faith, he did so because he was distracted by the high waves, which were engulfing him. Therefore, I am suggesting in following Jesus I know, that when I am overwhelmed in a sea of uncertainty that may cause my faith to waver and lead me to sink in despair, that I must focus on God and Jesus alone, rather than my own inadequacies.

So, I will have a preferred church base and a church family, but will avoid the waves of religiosity, constructs, movements, or human inconsistencies.

Instead focusing only on God and Jesus to orientate me back on course. I will keep my eyes firmly fixed on the Lord Jesus Christ. Father, Son, and Holy Spirit. For only He can still life's storms to a whisper and only He can hush the crashing waves of the sea. I had been called to embark upon this project and to spread the Good News. I have been called to send these words out into all the nations; and by getting this book published I was one step further down the road to doing just that. Yet, I always said that If I touched the heart of just one person. If my story resonated with just one person. If my words could help reconcile a fractured relationship or a mere element of our fragmented society. If this exploration changed, restored, and transformed the thinking of just one person. If just one person's life was made better and if just one person repented and could be saved by these words, then my writing would have been a success.

As written in Luke 15:10, "In the same way, I tell you, there is rejoicing in the presence of the angels of God over one sinner who repents."

CHAPTER 15:
BLENDEDNESS

(The Glass Palace, Madrid, 1887)

B ACK IN CHAPTER 8, I WROTE ABOUT The Crystal Palace (1851) and its undoubted influence relating to the design of many other prominent glasshouses throughout the world. One such instance, borrowing heavily from Paxton's design, is The Glass Palace (1887) in the Retiro Park, Madrid. It must be one of the finest examples of glass house structures in Spain. This metal and glass structure was constructed in 1887 for the Philippines Exhibition of that year. Designed by Ricardo Velázquez Bosco, the project was clearly inspired by Paxton's Crystal Palace. It was originally planned as a gigantic greenhouse to contain tropical plants but today it is, without irony, used only for exhibitions and art exhibitions. The Crystal Palace's influence is undeniable.

Moreover, the Anna Scripps Whitcomb Conservatory (1902) is a greenhouse and a botanical garden located on Belle Isle, a 982-acre island park located in the Detroit River between Detroit, Michigan and Windsor, Ontario near the Canada–United States border. The park consists of 13 acres of preserved land for the conservatory and its botanical garden. The Belle Isle Conservatory, along with the neighbouring Belle Isle Aquarium, was designed by the noted firm of George D. Mason and Albert Kahn.

Kahn modelled the building after architectural exhibitions and garden pavilions of the mid- to late-nineteenth century, most notably The Crystal Palace and the Palm House at Kew Gardens.

Also, in Buffalo and Erie County Botanical Gardens, there exists a tri-domed glass, wood, and steel conservatory (1900) that was designed by Lord & Burnham, who were among the premier conservatory designers of the time. Again, it is written in Wikipedia that construction methods were based upon the famous Crystal Palace and Kew Gardens Palm House in England. When built in 1897-1899, it was one of the largest public greenhouses in the country (at a cost of $130,000). Today there are fewer than a dozen large, prominent Victorian conservatories in America.

Another example of the Crystal Palace's global influence can be found at the Franklin Park Conservatory and Botanical Gardens in Columbus, Ohio (1895). The Chicago's World Fair and Columbian Exposition was an immensely influential social and cultural event. It inspired the city of Columbus to create a horticulture building modelled after the Glass Palace. This glass structure, built in the grand Victorian style, was erected in Franklin Park and opened to the public in 1895 as the Franklin Park Conservatory.

Furthermore, the Volunteer Park Conservatory is a botanical garden, conservatory, and Seattle landmark located in Seattle, Washington at the north end of Volunteer Park on Capitol Hill. Made up of 3,426 glass panes fitted into a wood and iron framework, this Victorian-style greenhouse structure is modelled on London's Crystal Palace. Inside, the Volunteer Park Conservatory is divided into five display houses: bromeliads, ferns, palms, seasonal, and cacti/succulents. The conservatory was among the earliest additions to City/Volunteer Park. After the project was proposed in 1893, the City of Seattle purchased the conservatory design and framework from the Hitchings Company of New York before completing construction in 1902.

There are many other examples that we can discuss in detail in another book. But from Beijing to Belfast and from Berlin to Brazil, where you find beautiful botanical gardens invariably you will find glamourous glasshouses. My extensive desk-based research uncovered the fact that many of the glasshouses that exist throughout the world have been influenced by the design and construction methods of The Crystal Palace (1851) and or Kew Gardens (1848) and many of which I aspire to explore, moving forward. Yet, I often consider that our very own Palm House in Belfast (1840) was constructed before both aforementioned structures in England, given it has been described as a 'proto type' for The Palm House at Kew Gardens. Therefore, it cannot be glossed over that this microcosmic curvilinear glass house structure, which is iconic to Belfast, might also be acknowledged and recognized for its subtle global influence.

IT SEEMS THAT THERE IS no 'one size fits all' when it comes to worshipping God. This is something I can testify to, because growing up as a young cradle Catholic in the unorthodox little part of the world that is Northern Ireland, it is fair to say that inclusivity is something that there has historically been a distinct lack of.

In the world in which I grew up, the Catholic Church was regarded with utmost suspicion by many Protestant denominations, and it seems that suspicion may have been equally reciprocated by most Catholics. Often distracted, some have expended time and energy by begrudgingly trying to debunk each other's histories, doctrines, and dogmas. But often lacking an embodied knowledge or any empirical evidence to do so, both groups often preferred to simplistically believe that each other's churches were likely on the road to hell. That said, even with such perceptions still prevalent in society, Christian ecumenism and understanding has made astounding leaps. But today I like to believe, obscurely albeit strongly, (and many true Christians will agree) that the truth about God is far more complex and mysterious than any of those blinded by religiosity, can ever comprehend.

I read a commentary by Calvinist Peter Kreeft called Hauled onto the Ark, in which the writer suggested the following – "Then in a Church history class at Calvin, a professor gave me a way to investigate the claims of the Catholic Church on my own. The essential claim is historical: that Christ founded the Catholic Church, that there is historical continuity. If that were true, I would have to be a Catholic out of obedience to my one absolute, the will of my Lord. The teacher explained the Protestant belief. He said that Catholics accuse us Protestants of going back only to Luther and Calvin; but this is not true; we go back to Christ. Christ had never intended a Catholic-style Church, but a Protestant-style one. The Catholic additions to the simple, Protestant- style New Testament Church had grown up gradually in the Middle Ages like barnacles on the hull of a ship, and the Protestant Reformers had merely scraped off the barnacles, the alien, pagan accretions. The Catholics, on the other hand, believed that Christ established the Church Catholic from the start, and that the doctrines and practices that Protestants saw as barnacles were, in fact, the very living and inseparable parts of the planks and beams of the ship."

Moving forward and as one part of a 'mixed marriage', I can say with confidence that there is a 'blendedness' to our Christian bond that has ensured that we as a couple and we as a nuclear family, have realised many positive benefits and outcomes from our bi-cultural relationship.

In fact, Ephesians 4:1 unambiguously states, "Make every effort to keep the unity of spirit through the bond of peace." Put simply, it is my belief that inclusiveness and peace can be achieved if we start focusing on the many things that we as believers have in common and not on our differences, which of course will always exist. This is what I believe my household achieves successfully, and we do so respectfully by steering clear of bias, favouritism or judgementalism. Moreover, we do so by having Jesus at the centre of our ecumenical household and by living an authentic Christo-centric lifestyle. For 'a sovereign God doesn't want denominations, he wants men and women out of which something grows'.

In Rick Warren's 'A Purpose Driven Life', he suggests that we as believers share one Lord, one body, one purpose, one Father, one Spirit, one hope, one faith, one baptism, and one love. We share the same salvation, the same life, and the same future. We must remember that it was God who chose to give us different personalities, backgrounds, races, and preferences, so we should value and enjoy those differences, not merely tolerate them.

These sentiments are highlighted in Proverbs 22:2 which states, 'The rich and the poor meet together; the Lord is the maker of them all.' Whilst Colossians 3:11 highlights, that 'here there is not Greek and Jew, circumcised and uncircumcised, barbarian, Scythian, slave, free; but Christ is all, and in all.' Unity and inclusiveness are a symbol of the Holy Spirit that can enable us to become disciples and authentic followers of Jesus, interconnecting at a spiritual level. For when we start being eternity conscious all our values and interests change, no longer seduced by worldly trivia. In fact, I have discovered that the term interconnectedness has its foundation in the very nature of the Holy Trinity - God the Father, God the Son, and God the Holy Spirit.

When the Lord tells us in Luke 5:27 to 'Come as you are' he requires his Church and his disciples to be authentic, welcoming, and inclusive, not haughty, or exclusive; with our lips saying one thing and our hearts another. He wants His children to know that we are welcome to 'come as we are' in our scruffy jeans and trainers but of course, above all else, to 'come as we are', with our darkest sins, guilt and shame, the yokes of which enslave and burden us so heavily.

This is what Jesus did when he walked the earth more than two thousand years ago. He assembled his team of very ordinary boys (and girls) who were blended together from differing backgrounds, before transforming them without cultural bias, into influential ambassadors for Christ. By accepting Jesus's invitation to discipleship, he converted them via the power of the Holy Spirit, where they grew to work alongside those from other cultures, in partnership with God. Thus playing a significant role in the redemption of the world, by leading others to Christ. Knowing this, there is still much work to be done because biblically speaking the inclusion of people who were previously excluded, is a constant theme running throughout scripture.

For instance, in Acts chapter 8 we meet the Ethiopian eunuch, who converts to Christianity and who it seems is given full membership in the Christian community just as he was— without having to modify anything about his gender or his sexuality. Moreover, in the beginning of the book of Ruth, we're told that Ruth herself is a Moabite but that she's taken in by her mother-in-law Naomi and made part of the Israelite family. Actually, Ruth is given the privilege of being one of the four women mentioned in Jesus' genealogy in Matthew.

In fact, if Jesus had not converted 'outsiders' from differing backgrounds such as Matthew (Gentile) or Paul (Jew) or used Luke (Greek), then these men would not have been inspired by the Holy Spirit and would not have contributed towards compiling the Bible. In John's Gospel, Jesus addresses the church leaders by stating "I have other sheep that do not belong to this fold. I must bring them also, and they will listen to my voice. So, there will be one flock, one shepherd." This emphasizes there can be no dividing lines and that we as genuine disciples, like Jesus, must work with love and grace towards inclusion for *all* people.

In Romans 10:1-21 the Apostle Paul writes, for it is by believing in your heart that you are made right with God, and it is by confessing with your mouth that you are saved...Anyone who believes in Him will not be disappointed. Jew and gentile are the same in this respect. They all have the same Lord... For anyone who calls on the name of the Lord will be saved. But how can they call on Him to save them unless they believe in Him? And how can they believe in Him if they have never heard about Him? And how can they hear about Him unless someone tells them? This is what Scriptures mean when they say, "How beautiful are the feet of those who bring the good news!"

Today, the Holy Spirit continues to use me to reach the lost, the atheist, the unbeliever, and the backslider alike. For my part, I can say with confidence that with the help of the Holy Spirit, I have become not only a 'hearer and a sayer of God's word, but also a doer of God's Word'. I have grown to despise hate and I have grown to hate all types of sin. As Jesus states, 'if any man come to me… and hate not his own life, he cannot be my disciple' (Luke 14:33). Moreover, in Matthew 5 it confirms, 'Blessed are they who mourn for they will be comforted'. In this sermon was a collection of truths designed to prepare Jesus followers for His kingdom, encouraging a radically different lifestyle from the world's. This verse relates to one's willingness to mourn over one's sinfulness. It relates to those willing to be honest about their own sins and humble enough to ask for healing and forgiveness. This verse relates to me; and I would suggest it might relate to you too.

Realising this became a pivotal moment and one that resulted in me doing a seismic about-turn. Unbeknown to me, there had been a spiritual battle raging inside of me my whole adult life. It was crossroads time. It was time for me to trust in Christ and to turn away from a life of sin and disobedience and towards a more Christocentric lifestyle. It was time to pick up and carry my cross. Like a supply of second-hand bricks salvaged from a war-torn city, the Lord was about to reconstruct and reuse me in a mighty way. It was this time when I realised that to truly love and worship, we must give up something in return. We must serve.

Now, I am always fully aware that 'good works' alone do not get us to heaven, that it is in the hands of God's mercy and His Grace. But I discovered that Grace builds on nature, because so transformed was I, that I found myself leaving my office at lunchtime to walk through Belfast city centre alone to crouch down to speak with some of the homeless people existing on our streets.

I knew where they would be located. Sometimes I gave money, sometimes I gave food or advice on the location of the nearest homeless shelters, but generally I gave strangers time, love, and respect. Which was something I hadn't historically ever done before.

I asked every one of the people I spoke with the same question, 'How did you get to be here today? The responses were often diverse. Marital breakdown, relationship breakdown, alcoholism, or drug addiction and even on one occasion a girl with an inverted cross on her wrist confirmed she had been a former member of a satanic cult. Regardless of background, I offered the same message. That Jesus loves them, and that he has a plan for their lives. I also prayed for those individuals. For their healing and reconciliation. As emphasised in the Gospel according to Mark, are those stories of Christ healing the vulnerable on the margins. In doing so, he assured those on the margins that they too are called into the kingdom of God. I listened to a powerful online sermon where people on the margins were described as sinners, the poor, the unclean and those separated from conventional religion. They were sheep without a shepherd. They were people on the fringe of society desperately looking to touch the fringes of Christ's cloak. Reaching out for love; reaching for healing to their mind and bodies and direction towards God's Kingdom. I had learned that when you are hanging on by a thread, it is important to make sure that it is the thread of Jesus's garment.

I believe this challenges us as believers to ponder, are the poor on our streets like Jesus, encouraging us to serve in the spirit of discipleship and inclusivity, or do they merely inconvenience our comfortable outward lives? It was a time when I literally started to ask myself, what if that person I have just walked past today was Jesus or an angel disguised as a homeless person? And I, as a purported Christian, did not stop to talk or help?

Furthermore, before embarking upon this exploration, it was in 2018 that I received the necessary approval to proceed with a proposal to design and develop a free pocket-sized daily bible reading guide for the people of my local parish, pastoral community and beyond. This scripture-focused project was carried out in partnership with the Bible Society of Northern Ireland, who subsequently described our inclusive collaboration, as "ground-breaking".

I was concerned, from my personal experience, that it was a long time from one Sunday sermon to the next. I recognised, having been there, that there is a lot of secular worldly living, risk and temptation that happens between one Sunday service and the next. So, my aim was to encourage my fellow Catholics to pick up a bible and get better acquainted with reading scripture at home and to reap the spiritual benefits of doing so. A. W. Tozer wrote, "As we come to the Word of God, we do not come just for information; we come for an encounter with the living Word of God... I will not settle for just the text. I want to see beyond that text and encounter the Christ - the Word of Life. So, the next time you open your Bible, think of it as a conversation in which the Author is speaking through His Book personally to you."

With the Daily Bible Reading Guide, there was absolutely no reinvention of the wheel. This had been tried and tested in many reformed churches but having gotten hold of such a guide, I had found it of great benefit to me on my spiritual journey and so I knew, that it might also be of benefit to others. To accompany the Guides, I also got approval to sell Good News Catholic Bibles, within my church and the small amount I ordered were eagerly snapped up by parishioners. The first year of the project, the 2000 Guides that were in circulation were taken up by households and families within my parish. But by the second year the output had quadrupled to 8,000 units as these were circulated to homes, schools, prisons and to different parishes throughout the diocese, north and south of

Ireland. These numbers are, of course, very modest, but that project will now be in its third year and having passed the baton on to others to keep up the good works, I fully expect that the aspiration should one day be to have those Guides issued diocese wide, if not Island- wide. Never has the need for such a project been so great, with the rampant secularisation of the island of Ireland ongoing at a ferocious pace.

Also, during the global pandemic, I was invited to contribute chapters for not one, but two Christian books, that were both published 'Worship in Cyber Churches', by Dr P. Mann and David Wong. I wanted those who needed to know that to me, Scripture wasn't any ordinary book. In Scott Hann's book 'Consuming the Word', he states, "Scripture is the Word inspired and that Jesus is the Word incarnate. The Bible is the divine Word expressed in human language; and in Jesus the divine Word takes flesh in human nature. The two mysteries illuminate each other." For me it is the only book we can never finish because it is fully alive. For every time we open it, we will discover something new or something we haven't noticed before.

In St Paul's second letter to Timothy he states, 'All scripture is inspired by God…this is how the man who is dedicated to God becomes fully equipped and ready for any good work…' Similarly, St Theresa of Avila once stated, 'if you want to hear God talk to you, read scripture.' In fact, it was through immersing myself in scripture that the flame that had dwelt in me since baptism, was fully reignited. It was at that time that I decided to commit, to having that change of heart, that change of mind, that change of spirit, that change of culture, that change of lifestyle that is required - to enable the shift away from modern day idols such as consumerism, individualism, materialism, and secularism, towards a God-focused existence and a personal relationship with Jesus.

Although not understood or accepted by everyone, it cannot be glossed over that Scripture, the Magisterium and Tradition are not opposing authorities but three pillars that support and inform each other, making God all the more present in us. For by taking in God's "saving truth" (ccc136) as our spiritual food on a daily basis, it can bring us true and lasting inner satisfaction; a calm transformation; by the renewal of our minds. This was amplified by Pope Francis who confirmed, that the 'relationship between the risen Lord, a community of believers, and sacred scripture is essential to who we are, as a member of many different Christian assemblies.' I echo these sentiments and fully and openly encourage everyone of us all, to 'open the way to the scripture's'. Scripture inspires a greater diligence, and it encouraged me to ask more questions relating to salvation. In life, so many of us are focused on improving our physical fitness or our mental fitness; and perhaps rightly so. However, scripture offers us all an opportunity for us to work on and improve our spiritual fitness. For as stated in 1st Timothy Chapter 4, "Physical training is good, but training for godliness is much better, promising benefits in this life and in the life to come."

Each of us can learn a lot of lessons about how to manage our memories, how to edit them and to learn by our mistakes. I am not for one moment suggesting that the good that comes can justify the bad that happened. But the good is the outcome of authentically living a life of faith and the bad reflects the fallibility of fallen human beings, born of original sin. For if we drift away from the truth, blind to the wrongfulness that we do, then we deceive and delude ourselves. But St Paul reminds us that the whole human race is sin. Yet Jesus stated that if anyone declares me in the presence of people, I will declare them in the presence of my father that he may stand up for us in front of our father in heaven. Witnessing for Christ helps others in the crowd who lack the courage to follow their calling, because none of us will leave this earth, perfectly fit. Yet so many are held back because of what people might think of their change. But again, scripture says it perfectly in Proverbs 29:25 when it states, 'Fear of man will prove to be a snare, but whoever trusts in the Lord is kept safe.'

In an interview with the National Catholic Register, a female former Protestant Pastor, Barbara Heil affirmed that it is by our baptism that we've been commissioned by Jesus himself, if we believe the words of the apostles, that we will go into other worlds and share the Gospel. That's for the believer; that's for the average Catholic. That's for the Christian. If you believe, then you're called to go. You're called to pray for people. So, this work is my admission that I understand that I, as a baptised (Catholic) Christian, am commissioned by God to share my faith whilst testifying to the transformational power of the Gospels.

That said, once one answers a call, it isn't all plain sailing. There is no metaphorical lottery win – not that being spoilt by material gain is at the forefront of one's mind anymore. I recall one bright sunny summer morning at 7.30am in June when I had a momentary lapse of judgement. I pulled my car out of a junction, before suddenly seeing a speeding car hurtle towards my driver's door. As I gripped the steering wheel, I screamed out the name of Jesus! Just at that second as I braced myself for impact, the oncoming car seemed to swerve fractionally away from my driver's door, smashing into my front driver's wing. The collision sent bits of car flying, my head juddering and my vehicle spinning violently into a quadruple spin. My car was a write off. The other car ended up on a grass verge by the roadside, with a damaged grill and bonnet. I was subsequently taken to hospital with light damage to my head, alongside injuries to my ribs and leg. I would be out of work for eleven weeks to convalesce and recover. The Police and ambulance people both later agreed that, if the car had crashed a few inches further over and into my driver's door, then I would have been dead, or they would have been 'putting me back together' at best.

Yet that accident brought home to me that we are all capable of having momentary lapses in judgement at any moment – albeit some more costly than others. This event could have created major challenges for me both personally and professionally, because my office was a daily round trip of almost ninety miles away from my home, and I had a new baby daughter who was only six weeks old at the time. However, from a personal perspective, I started praying hard to God for peace of mind. It could have also been a challenge spiritually, but I was incredibly relaxed about the whole scenario.

My point is, in situations like this, one might be discouraged or angry with God at the cards we are dealt. After all of my life experiences, I could have done without experiencing a serious car accident, physical injuries and all of the insurance related pressures that came with it. So, I know I'd be forgiven for asking, when do these tribulations end? Now, I am not suggesting for a moment that I am a righteous man like Job, having been on the receiving end of yet another one of life's stark lessons. Yet, I didn't feel anger or self-pity. In fact, I continued to pray, to read scripture and to carry out good works and circulate with likeminded souls during that time. I was very honest about it all. I was able to gain help from the Book of Job 19 and by reading his experiences it helped me to react in the right way to this latest tribulation. You see a lot of things happened to Job in his life. Yet he realised that he had ultimately lost nothing of meaning or lasting value, other than the temporal and material. Job knew he had lost nothing, and because he was a righteous man, he didn't have a victim mentality. He knew there was another life to come, knowing that Jesus would be the ultimate victim for us. Until Job had been on the receiving end of these tests, he had been given protection by God with his righteous faith and his material and worldly success. But unusually, God gave Satan permission to do as he pleased with Job. He could literally do anything he wanted to negatively affect Job's life – except kill him. Job encountered the Chaldeans, the Sabaeans, a cyclone and a fire but behind all the aforementioned trials was Satan, and the Book of Job is to me a demonstration of how powerful and damaging Satan can be. Job's faith and righteousness were laudable, but this was yet another example of the power of God's Word and how He can help us live at peace in troubled times.

As Charles Spurgeon once stated, to trust God in the light is nothing, but to trust him in the dark that is faith. It is sometimes as though God allows us to experience such challenges, so that our faith can be tested, and we can demonstrate by our actions, how his healing hand brings us through those sufferings. That we have our eyes fixed not on this temporal world but on the world to come. For we walk by faith, not by sight. A number of months after that accident, I got a *chance* text from a company one day, offering a random opportunity that interested me. I immediately got an interview and rapidly received the offer of a new job. My new office would be located six miles from my home. Better still, all my new projects would be within walking distance or a short drive from my new office. No more lengthy, rural journeys. I believe it was yet another obvious answer to prayer, and yet more evidence of Divine Providence and God's hand playing a demonstrable part in my life.

You see, as Christians, we still get challenged by unforeseen events or even by unsaid words. We might be subject to ugly attacks of professional jealousy, envy or "unhealthy competition" in the office; or get mocked and ridiculed by doubters and unbelievers trying to derail our progress and development. We may even lose 'friends' or grow apart from family members, but with God's Word we become fully equipped to deal with all worldly challenges. In my limited experience we must always forgive them anyway, for what we feed grows! If, we touch on some biblical examples - Who killed Abel? - His brother. Who sold Joseph? - His brothers. Who expelled Jephthah? - His brothers. Who was jealous of David? - His brother. Who was not happy with the return of the prodigal son and the reconciliation with his father? - His brother. For as the weeping

Prophet Jeremiah warned us – disparaging me, denouncing me, those who used to be my friends. Among so many examples in scripture, we perceive that all those who have been betrayed and mistreated by their own brethren, have been greatly blessed and kept by God. In life, people you have considered your family or friends may turn their backs on you, but their rejection may be a path God has planned for our glory. For God not only opens doors with purpose, but he can close doors with purpose too! In reality, I have learned that what others do and say is not really under my control. I quickly discovered that the best way to handle who and what we can't control is to live a life under the control of the Holy Spirit. When we are led by the Spirit of God, we are led by One who loves us and provides for us in every situation; the one who allows us to manifest love and other virtues in every situation (Galatians 5:22-23). So, I gave up spending my days worrying about what I could not control. Instead, yielding to the control of the Holy Spirit. For as Christians with the Holy Spirit working within us, we can quickly become blessed with the gift of discernment. Discernment can initially be a tad confusing for Christian's and non-Christians alike, but it need not be. In his wonderful book, Gaudette et Exsultate, Pope Francis asks, 'how can we know if something comes from the Holy Spirit or if it stems from the spirit of the world or the spirit of the devil? The only way is through discernment, which calls for something more than intelligence or common sense. It is a gift which we must implore. The gift and grace of discernment has become all the more necessary today, since contemporary life offers immense possibilities for action and distraction, and the world presents all of them as valid and good... Without the wisdom of discernment, we can easily become prey to every worldly, liberal passing trend.

Yet, we can *still* suffer and experience suffering. I listened to a sermon in which Lutheran theologian, Detrich Bonhoffer described suffering as the badge of true discipleship. Since Christ suffered in his body, we must not be surprised at the painful issues we suffer, whilst living in this world. In the Book of Genesis, didn't Adam and Eve immediately suffer for their sin and disobedience. Didn't Cain suffer because of Abel's jealousy? Didn't the wicked who never made it onto Noah's Ark suffer? One only need consult the Book of Job to see how even the most faithful believer can have his faith put to the test and be allowed to suffer, even by God. Ultimately, we must look to the cross of Christ as the benchmark of suffering and a model of Christian living. The Gospel Good News will always have enemies who will attempt to inflict suffering. Although, as Fulton J Sheen reminds us, what a lesson for us to remember; that those who do us harm, may, too, be the same type of misguided consciences as those who crucified Christ.

"Amazing Grace how sweet the sound, that *saved* a *wretch* like me. I once was lost but now I am found, 'twas blind but now I see..." Trust me when I say that it is not the case that I have been irrationally obsessed by my sinful past, far from it. But it was an understanding of the reservoir of God's grace that effortlessly enabled me to unburden any shackles of embarrassment, fear, guilt, insecurity, and shame that may have unknowingly hounded me, throughout many of my first thirty or so years on earth. The combination of confession, repentance, faith, grace, and good works as second nature has empowered me with confidence and compassion. It has restored and transformed me in such a radical way that I not only embrace life, but now also embrace the forthcoming reality of death. My road to change was that I had an open willingness to change. However, I know many are afraid of changing the ways of their daily lives. In my experience, it seems as though those who rise highest in holiness are those brave enough to fight against whatever it is that holds them back; and be willing to testify publicly to that rise, one way or another. The more you master your feelings and blind desires the greater the graces Christ will offer you. However, trust me, old habits die hard, and these feelings will continue to rebel against you.

That said, faith and healing are intertwined. I love that well-worn phrase that a church is not a building for the well but a hospital for the sick, the sick being the unclean and the sinner. I once heard of an old church tradition that regarded priests as the 'physicians of the soul'. It is a deep concept that is related to the word curate, in reference to priests being tasked with helping with the cure of souls. Just as the day of Pentecost signals the end of Easter and the beginning of ordinary time, bringing about the shoots of hope and new birth and a new life from nothingness. Our Priests, Pastors and Ministers show how through repentance, we too can avail of the opportunity to experience a restoration and a transformation.

As a boy who grew up in the 1980s, I see my life as being a bit like that art-game, Etcha-Sketch. When we start twiddling the white plastic knobs, with a view to creating a picture on the plastic screen, we start off with a nice straight line but with the merest lack of focus, our original straight-lined plan becomes derailed. As we twist and turn the knobs to get back online, we find what was once a straight line can quickly become an unrecognisable, embarrassing squiggly mess. This is life. However, with one swipe of a plastic lever the squiggly mess is immediately erased, and the screen is once again completely clear. At this point we have the opportunity to learn lessons from our previous mistakes and immediately start afresh. This is the power of Christ and the power of conversion. It is through His Word that we can discover that He can make all things new. He can restore us by erasing our embarrassing squiggly messes and by offering us all a clean start. The most beautiful thing is that this opportunity is available to us all every second of every day – and it's completely free.

> *"Now you must repent and turn to God, so that your sins may be wiped out, and so that the Lord may send the time of comfort"*
>
> —Acts 3:19

CHAPTER 16:
RISK MANAGEMENT

Conclusion

L ET ME TAKE THIS MOMENT to assure you, the reader, that the last thing I wanted to do in this book was become 'Preachy McPreacherson' preaching like a preacher to all and sundry! Rather, I wanted to use these final chapters to share with you my experiences and what I found worked for me, once I let God take control, and tried to live my life according to His Will. In my experience there is no shame in changing your mind or your point of view if new, reliable information comes to light. However, for so many 'pride comes before a fall'. The idea of changing their minds, hearts, spirits, cultures, and lifestyles petrifies them, because they are still living a life pleasing to the petty feelings of the confused people of this world.

I am satisfied now with the course my life has taken, but it was after an introspective deep dive that I was able to confront my defects and flaws and achieve a more peaceful outlook. I have experienced everything the world has had to offer. Its relative successes, joys and pleasures alongside its sorrows and struggles. I have helped and served but have also hurt and ignored.

During my surveying career I have discovered many parallels between the project management of construction projects and the project management of a lifecycle. Let me briefly explain what I mean. I once read an enjoyable essay from a Professor David Coley who posed the question, "Are buildings evil?" He argued that "designing and constructing energy-intensive buildings fuels global climate injustice and is therefore morally offensive, and

233

potentially a form of unconscious institutional racism" as he put it. "We know how to build, and have built, some exemplary low-energy buildings, so our failure to adopt them as the norm can be viewed as deliberate. In short, rather than seeing low-energy design as an engineering issue, we need to focus on the truth—it is a moral issue", he stated. Once energy use and carbon emissions are linked to morality and aesthetics, they become reputational and legacy issues, not engineering ones."

Although the construction industry's battle against carbon emissions and rethinking construction is nothing new, this essay's overarching point was one of ethics, ethical dilemmas, and morals. By highlighting how the construction industry accounts for a reputed 40% of all carbon emissions in industrialised nations such as the UK, the writer calls-out those experienced and qualified enough to know better. He is urging them to no longer giving consideration to knowingly, wilfully designing and constructing structures using methods and materials that they know are damaging the environment and greatly contributing to our transforming climate. For me, the construction industries attitude to carbon emissions is akin to a human being's attitude to knowingly and wilfully committing habitual sin.

As a construction project manager with almost twenty years' experience, I believe that our lives can be like a construction project. I can see good and bad at work in everything. Project management is centred around a triangle of three key parameters—Time (duration) Cost (budget) and quality (excellence of outcome) but this can also extend to functionality, which ensures that the outcome of any given project is 'fit for purpose' upon completion. Following our project inception, the project lifecycle usually commences with a hubbub of excitement and expectation before it all usually ends around an anticipated completion date. However, for believers, the project does not end upon completion because what happens 'post completion', will be equally as important. Between the key milestones of commencement and completion, is where the real fun, risk, mistakes and fall outs usually happen.

Even with an array of project team experts offering sage advice, guidance, and recommendations throughout the duration of the project, there are constant risks and would-be changes to our project which must be managed effectively. However, no matter how diligently risk, and change are managed, the risk of an 'unforeseen circumstance' occurring, always looms. It's those unknown unknowns in life that can create the type of risk that negatively impacts upon our time and our quality, but this can also come at a great cost.

Be it personal, monetary, societal, environmental, governmental, or spiritual, the risk of a risk impacting upon our project and derailing our progress and our quality of life, is moderate to high. Yet, in life if the likelihood of a risk occurring is low, moderate, or high, there are often those key stakeholders in our lives qualified to help us manage those risks, by showing us how to safely transfer or avoid those risks that might cause irreparable damage to the project. Be they parents, family, friends, Bishops, priests, pastors, ministers, or elders, we trust they can help us circumvent or control any risk—even though they too live in the limitations of weakness (Hebrews 5).

There will be those members or stakeholders on your project team, who will add value to your project, helping to ensure that your project is a successful one. By operating in the correct spirit that is the spirit of openness, honesty, and transparency, and by way of a benchmark, they will help you 'learn lessons' from mistakes they made during their own personal projects – knowingly and wilfully ensuring that history does not repeat itself. They will also affirm what went well.

There will, of course, also be those with different agendas, perceptions, and outlooks. Like wolves in sheep's clothing or a brood of vipers, they will knowingly negatively impact upon your time. Snake-like and egotistical they will place blockages in systems and create cost implications that impact upon the quality of your journey. With my own personal project still ongoing, I can say with confidence that I didn't always have the best project team on my side. Sage advice, guidance and sound recommendations were often lacking, with strategic and robust risk management often non-existent. On those costly occasions when my project programme was affected and my quality of life derailed, I found that unlike many others who have lived out similar scenarios, that I had no contingency plan and therefore no safety net in place. Having taken risks, I was often unaware of the severity of outcome, and left to my own devices, things did not go well.

However, if one were to procure me to provide consultancy on a personal project today, then my advice would be that there is no better project team in life, than one driven by God the Father, Son, and Holy Spirit. Perhaps you might also believe there is no better strength in depth, than having a 'posse' of angels, apostles, and saints as the "great cloud of witnesses" (Hebrews 12) to whom you can pray to? There is no better form of contract than Baptism (from birth or as an adult) and no better contract clauses than those found in the sacraments, the Ten Commandments (regardless of perceptions surrounding apparent tweaks to those commandments) or the hundreds of commands and decrees found in God's Word (regardless of preferred biblical translation). For our personal project of health and safety, we must be risk adverse by outsourcing all risk to Jesus. Help to eliminate life's risks by transferring them to the foot of the cross, for only He can provide us with the assurance we need that ensures that our time on earth meets functionality requirements and that we are fit for purpose as ambassadors or witnesses for Christ. There is no better commitment than desiring to use our time to live a Christo-centric lifecycle. For after our project ends, we will have to give a post project appraisal at which point our time on earth will be evaluated.

I have highlighted in my writing that over many years, some glasshouses and many buildings have been adapted to serve a vast range of alternative uses. The same principle can be applied to you and me. With the Holy Spirit as the new project manager tasked with driving my personal project, I have been adapted and restored and reused by God in a mighty way. As a husband, a father, a project manager, a chartered professional, a member of the body of the church and now as an author, I have become multi-functional in the extreme. I feel as if I have become like the palms described in Amelia Stein's stunning book, 'The Palm House' in which she eloquently states, 'Throughout the world, palms are closely linked to human activity. Their stems are used to construct, their leaves to thatch, weave and clothe, their seed for food, fodder, and oil. Even today, their parts are sculpted, carved, and harvested for trade. They range from small under-storey plants that inhabit the darkened jungle floor to giants that dominate the forest canopy. Their great fans have inspired designers, architects, and builders since the age of the Pharaohs.'

Moreover, and by way of a summary, so too can glasshouses be linked to human activity and multi-functionality. For I have discovered that glasshouses not only house plants and botany but can be used for educational purposes, for dining under the stars, for practicing yoga and for dancing, for celebrations and for weddings; for corporate events and private functions, for ceremony and for evangelising, for book launches and for musical gigs, for market stalls and for poetry readings, for light shows and Christmas festivals, for developing botanical products and for growing edible foods, for wine tastings and relaxation, and for enjoying all seasonal, key milestones throughout the year.

Although my project has yet to reach full completion, I now have great confidence that the end result will be a successful one. For God and Jesus have enabled me to avoid the risk and the cost that comes from living a life of sin. In the project management and construction world, with residual risk, finance often follows fear. However, if we look at the probability of risk of sinful behaviour versus the severity of outcome, then I am urging you as a reader to no longer giving consideration to living a risky life of habitual sin (a sin that we keep coming back to) and disobedience. For as Scripture warns us, the wages of sin is death. Not a surprise physical death, although there is always a risk of that. But the risk of a spiritual and an eternal death, with permanent separation from God. Therefore, the cost of living a life without God is, put simply, risk filled beyond belief. There can be no fudging. A life of living for the self, without Jesus, will not bring about project success. It will ensure that our project ends in misery.

For many of us are so comprehensively trapped in ourselves that we cannot possibly live an authentic Christian life. Making pride-driven decisions for ourselves, working egotistically for ourselves, or dreaming for ourselves. In doing this we are not emphasising that something greater than ourselves exists. If we do not manage the risk of living for the self then we may not hear those words, 'good and faithful servant' and we may not be in a position to collect those 'rewards' that scripture confirms, 'awaits us followers in heaven'. There will be no heavenly, eternal life after death. There may be a purgatorial second chance or there may only be hell; and there-in lies further risks that need to be managed.

Speaking from my own very limited perspective, as a non-subject matter specialist, laity are often guided and driven by subject matter specialists such as our Bishops, pastors, priests and ministers or expert theologians. This of course requires much trust on our part because such individuals are obviously also human beings born of original sin, who grapple with all of the exact same daily risks that we do. But, let me ask you these questions - what sinful behaviour do you currently, knowingly embark upon that might separate you from God? With risk awareness, what actions might you take to enable you to escape your corruption and become reconciled with God? For me, the bridge that spans the chasm between God and mankind, is the gift of God's Word and the Gospel. The Bible states that everyone who calls on the name of the Lord will be saved (Romans 10:12). Note that the promise is for everyone. However, like an offer of any gift that we do not work for, earn, or even deserve, there may inevitably be those who feel compelled to consider or indeed refuse the offer of that gift. However, when the gift in question is the gift of eternal life, then I suggest there can be no time for consideration, and certainly no thought given to refusal. Why?

Well, I recall reading from the book of Wisdom which stated, 'it was the devil's envy that brought death into the world, as those who are his partners will discover.' So, who are his partners and what exactly will they discover? Well, there is a perception that the devil's partners may be those who have heard the Gospel but chose not to trust it. They may be those who faced with a choice, who knowingly and wilfully chose to live a temporal, immoral, unethical existence. It may be the downright wicked or those who despite constant warnings, chose to worship other gods. It may be those who simply turned a blind eye to their brothers and sisters stranded on the margins. Or... is the author simply threatening us all with hell?

I mean, it is really challenging to imagine the horrors of hell that apparently await the wicked, the unbeliever or unrepentant sinner, but that doesn't mean we shouldn't try. Sure, we can draw help from the perceptions highlighted in Dante's cadaverous writing or Giotto's macabre paintings, which depict a gluttonous horned demon devouring petrified lost souls. But I once listened to an American theologian, who described Jesus as a 'hell fire' preacher. It seems Jesus spoke about hell a lot. He spoke about hell more than any person in the Bible and he spoke about it more than Heaven.

In Luke 16:23, hell is described as 'a place of eternal torment.' In Mark 9:43 it's highlighted as 'a place of unquenchable fire' and in Mark 9:48 'Where the worm does not die'. In Matthew 13:42 it states that people will nash their teeth in anguish and regret and in Luke 16-19:35 it is described as a place from which there is no return even to warn loved ones.' It is defined as a place of outer darkness in Matthew 25:30, and in Matthew 10:28 he compares it to a place called Gehenna, which was a trash heap, which burned indefinitely outside of the walls of Jerusalem where all sorts of filth and vermin abounded.

Furthermore, in Matthew 25:31:33 it states, when the Son of Man comes in His glory, and all the angels with Him, he will sit on His glorious throne. All the nations will be gathered before Him, and He will separate the people one from another as a shepherd separates the sheep from the goats. He will put the sheep on his right and the goats on His left. Yet one of the scariest verses in scripture has to be Matthew 7-21:23, where the Lord warns, 'Not everyone who says to Me, 'Lord, Lord,' shall enter the kingdom of heaven, but he who does *the will* of My Father in heaven. Many will say to Me in that day, 'Lord, Lord, have we not prophesied in Your name, cast out demons in Your name, and done many wonders in Your name?' And then I will declare to them, 'I never knew you; depart from Me, you who practice lawlessness!'

For my part, I always try to remember that it is not the sin that's going to hell, but the sinner tempted into committing those sins who is going to hell. From the day I first received that wonderful gift of a Bible from my wife, I put it to good use. And very quickly it was clear that I needed to get right with God. It was through reading the gospel that I believed that I might well be on my way to hell. That moment the penny dropped, I was literally terrified that I might fall into the hands of a living God and encounter His wrath for my repetitive sinful disobedience. That is why I implore everyone to pick up God's Word and read it because you will find that words, verses, psalms, and parables will spring up off the page and relate specifically to you, your demons, your plight, your transgressions, and your inequities. It will sound out an urgent call for conversion and enable you to see clearly. For as Jesus said, "unless you repent you will all likewise perish" (Luke 13:5).

Let me use this moment to share with you a vivid dream that I had about my *father* several years after he had passed away. I dreamt that he was dirty and emaciated, wearing only a filthy loin cloth and he was pushing a huge millstone round in a circle. His eyes were glazed, and he was exasperated, grimacing and beyond exhausted. He looked like he hadn't been allowed to sleep in years. He was surrounded by red smoke and flames. Was this an unrepentant sinner in hell or was this a vision of a purification process ongoing in purgatory? Or was it just a random dream? I much later discovered that theologian and author, Diarmuid MacCullouch, described purgatory as being like hell, full of fire and pain but it is a process that has an end. "Purgatory, he elaborated, has an exit door that leads only to heaven because after purgatory we are suitably purified which enables us to go to heaven -

therefore we do not go to hell. It is an optimistic, hopeful doctrine." Whether you believe in it or not, I do not judge either way. People in glass houses...

As Charles Spurgeon once quoted, 'Better a brief warfare and eternal rest, than false peace and everlasting torment.' Generally speaking, this quotation always makes me think of those 'Christians' who consistently sit front row centre in their usual church pew. Piously and sanctimoniously, they are often active in their church or parish, readily willing to go to the opening of a 'church envelope'. Yet, behind the scenes they have no personal relationship with God. They are unfamiliar with His Word, with hearts of stone and with minds darkened with bitterness and resentment. It was RC Sproul who stated, "people go to church every Sunday and go through the motions of religion while their hearts are far from God. They act out their religion, as actors in a play, but without faith and without any real personal commitment to God." Unreconciled, they are unable to offer love and or forgiveness, instead living a hypocritical life of doublemindedness, never really doing what Jesus would do. They are what the Apostle Paul referred to in Corinthians 13:1 as, gongs booming or cymbals clashing. As outward people misunderstanding our roles as Christians. Do I judge such people? Certainly not, I was one. People in glass houses...

In Luke 14:15, Jesus used a common every-day story to illustrate a spiritual truth. This story was about a supper invitation where Jesus invited many guests to a great banquet. In reality, those guests were you and I, and the 'banquet' was an invitation to the cross for repentance and salvation and to have our names written in the book of life. Unfortunately, the characters highlighted in the parable, in not wanting to change their lives or their sinful ways, individually offered a raft of excuses to politely decline the invitation.

On the other hand, the moment I realised I was being offered the same invitation, I no longer wanted to make excuses but instead readily and gratefully accept the grace.

Yet, if you are one of the dear readers who are making your way through this book, then I would suggest with confidence that you may be seeking God in some capacity and longing to ask Him to come into your life; or the life of someone near or dear to you. You reading this book is not an accident. The Holy Spirit is leading you. You must believe that when you seek and find, and when you've been healed by God, and you know you've been healed, then you must never let the enemy or any of his dogs or swine convince you that you haven't. We must never allow the marauding enemy (Satan) to convince us that we are irreparably damaged and beyond restoration. We must never allow him to drag us back into "the pit" after God has called and taken us out of it. For this will be the enemy's attempt to deny the great work that the Lord has done for us. God's Word invites us to restore our hearts, from existing hearts of stone to beating hearts of flesh (Ezekiel 36:26). God offers us the opportunity, every second of every day, to abandon compromises with evil and hypocrisy, which all of us as 'PIGs' have, and to take the path of purification and enlightenment of the gospel.

One Saturday at Mass, I listened intently to a powerful sermon from my parish priest who waxed about scriptural metaphor. When he spoke, his words resonated with me on several levels because he spoke of "bruised reeds". It resounded with me because I was once what scripture would describe as a "bruised reed". I still am in fact. Yet it is written that a bruised reed he will not break, and a smouldering wick he will not snuff out" (Matthew 12:20).

When Matthew wrote these words, he was quoting a prophecy from Isaiah 42:1–4. This prophecy pointed to the actions and demeanour of the coming Messiah, now revealed as Jesus Christ. In the prophecy, the "bruised reed" and the "smouldering wick" refer to the spiritually, physically, or morally weak. A reed that is bruised may be damaged, but the harm is not irreparable. A "smouldering wick" may be about to lose its fire altogether, but it can still be reignited.

To the world, a bruised reed is a worthless thing. It has no power, no stability, no purpose. It is good for nothing but to be cut down and discarded. Yet, in the world there are a great many bruised people, individuals who have been wounded emotionally, mentally, spiritually, or physically. They are exhausted and feeble, and to most of the world, they are dispensable. But not to God. The prophecy that Jesus fulfilled is that the bruised reed He would not break. It's a prophecy that speaks of Christ's tender, compassionate care for the weak and downtrodden.

The disfigured man whom Jesus met in Matthew 12 was a "bruised reed," and Jesus gave him strength and cured his shrivelled hand. The woman taken in adultery was a "bruised reed" in John 8, and Jesus saved her from stoning and forgave her sin. Jairus was a "bruised reed" as he mourned his daughter's death, but Jesus strengthened his faith and raised his daughter from the dead (Mark 5). The woman with the issue of blood in Luke 8 was a "bruised reed," and Jesus restored her to full health. The disciple Peter was a "bruised reed" after his denial of the Lord, but Jesus gently and lovingly renewed him to fellowship after the resurrection. Over and over in the gospels, we see Jesus caring for the "bruised reeds" of the world. Levi (Matthew) and Saul of Tarsus (Apostle Paul), King David, Solomon, Zacchaeus etc were all bruised reeds, yet Jesus used them all mightily in differing ways.

Jesus understands the bruised reed because he was "bruised for our iniquities" (Isaiah 53:5). In other words, He was bruised on the cross on behalf of those bruised by sin. Those who come to Christ He will not despise. They have this promise from Jesus: "[God] has sent me to bind up the broken-hearted" (Isaiah 61:1). 'You may be a "bruised reed" in some way today. You may be pressed down with the troubles of this world. You may be struggling with some of the many thematics of sin that I highlighted in the earlier chapters of this book. You may be feeble and disheartened and ready to break. But know this: Jesus cares. He will have pity for the broken-hearted, compassion for the humble, affection for the penitent, and healing for the afflicted. Come to Him in faith, humbly trusting His strength, and find that He is gracious to all.'

That said, in this world and in our culture and often in our own minds, I have discovered that we can have a warped sense of what sin is. The world will often explain away sin, giving a sense that our sinful behaviour that often harms others, can be carried out without immediate consequences or even deferred consequences, is commonplace. When in reality scripture is clear that we are getting away with nothing. You and I are not getting away with anything. No sin with the lips, no sin in the mind, nothing. And we will have to give account of absolutely everything we have done. For it is also written that what is hidden in the darkness of our minds and our hearts, will come to light. Whether now or in the future or after we die, our darkness will be exposed by light.

I draw on the words of Ezekiel 33:7-9, which states, "The word of the Lord was addressed to me as follows, "Son of man, I have appointed you as sentry to the house of Israel. When you hear a word from my mouth, warn them in my name. If I say to a wicked man: Wicked wretch, you are to die, and you do not speak to warn the wicked man to renounce his ways, then he shall die for his sin, but I will hold you responsible for his death. If, however, you do warn the wicked man to renounce his ways and repent, and he does not repent, then he shall die for his sin, but you yourself will have saved your life." This verse sets the prophet Ezekiel as a watchman sent not only to warn of the righteous judgement of God but also to preach a message of hope. In other words, those who persist in rebelling against God by continuing to live a life of habitual sin and disobedience, should take warning. Whilst those who authentically believe in and are faithful to God, should find encouragement and hope. For as evangelical preacher Leonard Ravenhill once put it, there are two kinds of people in the world – only two kinds. Not black or white, rich or poor (or Catholic or Protestant) but those either deceived, dead in sin or dead to sin.

I had some pivotal experiences in my life but, in this book, I have been called to bring them to light. By being an active witness for Jesus and giving my testimony to as many people as possible, I pray it will give encouragement and hope to the great many who need it, so that those who have, or have yet to have, similar or differing sinful experiences to mine, can know that they do not have to die in their sin. I have discovered that we can kill all manner of sinfulness if we do not sow it. So, an element of this book is my method of sharing with you where it is that I believe I am headed, and what I believe I need to do to get there.

You see, it is not enough for a Christian to repent of his sins and to have his life restored and transformed, if he is then to hide his light under a bushel (Matthew 5:15). In St. Paul's letter to the Romans (13:8-10) he states, avoid getting into debt, except the debt of mutual love. If you love your fellow man you have carried out your obligations… you must love your neighbour as yourself… love is the one thing that cannot hurt your neighbour… ' and it is by writing these words and through love, I am sharing my repentance and testifying publicly offering hope to the many who desperately need to hear it; because every person called by Jesus in the new testament was called publicly. Just like Jesus hung on the cross… publicly.

Having listened to a great many testimonies in reformed churches, I can say with confidence that they gave me such wonderful encouragement and hope. What I loved about such testimonies was the constant theme of genuine humility that is weaved throughout them.

Humility is a vital characteristic in the life of a Christian. When I engage with humility, I accept that I am exactly where I am supposed to be.

Above all, I love God's Word and liturgy. It is a wonderful thing. I love the scale of the book and the layer upon layer of complexity and depth within it. Take Genesis 22, when God told Abraham to take his only son Isaac and offer him as a sacrifice and a burnt offering. Of course, even though it appeared as though Abraham was about to obey God's command, The Lord did not allow Abraham to carry through with the offering because it was enough for The Lord, that Abraham had demonstrated a fear of God and that he was willing to obey him at any cost. However, if we move forward to the New Testament, we see that God goes through with the sacrifice His only son whom He loves, for people who don't fear Him, who persecute Him and would literally crucify Him. Such a powerful message.

That said, as a self-confessed Person in a Glass house, let me share with you Psalm 91:13 (CTS) which proclaims, the just will flourish like a palm tree. Or as translated in Psalm 92:12 (NIV), But the godly will flourish like Palm trees. What message is hidden behind these eight words? Well, palm trees are known for their long lives. Therefore, to flourish like a palm tree means to stand tall and to live long and healthily. The cedars of Lebanon could grow to 120 feet high and 30 feet in circumference. Making them solid, strong, and immovable. The Psalmist saw believers, Christians, as upright strong, healthy people, unmoved by the winds of circumstance. That those who have their faith firmly in God, can have this strength and vitality that can lead to something quite extraordinary.

For me, this verse always evokes powerful images of those palm trees in Miami or wherever in the world they might be, getting battered by storms and hurricanes. Tall palm trees being flapped and shaken violently, bent over at times to the point of snapping. But they don't snap. In this verse the palm tree is representative of the solid back bone of the upright Christian man or woman, who will invariably get battered by the suffering that comes from the storms of life. They are people who will experience the confusion of grief, pain, and agony and all of whom will face the inevitability of death. Yet regardless, they remain as upright people of faith. Steadfast they remain godly and righteous, as fearless people of hope who are utterly engulfed by the love of God. God never said that storms wouldn't come. In fact, he stated that persecution would. Therefore, my hope is not in the absence of storms, but that God will keep with me – and so I keep abiding.

This everchanging life can be difficult, and today we are living in very dark and troubled times, with several unprecedented, phased, global shocks that have led to great risk and uncertainty. But with ears to hear, eyes to see and discernment in our hearts we can begin to perceive the direction in which things appear to be headed. We live in a sophisticated and scientific world that I believe may drive us towards an inflection point. With the risk of many nefarious changes unfolding overtly at a societal level, *and* at a mainstream media-driven, level. These include strange leftfield ideologies that are subverting the thought processes of our young and vulnerable. By creating delusion and unnecessary confusion, we appear to have an unconscious element of human society who have fallen into a sink hole. We have proud "liberal" forces, who continue to rebel against and scoff at tradition, with the ultimate goal of trying to remove God and Christianity from our society. I say "liberal" because the trend in question does not appear to be liberal. Because true liberalism in my experience, demonstrates an open, relaxed willingness to accept or respect behaviours, which might differ from one's own.

Instead, we appear to have a militant, atheistic and pluralistic movement that appears to have devolved into a radical, political, and social ideology that flirts with authoritarianism and intolerance, yet wears a mask of virtue whilst doing so. It is a societal fad that less reflects authentic awakening, but more introduces an intolerant rigidity constructed on a pretence of weaponised bitterness and resentment. Where denial of reality, dishonesty and inauthenticity is the order of the day. To put it another way, it is 'gaslighting' or pretence on a mass scale. That is, it is a movement which is disguised as the opposite of what it purports to be. But one with its own vivid imagination, that dangerously deceives and socialises its young followers to such an extent, that they actually lose touch with their own authentic being. It kills what is real and true. So once again, I say with love, if we *truly* walk in the spirit of truth, then we cannot be offended by the truth.

Knowing this, can we stand by and wilfully allow the emotional, mental, physical, and spiritual ruination of a generation, at the expense of a movement that appears to make little in the way of logical sense, and conveys no reason? An enforced ideology that assails the rational, where a movement of misinformation confuses people to such an extent that it leaves them certain about nothing, but seemingly offended by everything? Again, there is so much dangerous corruption, deception, inversion, manipulation, perversion, and subversion in the world. For as written in Isaiah 5:20 "Woe unto them that call evil good, and good evil; that put darkness for light, and light for darkness; that put bitter for sweet, and sweet for bitter".

Under such conditions, such an individualistic society may either destroy itself, or perhaps God will bring it to an end. But there is another way—God can still save such a people. Remember Nineveh? Only with the help of Our Lord Jesus Christ Himself can we defeat the Darkness in the World and help save the Souls of our wayward Brethren. If these are the Signs of the Times, then I suggest things might worsen substantially before they get better. For as written in Timothy 4:4, Many Are Turning Away from The Truth & Wandering into Myths.

Yet, what a futile exercise it must be, trying to remove something as sublime, mysterious and incomprehensible as God from our lives. Because God and His Word are life and the only solid

Truth in these troubled times. In what appears akin to the Days of Noah, or a Nimrod-driven-Babylon, where corruption, deceit and the worship of false Gods abounds, one thing remains clear and constant. We all need Christ, because without Christ and Christianity underpinning our society, it can never work. We humans for many thousands of years have had religion, which has served our deep human need and our human nature, by embedding Christ in our consciousness. Christ is our existing spiritual ark and only once the doors are shut and we are safely inside, are we sheltered and protected from a changing world that, quite frankly, appears insane. Yet, during all these personal, governmental, ideological, societal, and technological changes, there are certain things that have not changed and will never change. For in Malachi 3:6 it states very clearly, I am the Lord I change not.

If ten years ago you'd ask me what I hoped for in life, my response would have been wholly grounded in worldly success and materialism, and not in love, service, and a life eternal. Now, my head and heart are content in the knowledge that by praying comfortably into God's silence, that he hears my prayers because as I have already unambiguously confirmed in writing, He has demonstrably answered many of those prayers. I thank God every day for saving me from the things I thought were important; from the things that were governing my life; and from the things I thought I needed. He answered my call and in doing so he increased my faith by igniting the flame that is the Holy Spirit, who had dwelt within me since my baptism. He saved me from a life of worldly distraction in which I was suffocating. Therefore, "It is truly right and just, our duty and our salvation, always and everywhere to give thanks."

Yet I am under no illusion. For the verse, many are called but few are chosen, (Matthew 22:14) always rings loudly in my ears. For as a mere member of the laity, let me assure you, that I have *never* professed to be some expert theologian or guru, who knows all about scripture and all about God. And nor do I purport to be, for I am anything but an expert! Far from it. In fact, I very much know my place. I am not super-religious, and I tend to steer clear of pointless, pious, and sanctimonious religiosity. What I am is a simple but very imperfect, follower of Christ, who desires to use his time in this life to know Him better. He is everlasting, the Alpha and the Omega the Beginning and the End. I absolutely do not understand it, but I have authentic faith and backed by scripture, prayer, and the Holy Spirit, I accept it. I do not have all the answers, but acknowledge He is the answer to each one of my needs. I simply love God's Word and through that I now know God and believe in his promise (Daniel 12:3) that those who are wise will shine like the brightness of the heavens, and those who lead many to righteousness, like the stars for ever and ever.

This book is not written as some self-pitying, rumination of the pain from the past and I do not call upon some bizarre form of victim mentality. I do not justify my wrongdoing by pointing at the wrongdoing of another or by painting myself as a victim. If I were to go down this route, I would in effect be excusing myself for my actions and diminishing or avoiding the astonishing immorality of those actions. I am not doing this. I am not doing this because morality is not a zero-sum game. The wickedness of one individual does not excuse another. Yet one thing about the Bible that you will notice is that God has a way of using imperfect, majorly flawed people. People in glass houses, just like you and me.

Finally, what was on my mind at the time of writing was this, was that the Bible still speaks to us today. Scripture is relevant, reliable, and sufficient and it gives the wisdom we need especially in times such as these. There is a saying in law and its, res ipsa loquitur, which means, the thing speaks for itself. It is God's Word. In particular, it reads like sage advice for life. A blueprint for our culture and our environment, it is more empowering and offers more power than anything else I have ever read. Why? It is the Word of God. In Hebrews Chapter 4 it states, it is a sword that pierces to the joining of the soul and spirit, right to the joints and marrow, judging the thoughts and intentions of the heart. To put it another way, I found that reading the Bible as a habit, was a way of getting to know the true me; and for anyone who has known me for the last ten years or more, then congratulations. You have experienced the true me.

To rubberstamp this claim, it also says in James Chapter 1 that it (Gods Word) is a mirror. When I looked in, my issues looked back out at me, and it showed me what I needed to do to change. It also says we are to humbly receive the implanted Word, which *can save us*. This, again, is true because I have discovered that when we read it, it can dwell in us and spring up exactly when we need it. It is a light in the dark, the darkness of this world. It is the law of liberty. It is the law of God, which is for our good. Jesus said If you are truly my disciples you will abide in my Word and the Truth will set you free… by living within its parameters and abiding by it, we can be fit to handle real oppression, which is sin.

Among all of the world's most beautiful structures, Victorian curvilinear glasshouses must be amongst the most beloved. Wherever you are geographically based on this earth and whatever stage of your lifecycle you are at, please take time to visit, some of the historic Victorian glass houses that may be close by. You will not regret it. When you visit, by all means marvel at the architectural splendour and the detail rich construction. Wonder at the multi-functionality. But also use that moment to stare into the glazing and reflect upon your life and on what is being mirrored back at you. Are we what we say we are? What is our purpose? Are we using our time meaningfully? Please also relax in the breeze, listen to the bird song, and think of God and his awesome and incredible creation. Ponder on the lives of those flourishing palms and use the time to pray and to explore the reality of God's existence. Also, remember, to make God's love visible, and weave it into our lives and our actions, each and every day. For, when our pilgrimage's draw to a close and we arrive at Eternity's shores, as people in glass houses, regardless of what we have done, what we are doing or what we will do, a merciful God has already confirmed by His Word, that the righteous man will flourish like a Palm tree.

BIBLIOGRAPHY

Alexandre, L and Besnier, J. (2018) Do Robots Make Love. Octopus Publishing. London

Ballard, P. (1983 and 2003) An Oasis of Delight. Brewin Books. Warwickshire

Banville, J; Sayers, B; and Stein, A. (2012) The Palm House. The Lilliput Press Ltd. Dublin

Bible. English. New Living Translation. (1996) Tyndale House Publishers, Inc. Illinois

Brakke, D. (2009) Evagrius of Pontus Talking Back. Cisterian Publications. Kentucky

Cahill, Rev E. (1959)

Chesterton, GK. (1908) All Things Considered. Methuan and Co. London

CTS, The. (2012) New Catholic Bible. The Catholic Truth Society. London

Curtis, E. (1999) Kibble's Palace. Argyll Publishing. Argyll

Curtis, E. (2006) The Story of Glasgow's Botanic Gardens. Argyll Publishing. Argyll

Coll, N (2015) Ireland & Vatican II. The Columba Press. Dublin

D'Arcy B. (2019) It has to be said. Sliah Ban Productions

Desmond, R. (2007) The History of Kew. 2nd Ed. Royal Botanic Gardens, Kew

Dunleath, V. (2008-2009) The restoration of the conservatory at Ballywalter Park. Blurb

Evans, D and Weatherall, N. (2002) South Belfast Terrace and Villa. Cottage Publications

Fahey, Fr D (1939) The Mystical Body of Christ in the Modern World. Dublin Regina Publications

Francis, Pope. (2018) Rejoice and Be Glad. The Word Among Us Press. Maryland

Grant, F. (2013) Glasshouses. Shire Publications. Oxford

Haddick-Flynn K. (2002) A Short History of Orangeism. Mercier Press. Dublin

Hann, S (2020) Hope to Die. Blue Vase Books. USA

Hix, J. (1996) The Glasshouse. Phaidon Press Limited. London

Hobson I and Edmundson E. (2018) Glasshouse Greenhouse. Pavillion books Company Ltd

Howard R and Addison A. (1998) The Enneagram and Kabbalah. Jewish Lights Publishing. Vermont

Leo, Pope. (1978) Humanus Genus – On Freemasonry, Par.2, 12, 14, 15, 16

Marshall, Dr T. (2019) Infiltration – The Plot to Destroy the Church from within. Crisis Publications. USA

McCracken, E. (1971) The Palm House and Botanic Garden, Belfast. Ulster Architectural Heritage Society

Miceli SJ, Fr V. ( ) The Antichrist. Harrison NY

Mirala, P (2007) Freemasonry in Ulster 1733-1813. Four Courts Press. Dublin

Mulligan, K V (2018) Ballyfin The Restoration of and Irish House and Demense. Churchill House Press

Nonaka, I. (1998) The Knowledge-Creating Company. Harvard Business School Press. USA

Novak, M. (1966) Belief and Unbelief, Darton, Longman and Todd. London

Paterson, L. (2013) How the Garden Grew. Royal Botanic Garden Edinburgh. Edinburgh

Piatigorsky, A. (1997) Freemasonry. The Harvill Press. London

Pike, A. (1871) Morals and Dogma of the Ancient and Accepted Scottish Rite of Freemasonry, Martino Fine Books

The thief on the cross, the comma & Christ | Bibleinfo.com

https://www.alastaircoeyarchitects.com/allprojects/bwp23/portfolio-item-bwp23.html

https://www.annacastle.com/pix-quotes-chelsea-physic-garden/

https://www.artvoice.com/2019/03/09/the-veiled-threat-of-freemasonry-part-1-blood-oaths-bloodshed-obstruction-of-justice/

https://www.arthurroadlandscapes.co.uk/blog/2018/3/9/the-palm-house-at-kew

https://ballywalterpark.com/lanyons-conservatories/
http://www.bgci.org/worldwide/article/0175/
https://www.bilan.ch/opinions/garry-

https://www.buildingcentre.co.uk/news/articles/restoration-of-the-historical-three-glasshouses-fota- arboretum-ireland

littman/switzerland_gateway_to_the_alps_and_gateway_to_hell
http://www.billingsdesign.ie/turner-curvili
https://www.birminghambotanicalgardens.org.uk/the-glasshouses/
https://www.birminghambotanicalgardens.org.uk/the-gardens-history/
https://blessingsyou.com/ http://botanicgardens.ie/glasnevin/glasshouses/

http://www.buildingconservation.com/articles/glasshouse-conservation/glasshouse-conservation.htm
http://www.cardiffparks.org.uk/roathpark/info/conservatory.shtml

5 Reasons To Read The Word Of God Daily - Catholic-Link
https://www.chatsworth.org/garden/history-of-the-garden/6th-duke-paxton/great-conservatory/ https://www.chelseaphysicgarden.co.uk/place

https://www.christiesrealestate.com/blog/global-greenhouses-an-antidote-to-the-winter-chill/ https://classroom.synonym.com/significance-skull-masonic-symbolism-7949.html
http://www.collenconstruction.co.uk/Conservation/Abbey_Lea_Glasshouse_Restoration.aspx http://www.crystalpalacefoundation.org.uk/history/the-complete-guide-to-crystal-palaces
https://www.dia.ie/architects/view/5405/turner%2C+richard+%2A
https://distillery.bombaysapphire.com/experiences

https://enduringword.com/bible-commentary/nehemiah-3/
http://www.engineering-timelines.com/scripts/engineeringItem.
https://www.esmadrid.com/en/tourist-information/palacio-de-cristal?utm_referrer=https%3A%2F%2Fwww.google.com%2
https://www.evangelicaltruth.com/orange-order-pagan-rites-under-attack

https://www.forbes.com/sites/alisoncoleman/2018/08/25/how-ireland-is-fast-becoming-the-ai-island/ https://www.ft.com/content/86e5edb4-1baf-

11e8-a748-5da7d696ccab https://gardencollage.com/wander/gardens-parks/palm-trees/

http://www.gardens-guide.com/gardenpages/_0482.htm George Washington becomes a Master Mason - HIST https://glasspaint.com/iconic-glass-structures-the-botanical-garden-of-curitiba/ https://www.gospeltruth.net/1868_75Independent/680409_freemasonryl.htm https://www.gotquestions.org/pearls-before-swine.html

https://www.theguardian.com/cities/2016/may/06/story-of-cities-37-mayor-jaime-lerner-curitiba-brazil- green-capital-global-icon

https://www.theguardian.com/cities/2014/sep/17/truth-property-developers-builders-exploit-planning-cities https://www.theguardian.com/science/2018/may/03/kew-gardens-temperate-house-reopens-after- restoration

https://www.theguardian.com/fashion/2021/apr/16/hail-satan-shoes-why-did-the-banksy-of-the-internet- put-blood-in-666-nike-air-max

https://www.theguardian.com/uk/1999/oct/24/northernireland.theobserver 1 http://www.glasgowbotanicgardens.com/the-gardens/history/kibble-palace/ https://www.gotquestions.org/bruised-reed-not-break.html

https://hartley-botanic.co.uk/magazine/a-history-of-the-english-glasshouse/

https://historicengland.org.uk/listing/the-list/list-entry/1000147ORY

https://www.historyireland.com/18th-19th-century-history/the-men-of-no-popery-the-origins-of-the-orange- order/

https://www.independent.co.uk/news/uk/psni-christian-rebecca-black-work-orange-order-b2023133.html https://www.irishheritagetrust.ie/our-properties/fota-house/

https://www.irishtimes.com/news/a-horticultural-pick-me-up-1.43410

https://www.irishtimes.com/life-and-style/homes-and-property/helping-ireland-s-old-conservatories-to- shine-in-all-their-glory-

https://www.irishtimes.com/culture/order-s-80-000-members-bound-by-oaths-1.59166

http://www.Irish hotel named best in the world by Condé Nast – The Irish Times http://www. Helping Ireland's old conservatories to shine in all their glory – The Irish Times

The Three Degrees of Freemasonry (jjcrowder743.com) https://jewishaction.com/religion/jewish-thought/legalease_tuesday_weddings/ https://www.joc-architects.ie/fota-c19th-glasshouses-restoration https://www.kew.org/blogs/kew-science/the-secret-sex-life-of-anthropomorphic-orchids http://klangchurchofchrist.org/ephesians-610-17-put-on-the-whole-armor-of-god www.knowyourlondon.wordpress.com

http://laist.com/2016/04/07/palm_city.php http://lanyonhotel.co.uk/charles-lanyon-impressive-buildings/ https://lareviewofbooks.org/article/piety-perversity-palms-los-angeles#! https://www.learnreligions.com/paganism-wicca-4684806 https://www.luomus.fi/en/kaisaniemi-botanic-garden/introduction

http://www.missouribotanicalgarden.org/gardens-gardening/our-garden/notable-plant-collections/biblical- plants.aspx

https://www.thenatureofcities.com/2012/07/24/let-us-champion-biodiversinesque-landscape-design-for-the-21st-century/

https://www.nationaltrust.org.uk/quarry-bank/features/the-glasshouse-at-quarry-bank https://www.nytimes.com/1988/01/31/style/gardening-the-era-of-palms-and-ferns.html https://www.oldhouseonline.com/gardens-and-exteriors/classic-greenhouses-and-conservatories https://www.orbcfamily.org/blog/faith/our-heavenly-father-vs-our-earthly-fathers/ https://palmhouse.org.uk/the-plants/ https://cdn.preterhuman.net/texts/conspiracy/Why%20I%20Left%20Freemasonry.pdf https://www.prolificnorth.co.uk/digital/featured/2017/06/chatsworth-glasshouse-recreated-virtual-reality http://www.ptno.ogr.ar.krakow.pl/Wydawn/FoliaHorticulturae/Spisy/FH2004/PDF16022004/fh1602p18.pdf https://realbiblebelievers.com/underworld-tartarus-sheol-paradise-gehenna/

https://www.sacred-texts.com/mas/dun/dun04.htm http://scienceofbeing.com https://stories.rbge.org.uk/archives/28717

http://searchresearch1.blogspot.com/2015/05/answer-victorians-and-palms-trees-thing.html http://www.skibbereeneagle.ie/ireland/richard-turners-glasshouses/ http://www.soane.co.uk/journal/palm-house-pleasure

https://www.state.gov/the-abraham-accords/
http://tanglewoodconservatories.com/heritage/conservatory-of-flowers/
https://www.thecarriagerooms.com/

http://themuseinthemirror.com https://www.theosophy.world/

Fatherless mice raise possibility of virgin births in humans | News | The Times https://www.timesofisrael.com/uae-reveals-progress-on-interfaith-complex-to-house-synagogue-mosque- church/

https://www.viator.com/Curitiba-attractions/Curitiba-Botanical-Garden-Jardim-Botanico/d23058-a21785
https://www.westburygardenrooms.com/blog/westburys-pick-botanical-garden-curitiba/ https://en.wikipedia.org/wiki/Belle_Isle_Conservatory
https://en.wikipedia.org/wiki/Fota_Island#Fota_Gardens
https://en.wikipedia.org/wiki/The_Crystal_Palace
https://en.wikipedia.org/wiki/Enid_A._Haupt_Conservatory
https://en.wikipedia.org/wiki/Rodef_Shalom_Biblical_Botanical_Garden
https://wondersoftransylvania.com/wonder/the-1568-session-of-the-transylvanian-diet